THE FIRST COMING

THE FIRST COMING

*How the
Kingdom of God
Became
Christianity*

THOMAS SHEEHAN

DORSET PRESS
New York

Grateful acknowledgment is made to The Crossroad Publishing Company
for permission to reprint excerpts from *Jesus: An Experiment in Christology*
by Edward Schillebeeckx. English translation copyright © 1979 by
William Collins & Sons Ltd. Reprinted by permission of
The Crossroad Publishing Company. Open Market rights
administered by William Collins & Sons Ltd.

This edition published by Dorset Press
a division of Marboro Books Corporation,
by arrangement with Random House, Inc., New York
1990 Dorset Press

ISBN 0-88029-475-2

Printed in the United States of America

M 9 8 7 6 5 4 3 2 1

For
Robert F. Giguere
and
Frank B. Norris
with respect and gratitude

These and similar prophesies, Trypho,
speak of the First Coming of Christ
when he appeared bereft of privilege
and divine form, a mortal man.

SAINT JUSTIN,
Philosopher and Martyr,
Dialogue With Trypho

Contents

INTRODUCTION: HOW CHRISTIANITY CAME INTO CRISIS   3

1. Liberal Protestantism and the Jesus of History (1800–1900)   10
2. Rudolf Bultmann and the Christ of Faith (1920–1950)   18
3. The New Quest for the Historical Jesus (1950 to Today)   23

ONE: HOW JESUS LIVED AND DIED   29

1. The End of the World   33
2. The Making of a Prophet   49
3. The Kingdom of God   57
4. God's Word at Work   70
5. Rejection and Death   77

TWO: HOW JESUS WAS RAISED FROM THE DEAD   89

SIMON'S EXPERIENCE   93
1. The Myth of Easter   95
2. The Birth of Christianity   101
3. An Early Formula of Faith   110
4. The Denial of Jesus   119

THE EMPTY TOMB   127
1. Easter According to Mark   131
2. An Earlier Legend   135
3. What Really Happened   147
4. An Apocalyptic Messenger   156
5. The Meaning of Easter   163

THREE: HOW JESUS BECAME GOD   *175*

1. The Apocalyptic Judge   *183*
2. The Reigning Lord and Christ   *192*
3. The Divine Son of God   *206*

CONCLUSION: RECOVERING THE KINGDOM   *219*

Appendix   *229*
Notes   *233*
Selected Bibliography   *275*

THE FIRST COMING

THE NEXT COMING

INTRODUCTION

HOW CHRISTIANITY CAME INTO CRISIS

TODAY, AT THE DAWN OF her third millennium, the Christian church is undergoing a theological crisis in what she thinks and believes about Jesus of Nazareth.

The crisis grows out of a fact now freely admitted by both Protestant and Catholic theologians and exegetes: that as far as can be discerned from the available historical data, Jesus of Nazareth did not think he was divine, did not assert any of the messianic claims that the New Testament attributes to him, and went to his death without intending to found a new religion called "Christianity." That is, the theological crisis has to do with the *prima facie* discrepancy between what Jesus of Nazareth apparently thought he was (a special but very human prophet) and what mainline Christian believers now take him to be (the divine Son of God, consubstantial with the Father and the Holy Spirit).[1]

The apparent difference between the "Jesus of history" and the "Christ of faith" is not a new problem in Christianity. Since the last century liberal Protestant scholars like Adolf von Harnack and agnostics like Ernest Renan have tried to strip away what they thought were the church's divinizing embellishments of Jesus of Nazareth so as to arrive at the "real" (that is, the human) prophet of Nazareth.

More recently Roman Catholic exegetes and theologians have joined the discussion.[2] With the encouragement of the Pontifical Biblical Commission, Catholic scholars now teach that the Gospels are not accurate "histories" of Jesus but religious testimonies produced by the second and third generations of Christians, whose faith that Jesus was their savior colored their memory of his days on earth.[3] Thus, even though all Catholic biblical scholars believe that Jesus is God, they do not necessarily maintain that Jesus himself thought he was the divine Son of God, who had existed from all eternity as the Second Person of the Trinity.[4]

Just as the question of discontinuity between the Jesus of history and the Christ of faith is not a new problem, so too solutions to it have long been available in Christian teaching. Today, however, those solutions and the presuppositions on which they rest are being called into question.

Did Jesus actually think that he was the divine Son of God? Christian theologians have traditionally answered this question by asserting that their savior, insofar as he was both God and man, was quite literally of two minds about himself. Relying on a complex distinction that ancient Hellenistic philosophy made between "nature" and "person" (or "rational hypostasis"), these theologians claim that Jesus, even though he was only one person, did have both a human and a divine nature, joined in "hypostatic union." Each of the two natures, they say, had a corresponding intellect, finite in the one case, infinite in the other. And therefore, even if in his human self-understanding Jesus was not aware of his own nature as God, in his divine mind he did know who and what he really was. And he chose to reveal his identity gradually and indirectly, in ways that believers came to fully comprehend only after Jesus' death and resurrection.[5]

How, then, do believers know that the Jesus of history is Christ and God? Some Christians assert that faith is a higher form of cognition than empirical, historical knowledge and therefore that Christian believers have a deeper insight into who Jesus really was than do nonbelievers. According to this thesis, historical research gives us only the "historiographical Jesus"—that is, only those aspects of him that are available via historico-critical method—but it cannot show us the authentic, *divine* Jesus of history, who actually lived and preached two millennia ago. To arrive at that real Jesus, so the theory goes, one must have faith; and unlike the scientific historian, the believing Christian supposedly knows that Jesus really was the Son of God, even if the historical evidence does not show that.

But this solution does not work. Faith provides the believer with no more data about who Jesus of Nazareth "really" was than does normal historical experience. There exists no revealed body of supernatural information that is given over to the Christian faithful while being kept hidden from nonbelievers. Christians have at their disposal only the same public evidence about Jesus that everyone else has—but they interpret the data differently. That is, Christianity is a "hermeneusis," or interpretation. Its beliefs and doctrines are but one of many possible and equally valid ways of understanding the universally available empirical data about Jesus of Nazareth. Christians may claim that their faith is based on revelation, but as far as one can tell empirically, such revelation is a name for the historically relative and culturally determined hermeneutical process in which Christians, confronting the humanly available information about Jesus of Nazareth, choose to interpret him as their savior, who reigns with God in heaven.

Despite these attempts at solving the problem, the critical fact remains: At the root of Christianity there lies the difference between how Jesus apparently understood himself while he was alive—as the eschatological *prophet*—and how the church came to interpret him within a half century of his death: as the divine *Son of God*.

Does this difference constitute a discrepancy, an incompatibility between the evidence of history and the claims of faith? On the one hand, no one can scientifically prove (and no believer would want to) that Jesus actually was the divine savior that Christianity eventually took him to be. On the other hand, it can be established with a high degree of historical certitude that the early church did not create her christological understanding of Jesus out of absolutely nothing, but rather based it on the earliest believers' firsthand impressions of Jesus' dramatically prophetic comportment. That is, Jesus spoke and acted with an extraordinary *authority* that he attributed to God, who was working through him. His disciples interpreted this authority as evidence that Jesus was God's final prophet, sent to prepare Israel for the end of time. Thus early christologies, which interpreted Jesus first as the Son of Man and eventually as Christ and God (see Part Three), were an extension and enhancement of what Simon Peter and the original disciples believed that Jesus had been, whether or not that belief corresponded to what Jesus actually thought of himself and (if this were knowable) who he ontologically was.

It is perhaps impossible and arguably unnecessary for Christianity to show any inevitable connection between Jesus' evaluation of himself when he was alive and Simon Peter's evaluation of Jesus both before and after the prophet's death. Christianity begins not with Jesus but with Simon Peter, and it maintains itself throughout history by staying in continuity with that first believer. Christianity essentially *is* its sense of history, its unique claim of historical continuity—but the continuum is with Peter and the first disciples rather than directly with Jesus. That is the meaning of the Catholic dictum *Ubi Petrus, ibi ecclesia*: Christianity is present wherever someone traces his or her faith back to that of Simon and the first believers. Those who choose to preserve continuity, in one way or another, with Simon Peter's evaluation of the prophet from Galilee can rightly lay claim to the title "Christian." Ultimately, Jesus' understanding of himself is not essential to Christianity. But Peter's is.

The gap that contemporary Christian exegetes have confirmed between the historical evidence about Jesus and the claims of faith about him is potentially salutary and illuminating. For one thing, this difference, once it is acknowledged, offers believers and nonbelievers alike an opportunity to reevaluate Christianity at its roots, not so as to destroy it out of hand or to salvage it at all costs, but in order to discover what Christianity intends to be about, to probe what it may have missed about Jesus, and to ask what kind of future lies ahead for it.

The present book is that kind of investigation, carried out along the border between the findings of empirical history and the questions that inspire faith. Working along that border, I take the devil's part, the role of *advocatus diaboli;* that is, I adopt the viewpoint of the historian, not that of the believer. I take the word "history" in the context of the original Greek verb that underlies it: *historein,* to search and inquire, using only the light of natural, empirical reason. My purpose is to bring the findings of modern historical and biblical research to bear on three questions that are central to the theological crisis in contemporary Christianity:

PART ONE: What Jesus preached about the kingdom of God
PART TWO: How belief in his resurrection evolved
PART THREE: How the earliest christologies developed in the first half
                       century after Jesus' death

At the heart of this theological crisis there lies a revolution in biblical studies—specifically, the emergence of historical-critical method—that began over a century ago and now dominates both Catholic and Protestant exegesis. The employment of the historical-critical method in scriptural research has often led to extraordinary shifts in the church's understanding of biblical texts; and since the testimony of the Bible is a major stone in the foundation of Christian faith, such shifts are bound to have repercussions in the theological edifice built on that foundation.

Therefore, we must preface our threefold study of Jesus, the resurrection, and the origins of christology with an overview of how the revolution in New Testament exegesis came about and what its major conclusions are. That is the task of the sections that immediately follow. Then, throughout the remainder of the book, I shall be drawing upon those conclusions—the results of contemporary (and quite orthodox) Christian exegesis—even though I shall be offering my own fundamentally variant interpretations of those conclusions. That is, I depend upon (and hope to show that I am faithful to) the scientifically controllable results of modern biblical scholarship; but then I go beyond that scholarship, by using its scientific results as data for my own theories.

Although Catholic scholars are relative latecomers to the revolution in biblical exegesis (their Protestant counterparts have been at it for almost 150 years), higher criticism of the New Testament is now the common activity and common property of both Protestants and Catholics. We turn now to the origins and development of that revolution.

1

LIBERAL
PROTESTANTISM
AND THE JESUS
OF HISTORY
(1800-1900)

THE BEGINNINGS of modern biblical exegesis go back to the birth of "historical consciousness" at the dawn of the nineteenth century; and the first stage in the Protestant development of that exegesis is roughly coextensive with what George Steiner has called "the summer of 1815–1915"—the century of bourgeois liberalism.[6]

Just as Newton's revolution in physics and Kant's in philosophy helped the eighteenth century to invent "nature" as the correlate of Enlightenment reason, so likewise the political revolutions in America and France and the enthronement of Hegelian philosophy in Germany contributed to the nineteenth century's invention of "history" as the correlate of bourgeois will. The more the world and events became transparent to human intellect and manageable by human praxis, the more the nineteenth-century bourgeoisie saw nature as a possible mirror of itself—as raw material to be shaped in its own image—and understood history as the medium of this self-making. As Marx noted in the Communist Manifesto, the bourgeoisie, in transforming the world, broke down the solid forms of unchanging substantiality and dissolved them into the fluidity of historical and social self-creation.

All fixed and frozen relations, with their train of ancient and vener-
able prejudices and opinions, are swept away, all new-formed ones
become antiquated before they can ossify. All that is solid melts into
air, all that is holy is profaned, and man is at last compelled to face
with sober senses his real conditions of life and his relations with his
kind.[7]

The rise of historical consciousness gave birth to a new approach to
humanistic studies *(Geisteswissenschaften)*. The notions that truth is
concrete and incarnate rather than abstract, that it develops in history
rather than being eternally given, and that each stage of its development reflects changing human needs and aspirations—these were some
of the presuppositions underlying the historical-critical method adum-
brated by Johann Gottfried von Herder and Wilhelm von Humboldt,
instituted by Leopold von Ranke, and adopted by biblical scholars.
After centuries of philosophical fascination with static being, the nineteenth century turned its attention to the adventure of historical
becoming, where, by the nature of the case, research had to focus on
the interrelations of concrete events rather than on universal essences
and could aspire only to probability rather than to necessarily certain
truth. Above all, against the Enlightenment's idea that historiography
established typical and recurring patterns of human character and
action, the passwords of historical studies now became the inevitability
of change and development.

Thus, historians or exegetes who wanted to get the meaning of a
text from the past had to forgo the desire to find in it a supposedly
eternal truth and restrain the urge to project their values into the past.
Instead, after scientifically establishing the primary evidence of the
text, they must devote themselves, first, to rigorously reconstructing
what the document meant to its author and original audience, and
second, to tracing how that meaning developed as it came into contact
with new communities. Only thereafter could they enter upon the task
of hermeneutics, that is, the interpretation of its possible meaning for
a reader today.

These presuppositions of historical consciousness and critical method
formed the background of the nineteenth century's revolution in biblical studies. Whether in the Hegelian orientation of the Tübingen

school or in the more empirical and philological work of the Cambridge school, the program with regard to the New Testament was the same: to investigate the Christian Scriptures as historical documents that bore witness not to eternal truths so much as to the religious beliefs of certain eastern Mediterranean communities in the first few decades after Jesus' death. This program entailed (1) the philological task of establishing the correct text of the New Testament; (2) the critical task of isolating the original sources of the Gospels; (3) the historical task of reconstructing the environments of the first Christian communities; and (4) the exegetical task of tracing the development of christology in the early church. This scientific work served as the foundation for (5) the theological-hermeneutical task of interpreting the relevance (or irrelevance) of early Christian beliefs for men and women of today.[8]

The current upheaval in Christian theology goes back to this project of constructing a scientific foundation of empirical, historical evidence for the edifice of theology. The two moments of the revolution—the scientific and the theological—are distinct but not totally separable. Tremors in the historical foundations often send shock waves through the upper stories of theology. Already in the nineteenth century some large cracks were beginning to show in the traditional doctrines about Jesus.

By the second half of the nineteenth century critical exegetes were virtually in agreement that, contrary to the traditional view, the Gospels were not written as neutral historical records of Jesus' words and deeds and that they offered no access to his inner thoughts or psychology. Rather, even if they preserve some historical recollection of Jesus, they more directly reflect the highly developed beliefs of Christian communities forty to sixty years after his death. Often enough, the critics showed, sentences that the Gospels put in Jesus' mouth (such as his claims to be Christ or the divine Son of God) had never been spoken by him but were invented by later believers.

Over the years New Testament critics have managed to identify at least three types of early Christian communities—two of them made up of Jews and one of Gentiles—each of which had its relatively distinct christology.[9] First came the *Aramaic-speaking Palestinian Jews* who were the earliest "Christians" (we should say more accurately: adherents of the "Jesus-movement" within Judaism). They took Jesus to be the eschatological prophet, God's final and authoritative spokes-man, who (1) had proclaimed the dawning kingdom of God, (2) had been vindicated by God after he died by being miraculously taken to heaven, and (3) had been designated to be the future apocalyptic judge who would appear at the imminent end of the world. Although these Aramaic-speaking Jewish believers saw Jesus as the prophet of God, they did not consider him to be ontologically divine. Nor did they think that he already was the messiah (Christ). Rather, they thought that he was only the messiah–designate and that he would come into his full power only at the end of time.

Secondly, there were the *Greek-speaking Jews* of Palestine and the Diaspora (for example, Syria) who had come to believe in Jesus and who were the first to be actually called "Christians" (Acts 6:1, 8:1, 11:26). As the parousia (Jesus' return to earth from heaven) continued to be delayed, these Hellenistic Jewish Christians began to stress not that Jesus would become the Christ at the end of time but that he already was the Christ and was currently reigning in heaven.

Thirdly, *Greek-speaking Gentiles* eventually converted to Christian-ity, beginning around 40 C.E., and they held that Jesus was the Son of God in the full divine sense: He had preexisted as God before his human incarnation, had been the true, if concealed, God-man during his life on earth, and after his death had been exalted to heaven and was currently reigning there.

The tremors that these discoveries sent through traditional theology took the form of a concatenation of questions: If Jesus did not declare he was Christ and God, and if such christology was a creation of later believers, what did the real, historical Jesus actually teach? What did he think about himself? Do his teachings have anything in common with traditional christology and, above all, do they have any relevance today? The nineteenth-century attempt to answer these questions gen-erally took the form of "the quest for the historical Jesus." In various ways, from Hermann Samuel Reimarus in the eighteenth century through David Strauss, Ernest Renan, and a score of others in the nineteenth century, this quest for the historical Jesus undertook the common task of searching for the "Jesus of history," who was con-cealed by and behind the "Christ of dogma."[10]

A classical statement of the liberal Protestant view of the Jesus of history can be found in the immensely popular lectures that Adolf von Harnack (1851–1930) delivered at the University of Berlin during the winter semester of 1899–1900 and published immediately thereafter as *Das Wesen des Christentums* (in English: *What is Christianity?*). For Harnack, Jesus was the ideal ethical humanist, and the essence of Christianity lay in a few timeless spiritual principles he had taught: the fatherhood of God, the brotherhood of man, and "the infinite value of the human soul." Above all, Jesus' message was meant for the interior man; it was, as Harnack put it, a question "of God and the soul, the soul and its God." He wrote:

> The kingdom of God comes . . . to the individual, by entering into his soul and laying hold of it. True, the kingdom of God is the rule of God; but it is the rule of the holy God in the hearts of individuals. . . .[11]

Looking back from the enlightened nineteenth century, Harnack saw christology, the doctrine that Jesus was the divine savior, as an invention of the early church, a crutch that weaker, more benighted generations had needed in order to hobble through their lives. Nonetheless, this christology had been a felicitous invention, Harnack thought, insofar as it had preserved the memory of Jesus for this more surefooted age; and now one could throw away the crutch and walk upright, shoulder to shoulder, with the Rotarian Jesus of history.

Twenty-five centuries earlier the Greek philosopher Xenophanes had observed that human beings, in depicting their gods, describe themselves (fragments 15 and 16). After reading Harnack's book, George Tyrell, the English Catholic modernist theologian, suggested that the liberal Protestant quest for the historical Jesus was comparable to looking down a well: Harnack and the others thought they had sighted Jesus, but they were seeing nothing but their own bourgeois reflection staring back up at them.

Harnack's book relied on the biblical scholarship of his day. In the nineteenth century exegetes had developed the science of "source criticism," the study of the literary relation between the relatively similar Gospels of Matthew, Mark, and Luke (the "synoptic" Gospels). As the name suggests, source criticism attempted to ferret out the *literary origins* of the Gospels, and by the 1860s it had succeeded in determining two things.[12]

First, by isolating the gospel verses that Matthew and Luke had borrowed from Mark (and by finding none that Mark had borrowed from them), source critics were able to establish that Mark's Gospel was the first one to be written (it is currently dated at ca. 70 C.E.) and that Matthew and Luke had used it as the principal written source of their own Gospels, which appeared about fifteen years later. Second, by isolating gospel verses that were common to Matthew and Luke but absent from Mark, the exegetes proposed the "two-source" hypothesis: that besides Mark there had been another, earlier source of gospel material, a collection composed mostly of sayings attributed to Jesus, which went back to the early Aramaic-speaking Christian communities of Palestine. This second source came to be known as "Q," which abbreviates the German word *Quelle* ("source"). Today, despite some disagreement about the exact contents of the Q-document, virtually all New Testament scholars accept the Q-hypothesis. However, the nineteenth-century theory of two sources—Q and Mark—has since been refined and expanded into the "four-source" theory (see accompanying chart), which postulates two other oral sources to account for materials that are unique to Matthew and to Luke.[13]

THE SOURCES OF THE SYNOPTIC GOSPELS

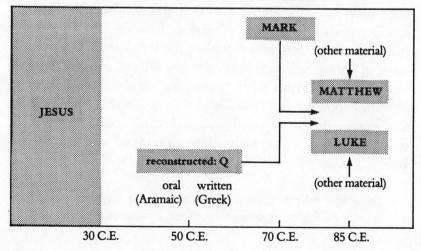

Harnack and other liberal Protestants thought that source criticism had established that Mark and Q were the earliest historical records of Jesus' life and preaching and therefore that exegetes could now peer through the christological embellishments of the later Gospels of Matthew and Luke and see in Mark and Q a more human Jesus—the real "Jesus of history." For example, Matthew and Luke assert that Jesus was conceived and born as the Christ, and John's Gospel, written around 100 C.E., goes even further and maintains that Jesus had preexisted as God before he was born. But source criticism had shown that the Gospels of Matthew and Luke developed out of Mark's earlier and more modest position, according to which Jesus was merely adopted as the Christ, indeed only when he had become an adult. By reading between the lines of Mark's Gospel, Harnack found—or reconstructed —an even simpler Jesus, an entirely human prophet whose message, as luck would have it, was entirely consonant with the religious sentiments of nineteenth-century liberal humanism.

Thus Christianity could finally bid adieu not only to the early church's divinization of Jesus but also, as Albrecht Ritschl (1822–1889) had earlier argued, even to the misguided doctrine of eschatology that Jesus himself had preached.[14] All that messy business about the imminent end of the world and God's unannounced (and frankly impolite) irruption into the tidy world of human self-improvement could be done away with. Christianity had at last found a place in sophisticated late-nineteenth-century society, even if it was a quiet and somewhat harmless place. For liberal Protestants, the contemporary meaning of Jesus' doctrine of the kingdom of God was not that some mythical apocalyptic judge was going to break in from the Beyond and take humanity to task for its sins. Rather, the kingdom of God was the result of human endeavor, "the corporate product of [the Christian] community," "a human product, springing out of an individual activity called forth by the divine 'seed.' "[15] In Ritschl's interpretation, Christianity became a purely interior community, an invisible, spiritual kingdom in the hearts of well-mannered men and women. Ritschl wrote:

> Those who believe in Christ . . . constitute the Kingdom of God
> in so far as, forgetting distinctions of sex, rank, or nationality, they

act reciprocally from love, and thus call into existence that fellowship of moral disposition and moral blessings which extends, through all possible gradations, to the limits of the human race.[16]

The historical Jesus came out of the pages of Scripture as a good bourgeois liberal, devoted to the preachment of self-improvement, love of one's neighbor, and religious freedom from ecclesiastical dogmatism. For Ritschl the kingdom of God was not an eschatological but an ethical and social affair: "the organization of humanity through action inspired by love."[17]

2

RUDOLF BULTMANN AND THE CHRIST OF FAITH (1920-1950)

B Y THE END OF World War I the liberals' reconstruction of Jesus, which for some years had been on shaky theological and exegetical grounds, came entirely unglued. As bourgeois optimism about the ethical improvability of mankind collapsed in the carnage of the war, a new generation of Protestant theologians came into their own, and they had little patience with the socially acceptable but innocuous Jesus who had been invented by their liberal forebears.

Already in 1892 the young scholar Johannes Weiss, who in fact was the son-in-law of Albrecht Ritschl, had profoundly shaken the liberal Protestant dogma that Jesus was merely an ethical teacher of the Fatherhood of God, the brotherhood of man, and the gradual growth of the kingdom of God in this world. His *Die Predigt Jesu vom Reiche Gottes (Jesus' Proclamation of the Kingdom of God)* burst on the scene, arguing that Jesus' teaching was entirely focused on the imminent arrival of God from outside the world and that Jesus had proclaimed not a bourgeois ethics of personal morality and civic duty but a radical "interim ethics" of preparation for the coming of the kingdom. For example, noting the distance between Jesus' passionate eschatological ethics and liberal Protestantism's accommodation to the world, Weiss declared that

> despite the explicit and earnest warning of Jesus that it is easier for a camel to go through the eye of a needle than for a rich man to enter the Kingdom of God, and although Jesus declared, "with men it is *impossible*," many rich Christians, indeed many rich churches have dared to remain rich. . . . It would be more truthful to take one's stand historically with respect to these matters, and to understand them from the perspective of Jesus' eschatological and dualistic viewpoint.[18]

This reassertion of the eschatological character of Jesus' message began to resonate strongly in Protestant circles after World War I. Karl Barth's powerful *Epistle to the Romans,* published in German in 1919, captured the religious imagination of the new generation by reproposing the traditional themes of man's sinfulness, God's transcendence, and the need for redemption from beyond, under the rubric "What was of grave importance [in Paul's time] is still so today."[19] Søren Kierkegaard, recently translated into German, began to make more sense with his call for an absurd "leap of faith" than did Ritschl and Harnack with their offer of a benign and well-mannered Jesus. The old Lutheran call for faith alone—without foundations in nature or history—found a resonance in those who were disillusioned with the March of Progress. While, of course, the worldwide Marxist revolution prompted many to look deeper within history for a solution to the social and political catastrophes of the age, others, like Rudolf Bultmann, found inspiration in Martin Heidegger's quasi-Lutheran turn to the individual and in his antihistoricist stress on the repeatability of the essential *(die Wiederholung des Gewesenen).* If liberal Protestants had abandoned the divine God-man of traditional doctrine in order to invent the humanitarian Jesus of history, Bultmann and others abandoned the liberal Jesus of history in order to invent the existential Christ of faith.[20]

After the war Protestant scholars began inventing sharper exegetical tools for probing the historical development of the Christian Scriptures and, in the eyes of many, for whittling away at the divinity of Jesus.

In the area of New Testament research, the watershed between liberal Protestant exegesis and what came after it can be dated to 1919–1921, the years in which Karl Ludwig Schmidt (1891–1956), Martin Dibelius (1883–1947), and Rudolf Bultmann (1884–1976) published groundbreaking works in the new area of biblical science called "form criticism."[21]

The source critics of the previous century had focused only on the *written* sources of the Gospels; and in postulating the Q-document and establishing the historical priority of Mark's Gospel among the Synoptics, they had gone as far back into early Christian history as they could. But with "form criticism" the focus shifted from the literary relationships among the Synoptic Gospels to the *preliterary* history of the material upon which those Gospels drew. Whereas source criticism goes back only to the period around 50 C.E., when the oral Aramaic Q was presumably written out in a Greek translation, form criticism traces the verses of the Gospels and of the hypothetical Q-document back to the period of their oral genesis and transmission between 30 and 50 C.E. (see chart).

One of the presuppositions of form criticism is that each Synoptic Gospel is like a mosaic composed of individual tesserae or a necklace made up of separate pearls strung together. Each Gospel is a creative compilation of earlier units of material (called "pericopes") which the church generated after Jesus died. These pericopes circulated in oral form as independent and self-contained sayings and stories before they were committed to writing (some of them in the Greek Q) and eventually organized into the Gospels. Form critics study the origins and development of the individual units, and they attempt to identify the particular forms those units take: for example, polemical or didactic sayings, proverbs, apocalyptic prophesies, community regulations, parables, miracle stories, and the like.[22] Some pericopes may well embody historical recollections of what Jesus said and did, whereas others contain words and deeds that the church, in retrospect, invented and attributed to him. In any case, at each stage of their reception and transmission these pericopes, according to the form critics, were freely adapted and creatively shaped by the Christian communities to fit their own particular needs, such as catechetics, liturgy, apologetics, and controversy with outsiders.[23]

THE NEW TESTAMENT PERIOD AND THE AREAS OF GOSPEL CRITICISM

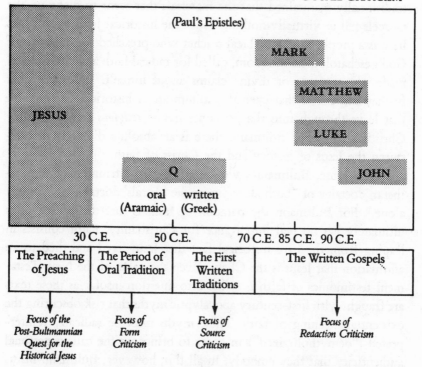

30 C.E.	50 C.E.	70 C.E. 85 C.E. 90 C.E.	
The Preaching of Jesus	The Period of Oral Tradition	The First Written Traditions	The Written Gospels

Focus of the Post-Bultmannian Quest for the Historical Jesus   *Focus of Form Criticism*   *Focus of Source Criticism*   *Focus of Redaction Criticism*

Therefore, the pericopes do not have an unadulterated historical value as neutral accounts of what Jesus said and did, but they do reveal in each case the particular life-situation *(Sitz im Leben)* of the communities that shaped them. And most important of all, they tell us how those communities understood the meaning of Jesus. The pericopes are not disinterested records of the life of Jesus but early testimonies of the community's faith in Jesus as the Christ.[24] In other words, form criticism takes the exegete further back into early Christianity than source criticism does, insofar as it sheds scientific light on the otherwise dark years between the death of Jesus (30 C.E.) and the emergence of the first written testimonies of faith (Paul's epistles and the Q-document, ca. 50 C.E., and the Gospels, ca. 70–95 C.E.). However, form criticism offers no direct access to the Jesus of history and his psychology—and least of all access to Harnack's humanitarian Jesus. Form criticism can get back only to the early oral traditions in which the first Christian generations passed down their faith in the prophet.

Form critics in general and Rudolf Bultmann in particular have traditionally maintained that the materials that went to make up the Gospels tell us virtually nothing about the historical Jesus except that he was a prophet and an ethical teacher who preached the dawning of God's eschatological kingdom, called for radical faith and charity, and made no messianic or divine claims about himself. Bultmann goes further and asserts that even this minimum of historical information that leaks through into the pericopes has *no religious significance* for Christian faith. For Bultmann there is an absolute discontinuity between the Jesus of history and the Christ of faith.

In this sense, Bultmann's work represents the triumph of the Lutheran doctrine of "faith alone" over the liberals' doctrine of "history alone." For Bultmann the paradox of faith is that the life of Jesus ultimately has no real importance for Christianity. Faith consists in leaping from the bare historical fact that Jesus lived and died to an affirmation that Jesus is the Christ. Even the value of the New Testament testimonies of faith is called into question insofar as these texts are fraught with first-century apocalyptic myths that risk obscuring the existential meaning of faith. These myths must be radically reinterpreted ("demythologized") in order to bring out the call to personal authenticity that they embody. In all this, however, Bultmann insists that Christianity (which in his hands looks more and more like a religious version of Heidegger's early philosophy) cannot dispense with christology, as the liberals thought it could, if only because, Bultmann claims, one needs christology (properly demythologized) for the existential challenge to authenticity that it conveys.

3

THE NEW QUEST
FOR THE
HISTORICAL JESUS
(1950 TO TODAY)

SINCE THE END OF World War II New Testament scholarship has undergone important developments both in critical method and in theological reflection. For one thing, while the method of form criticism continues to be used with some revisions by contemporary exegetes, it has been complemented since the late forties by "redaction criticism" (in German, *Redaktionsgeschichte*, "redaction history"), which attempts to sort out the differing theological conceptions that guided the four evangelists in reshaping earlier oral material into their written Gospels.[25]

But more important, some of the theological conclusions that Bultmann built upon form criticism have been called into question since World War II. In the early fifties a number of Protestant exegetes (among them, Ernst Käsemann, Günter Bornkamm, Hans Conzelmann, Gerhard Ebeling, and Ernst Fuchs, some of whom are former students of Bultmann's) argued that it was indeed possible, with the aid of exegetical criticism, to get behind the christological proclamations of the early church and to catch a glimpse not only of the actual words and deeds of the historical Jesus but also of the way he understood himself during his lifetime. With claims such as these it seemed that New Testament exegetes were coming around full circle. First, nineteenth-century liberalism had destroyed the divine Christ of faith and invented a humanitarian Jesus of history; then Bultmann virtually destroyed the Jesus of history and invented an existential Christ of faith; and now the "Post-Bultmannians" were advocating a "new quest for the historical Jesus." But the "new" quest has almost nothing in common with the nineteenth-century one. The Post-Bultmannians, for example, agree with Bultmann on a number of points: that there is no possibility of discovering an "uninterpreted Jesus of Nazareth," a Jesus untouched by Christian faith; that we cannot reconstruct Jesus' inner psychology and thoughts; that Christianity cannot do away with christology; that the post-Easter Christian community is (in large measure, at least) the seedbed of the Jesus-tradition; that faith cannot be reduced to history or reason and that *sola historia* cannot replace the Lutheran position of *sola fide*. [26]

But on the other hand, these new exegetes also take their distance from Bultmann. They point out that the historical recollections of Jesus found in the pericopes offer much more historical information about the prophet than Bultmann admits—and that this information does have some significance for faith. They argue, for example, that the authority that Jesus demonstrated in his words and deeds reveals, if not Jesus' inner psychology, at least his publicly enacted understanding of himself as a prophet.

Most important of all, the Post-Bultmannians deny that there is an unbridgeable chasm between the Jesus of history and the Christ of faith. Or, to put the matter positively and more accurately, they hold that there is a continuity between the meaning that the disciples attributed to Jesus during his life and the meaning they attributed to him after his death. In other words, the Post-Bultmannians do not see New Testament christology as a post-Easter invention on the part of the church but as a spelling out of the implicit christological claims that the disciples discerned in the authoritative words and deeds of Jesus during his lifetime. These exegetes point out that, after Easter, the disciples believed that it was Jesus—not some "X" but the Jesus they had known—who was the Christ. They claim that to deny this continuity of meaning, as Bultmann does, is to risk reducing Christianity to a modern myth with some generalized existential import.

Underlying and supporting these new theological positions are new, or at least revised, methods of scientific exegesis. Within form criticism, the Post-Bultmannians make use of at least four criteria for determining whether elements of the gospel material are authentically historical, that is, traceable to Jesus himself. First, the criterion of dissimilarity allows the exegete to attribute to Jesus at least those sayings which can be shown to be probably unique to him insofar as they are notably dissimilar from sayings that are provably typical of either the early church or ancient Judaism. Secondly, the criterion of coherence allows these exegetes to attribute to Jesus those sayings that are coherent with the material that has already been established to be "unique because dissimilar." Thirdly, the criterion of multiple attestation permits the exegete, within limits, to attribute to Jesus those deeds or kinds of behavior which are attested in all or many of the distinct gospel sources (for example, Mark and Q). Finally, according to the criterion of language and environment, any authentic saying of Jesus would have to reflect Aramaic speech and, in general, the cultural patterns of early Palestine—although it is possible that such characteristics might reflect only the earliest Palestinian churches.[27]

What, then, have the post-Bultmannian exegetes discovered about the historical Jesus by applying these criteria to the gospel material? Negatively, they have established that Jesus did not express his self-understanding in any christological titles—certainly not in the so-called higher titles (such as "God," or "Lord" in the full divine sense) and not even in the so-called lower titles (for example, "messiah," "[messianic eschatological] prophet," and "Son of Man"). On the positive side, what Jesus thought of himself can be seen indirectly and implicitly in the authoritative way he spoke and acted—for example, the way he bent the Law by eating with sinners and outcasts, or the way he declared that the kingdom of God was dawning in his words and deeds. In Jesus' assertion of his authority the scholars find the attitude of a prophet who seemed convinced that his word was God's word and that his will was at one with his Father's. They interpret this as an implicit claim to a unique relation with God—but only that and no more.

In other words, the "new quest" for the historical Jesus has discovered something more than Bultmann thought could be found, and something different from what the liberal quest thought it had discovered. It has found a Jesus who acts like an eschatological prophet with a sense of authority derived from his special relation to God. No doubt he did preach (to put it minimally) "the fatherhood of God and the brotherhood of man," as the liberals thought, but he did so in a number of ways the liberals overlooked. For one thing, there is an irreducible eschatological element to his preaching about the kingdom of God; for another, he preached the kingdom in a uniquely self-referential way: by acting as if he himself were the locus (if not the focus) of the dawning of that reign of God.

But, for all that, the question remains: What difference does this make? Even if we could establish (and we cannot) that Jesus actually thought he was God's eschatological prophet—or for that matter, God's divine Son—Jesus' opinion of himself would have no binding power on anyone else and so would make no real difference for faith. Jesus could have thought he was any number of things and still have been deluded. Regardless of what they have established about the Jesus of history, the Post-Bultmannians have not rendered the leap of faith any easier or more reasonable. Nor did they intend to do so. But neither, as it seems, have they raised the degree of Jesus' importance much higher than the liberals did. In fact, what real difference is there between Harnack's mild-mannered Jesus and the Post-Bultmannians' more self-assured and authoritative prophet? Have all three—Harnack, Bultmann, the Post-Bultmannians—been looking, with different exegetical spectacles, down the very same well and seeing only their own reflection?

We have seen how the revolution in New Testament exegesis has contributed to the theological crisis in Christianity. The rest of this book is an investigation of three major elements in that crisis: the content of Jesus' preaching, the doctrine of the resurrection, and the development of the first christologies. In what follows I shall be drawing upon the gains of contemporary exegesis that we have just studied. For example, I shall be employing the results of post-Bultmannian research into the authentic sayings of Jesus as I attempt to reconstruct the life and teachings of Jesus. But my purpose is to surpass rather than to repeat the mainline Christian interpretation of Jesus, both in its traditional and in its more modern "liberal" form. In appropriating and *ex*propriating the best of modern liberal exegesis of the New Testament, my goal is to contribute to the shaping of a postmodern and postliberal interpretation of the meaning of Jesus.

Fifteen hundred years ago the Christian philosopher Boethius described the perennial ideal of Christian thought and existence as a yoking together of faith and reason: *Fidem, si poteris, rationemque coniuge.* [28] Today we might paraphrase his dictum as follows: Faith, if it is possible and if it is to be responsible, can never escape from history or ignore the evidence that history provides. That very evidence is what has brought Christianity to the foundational crisis it is now living through. The time is ripe to muster the results of New Testament historians and exegetes, to use those findings in order to reread the origins of Christianity, and to see what this tradition can still say—or perhaps only whisper—on the other side of liberal Christianity.

ONE

HOW JESUS LIVED AND DIED

IN POPULAR CHRISTIAN TEACHING, Jesus often comes across as a divine visitor to our planet, a supernatural being who dropped into history disguised as a Jewish carpenter, performed some miracles, died on a cross to expiate sins, and miraculously departed again for the other world.

In official Church teaching this view of Jesus as a god who merely pretended to be human is a heresy, and the seriousness of the error is not mitigated by the fact that multitudes of the faithful, from catechists to cardinals, firmly believe and teach it. In earlier forms the heresy was called "Docetism" (from the Greek verb *dokei,* "he only seems to be"), and it has been condemned many times for maintaining, in effect, that Jesus merely appeared to be a human being but actually was not, that this heavenly savior merely "wore" flesh like a garment while he went about his divine task of redeeming the world. Church condemnations notwithstanding, this heresy continues to thrive in contemporary Christianity and remains one of the more common forms of christology in popular Roman Catholicism.[1]

But even in its official, orthodox form, Christianity tends to overlook the fact that, exceptional though he proved to be, Jesus was a young Jewish man of his times, as mortal and fallible as anyone before or after him. Whether this Galilean carpenter was also God is a matter of some debate. But no serious person doubts that he in fact lived as a human being in a certain place and at a certain time. Which means that one way to make sense of who he was and what he was about is to "materialize" him, to pull him out of his mythical eternity and reinsert him into the historical situation that shaped his mind and his message.

Jesus lived his brief and tragic life (from about 5 B.C.E. to 30 C.E.) at a time when Judaism was undergoing dramatic transformations in its social and political structures, and attempting to interpret Jesus in abstraction from that context would be like trying to make sense out of Dante without referring to medieval Florence. Therefore we begin the present chapter, which is devoted to understanding Jesus' message of the "kingdom of God," with some remarks on the historical development of Israel and, in particular, on the eschatological mood of the times.

1

THE END OF
THE WORLD

THE YEARS during which Jesus preached—probably 28–30 C.E.—
were moments of relative calm at the eye of a political hurricane.
Two hundred years earlier, the Maccabee brothers had revolted against
Syrian domination of Judea, and after a long struggle, the Jewish
people had won a brief hiatus of independence from foreign domi-
nation (142–63 B.C.E.). Those years of political freedom ended with
Pompey's conquest of Palestine, and thereafter the country lived under
the cloud of an uneasy Pax Romana that held until 66 C.E. In that year
Jewish revolutionaries, called Zealots, rebelled against the empire; but
Roman legions led by Titus crushed the insurrection and destroyed the
Jerusalem Temple in 70 C.E. In 135 C.E. a second Jewish revolt against
Rome ended with the razing of the Holy City.[2]

Those three hundred turbulent years, framed at both ends by violent
revolutions, mark one of the most creative eras in Western religious
and intellectual history, not only because they reshaped Judaism and
launched Christianity, but also because they delivered to the West the
notion of eschatology (the idea of an end to time), which, through
various transformations from millenarianism to Marxism, has profoundly influenced the Western concept of history.

THE HISTORY OF ISRAEL *(WITH APPROXIMATE DATES)*

1000 B.C.E.	**THE UNITED KINGDOM** Saul (1025–1000) David (1000–962) Solomon (961–922) **THE DIVIDED KINGDOM** North and South (922)	
		HELLENISTIC ERA (333–63) Ptolemies (333–200)
900 B.C.E.		**300 B.C.E.**
800 B.C.E.	PROPHETS: Elijah Elisha Amos Hosea Isaiah Northern kingdom falls (721)	**200 B.C.E.** Seleucids (200–142) Maccabee revolt begins (167) Book of Daniel (165) **HASMONEAN- MACCABEAN ERA** (142–63)
700 B.C.E.		**100 B.C.E.** Essenes Pharisees **ROMAN ERA** Pompey Conquers Palestine (63) Herod the Great (40–4)
600 B.C.E.	Jeremiah Southern kingdom falls Babylonian Exile (586–538) **PERSIAN DOMINATION OF PALESTINE** (539–333)	**1 C.E.** Jesus (5 B.C.E.–30 C.E.) Paul's Epistles (50–55) Jerusalem destroyed (70) Synoptic Gospels (70–85) John's Gospel (90–95)
500 B.C.E.		**100 C.E.** Bar Kokhba revolt crushed End of Jewish state (135)
400 B.C.E.	Ezra reasserts the Law	**200 C.E.**

What interests us about this axial period are the changes it engendered in Jewish religious consciousness just before and during Jesus' lifetime. One of the major accomplishments of the period was a radical shift in the Jewish conception of history and the emergence of an intense and pervasive expectation of "the end of the world." This eschatological mood dominated Jesus' lifetime and affected how people heard his message. Let us see how it came about.

FROM HISTORY TO THE LAW

The Jewish prophets who flourished before the Babylonian Exile (586–538 B.C.E.) had no clear doctrine of an end of time and certainly no hope that God would one day destroy the world. Rather, the uniqueness of the prophets' message lay in their insistence that *history* was the arena of God's salvation of Israel.[3]

Unlike many other religions, which located the manifestations of the divine in the mythical dawn of time or in the eternal cycles of nature, pre-exilic Judaism proclaimed that the realm of *human action* was the place where God revealed himself. Yahweh was a God of history who intervened on Israel's behalf through such concrete events as the Exodus, the conquest of Palestine, and the establishment of the Davidic kingdom. Israel's God was a political activist who established her rulers, toppled her enemies, and passed historical judgment on her good and bad actions. Long before Christians discovered Marx, the prophets preached a form of "liberation theology": faith as cooperation with God's intention to effect worldly justice and peace for mankind. Prophetism was an act of faith in the God of history.

Before the exile the Jews saw time as neither linear nor cyclical, neither teleological nor eschatological, but as *epiphantic,* the medium of God's revelation to and salvific presence with Israel. This faith that God was directing history (along with the later belief, derived from it, that he had created the world) prevented traditional Judaism from looking ahead to an apocalyptic end of history followed by a suprahistorical "new heaven and new earth." The classical prophets of the seventh and eighth centuries B.C.E. were neither pessimistic about history's course nor optimistic about transcending it, for theirs was a historical rather than an otherworldly hope. When Israel was beset by political and social sufferings, the prophets promised salvation not as a second life in the hereafter but as a temporal restoration of the nation under a future Davidic king. Salvation was not an escape *from* time through resurrection of the body or immortality of the soul, but a triumph *within* time in the form of peaceful social existence in a theocratic state.

But all that changed with conquest of the kingdom of Judah by Nebuchadnezzar in 586 B.C.E. and the subsequent exile in Babylon. When the Jewish people began returning to Palestine in 538 B.C.E. after a half century in captivity, they were allowed only limited political autonomy under Persian rule and, later, under Greek and Syrian domination. Deprived of her Davidic leaders and major prophets, Israel began to find her spiritual anchorage less in Yahweh's direction of her national history than in the revealed words of Scripture. But now the Bible was read not so much as an account of the *gesta dei,* God's interventions in Israel's past as a promise of further epiphanies to come. Rather, the emphasis was on the Law, which they thought had been given by God in the past and remained ever valid for the present, seemingly without the need of God's further interventions in time. This shift from history to hermeneutics, from faith in God's direction of history to scrupulous interpretation of legal codes, provided Israel with a tidier, if less dramatic, world.

For the next three and a half centuries Israel was a kingless theocracy governed by a timeless Law. Around 400 B.C.E., under the high priest Ezra ("a scribe skilled in the law of Moses," Ezra 7:6),[4] the five books of the Pentateuch, called the Torah, or Law, were edited in their final form and became the religious and legal constitution of the Jewish people.[5] Henceforth the guides of Israel would no longer be the prophets, who in pre-exilic times had called for fidelity to God's workings in history, and certainly not the Davidic kings, who were no more. Rather, her political and religious leaders would be the priests of the rebuilt Temple, the rabbis of the local synagogues, and in particular the scribes, the theological lawyers who delivered the casuistic and devotional embellishments on the Law that would eventually evolve into the Talmud.[6]

The Law, the index of Israel's fidelity to the Lord, became a complicated body of codes.[7] It was divided into the Written Law, or Torah
(torah she-biktab), which God had delivered to Moses—that is, the Ten
Commandments plus the myriad supplementary prescriptions found
throughout the Pentateuch—and the Oral Law, or "Sayings of the
Fathers," the hundreds of legal principles and devotional or ethical
interpretations that were generated by the scribes from the fourth
century B.C.E. onward as guiding rules for faithful Jews and that
eventually became codified as the Mishnah and the Gemara.

The purpose of the casuistic Oral Law was, as the scribes put it, to
"build a fence around the Torah,"[8] a bulwark of detailed codes which,
if properly observed, would guarantee that the scrupulous believer
could not have violated the Written Law. (Wearing a false tooth, for
example, might constitute carrying a heavy burden and thus violate the
commandment of Sabbath rest, whereas pulling a mule from a pit
might not.[9]) This elaborate "second Pentateuch," combined with the
already elaborate set of forty-one laws found in the Covenant Code
(Exodus 20:23–23:33), plus the seventy-eight laws of the Deutero-
nomic Code (Deuteronomy, chapters 12–26), and the strict regulation
of sex, feasts, and sacrifices in the Holiness Code (Leviticus, chapters
17–26), often gave the impression of a jurisprudential nightmare. And
the laws kept growing until, according to one tradition: "Six hundred
and thirteen commandments were communicated to Moses, three hundred and sixty-five prohibitions, corresponding to the number of days
in the solar year, and two hundred and forty-eight positive precepts,
corresponding to the number of the members of man's body"[10]—these
hundreds of statutes at the service of defining the ten rather simple
commandments revealed to Israel through Moses.

Moreover, by the time of Jesus Judaism was divided by sectarian
debates over the question of which Law was to be observed. The
conservative and aristocratic Sadducees were rigid literalists who observed only the ancient Written Law, whereas the fervent lay sect of
the Pharisees, who were aligned with the scribes, were considered
"liberals" because they not only followed the ancient Torah but also
observed and developed the more recent Oral Law with its scrupulous
attention to everyday life. The Pharisees of Jesus' day, who were
greatly respected by the ordinary people, were in turn divided into the

strict constructionists of the Shammai school and the more flexible adherents of the Hillel school. When we read in Mark's Gospel that the Pharisees approached Jesus with a question about the grounds for a legal divorce (10:1–12), we are witnessing an effort to get him to take a side in the debate between these two Pharisaic sects. The attempt, in fact, was unsuccessful, and as we shall see, much of the radical newness of Jesus' message consisted in his proclamation of a nonlegalistic relation to God.

In short, the period during and after the exile witnessed a major transformation in consciousness within Israel: a shift from history to hermeneutics, from a prophetic engagement with political events to a clerical exegesis of the Law. A historical contrast suggests itself here. The classical Greeks, in their confrontations with the Persian Empire from the battle of Marathon in 490 B.C.E. through the conquests of Alexander 150 years later, were led in a sense from religion to history, from mythical scripture (in their case, Homer) to political action. At roughly the same time Israel, reeling from her defeat by Babylon and humbled by her subjection to Persia, retreated from history to Scripture, from political action to religious legalism. As these two very different cultures collided with the empires of the Middle East, their paths took opposite directions. Greece, feeling its historical power, pushed beyond itself and became the worldwide cultural force of Hellenism. Israel, feeling its political impotence, turned within and became, for the first time, an institutionalized "religion."

THE BIRTH OF ESCHATOLOGY

Along with this post-exilic emphasis on the Law there went a transformation in the Jewish conception of Yahweh and his relation to his chosen people. Before the captivity in Babylon, Israel envisioned God's salvation as a future restoration of the glorious past under a new Davidic king. But after the exile, when Yahweh seemed to have fled to the higher heavens, leaving priests and scribes in his wake, the earlier hope for this-worldly theocratic restoration began to fade. Yahweh came to be seen less as the national deity who had intervened and would intervene again in Israel's political history, and more as an Oriental despot who ruled the entire universe, including the Gentile nations, from the distant and impersonal heights of metaphysical tran-scendence. From those heavens he governed the world no longer by direct historical intervention as in the past, but by the ministrations of angelic mediators who, like the eternal Law, mediated his presence to mankind.

Israel's retreat from history took a dramatic step in the second century B.C.E. with the emergence of the radically new idea of *eschatology,* the doctrine of the end of the world. At the beginning of the Maccabean revolt, when Israel's fate seemed to be at its lowest point, pious Jews began to hope not for a new divine intervention *within* history but for a catastrophic *end* to history, when God would stop the trajectory of Israel's decline by destroying this sinful world and creating a new, supratemporal realm where the just would find their eternal reward.[11]

This eschatology, or doctrine of the end of time, found literary expression in the imaginative and very popular genre of *apocalypse,* in which pseudonymous authors spun out fanciful predictions of the coming end of the world and dramatic descriptions of the aftermath. Apocalyptic eschatology spelled the end of the prophets' hope for a future revival of the past and replaced it with mythical hopes for a cosmic cataclysm followed by the eternal *olam ha-ba,* the "new age to come." If prophetism had been an act of faith in God's workings in history, apocalypticism was an act of despair.[12]

This recasting of Yahweh as apocalyptic destroyer was strongly influenced by the Zoroastrian religion that the Israelites had encoun-tered during the Babylonian Exile. Zoroaster (ca. 630–550 B.C.E.) had taught that the world was the scene of a dramatic cosmic struggle between the forces of Good and Evil, led by the gods Ormazd and Ahriman. But this conflict was not to continue forever because, accord-ing to Zoroastrianism, history was not endless but finite and in fact dualistic, divided between the present age of darkness and the coming age of light. Time was devolving through four (or in some accounts seven) progressively worsening periods toward an eschatological cata-clysm when Good would finally annihilate Evil and the just would receive their otherworldly reward in an age of eternal bliss. Zoroastri-anism's profound pessimism about present history was thus answered by its eschatological optimism about a future eternity.

As Israel's political fortunes faded and as such Zoroastrian ideas as these took hold, Judaism shifted the focus of its religious hopes from the arena of the national and historical to that of the eschatological and cosmic, from political salvation in some future time to preternatural survival in an afterlife. This radical change can be seen in late Judaism's adoption of notions like the fall of Adam from paradisal grace at the beginning of time, the workings of Satan and other demons in the present age, and the Last Judgment and the resurrection at the end of history—all of which Christianity was to take over and turn into dogmas. But the clearest sign of this absorption of Persian ideas can be found in the eschatological visions of history that surfaced in apocalyptic literature during the two centuries before Jesus began to preach.

One such apocalyptic work was the Book of Daniel, composed around 165 B.C.E. during the Maccabean revolt against the oppressive Seleucid dynasty. The tyrannical King Antiochus IV, who ruled Palestine (175–163 B.C.E.) from Syria, had undertaken to force Hellenistic religion and culture on his Jewish subjects. He deposed the legitimate high priest, forbad ritual sacrifice and circumcision, plundered the Temple treasury, and, most shocking of all, set up the "Abomination of Desolation" (Daniel 11:31), an altar to Olympian Zeus, within the Temple precinct.

The Book of Daniel was written by an anonymous author in the second century B.C.E.; but in a way typical of apocalyptic works, the book purported to have been composed some four centuries earlier by a prophet named Daniel, and pretended to predict the catastrophic events that in fact were happening in the author's own lifetime. The work interpreted these events as "eschatological woes," a time of sufferings and troubles "such as never has been since there was a nation" (12:1). According to God's hidden plan, these woes marked the final stage before the destruction of the old and godless world and the final triumph of divine justice.

The Book of Daniel envisaged history as rushing downhill toward its eschatological end, which the author was convinced would come in his own lifetime. For example, the book told of a dream that the sixth-century Babylonian king Nebuchadnezzar supposedly had and that the prophet Daniel interpreted for him in terms of the succession of kingdoms (2:31–43). In the dream history was depicted as a giant statue with the head made of gold (representing the kingdom of Babylon), the chest and arms of silver (the kingdom of the Medes), the belly and thighs of bronze (the kingdom of Persia), the legs of iron (the empire of Alexander), and the feet made partly of iron and partly of clay (the divided kingdom of the Seleucids in Syria and the Ptolemies in Egypt). In the dream

> [a stone] smote the image on its feet of iron and clay, and broke them in pieces; then the iron, the clay, the bronze, the silver, and the gold, all together were broken in pieces, and became like the chaff of the summer threshing floors. (2:34–35)

The prophet Daniel predicted that when the Seleucid kingdom crumbled—as the author of the book believed was happening in his own day—the end of time would come. But before that, Israel had to pass through a time of eschatological woes when the final godless kingdom would "devour the whole earth, trample it down and break it to pieces" (7:23). At the climax of these sufferings a Great Beast— in this case the Seleucid king Antiochus IV—was to appear and "speak words against the Most High and wear out his saints" (7:25).[13]

According to Daniel the duration of these eschatological woes was limited, and at the end of this period God himself would arrive as the cosmic judge to annihilate the kingdom of the beast and to "set up a kingdom which shall never be destroyed" (2:44). The apocalyptic writer describes his vision of the imminent eschaton:

> As I looked, thrones were placed, and one that was ancient of days took his seat. . . . The court sat in judgment and the books were opened. . . . And as I looked, the beast was slain, and its body destroyed and given over to be burned with fire. (7:9–11)

At the climax of this apocalyptic drama a mysterious figure, "one like a man," appears from the heavens. This figure assumes the role of God's viceregent and ushers in the new and eternal kingdom.

> And behold, with the clouds of heaven there came one like a man, and he came to the Ancient of Days and was presented before him.

And to him was given dominion and glory and kingdom, so that
all peoples, nations and languages should serve him. His dominion
is an everlasting dominion, which shall not be destroyed. (7:13–14)

This strange eschatological figure, who came to be called "the Son
of Man," has been the subject of much scholarly debate.[14] One plausible hypothesis explains him as a collective symbol of the Jewish people
themselves, represented in the form of an *angel* ("one *like* a man")
whom God had appointed as Israel's protector and advocate in God's
sight. However, later (probably in the first century B.C.E.) this collective symbol of Israel became concretized as a specific individual savior
who was expected to descend from heaven at the end of time. Apocalyptic writers took the phrase from the Book of Daniel ("one *like* a
man") and turned it into an eschatological title: "the Son of Man." For
example, the First (Ethiopic) Book of Enoch 46 (ca. 100 B.C.E.?)
interprets this savior as having existed from all eternity, hidden in
God's presence since before the creation. The apocalyptic visionary,
swept up to heaven and to the beginning of everything, writes:

At that hour, that Son of Man was given a name in the presence of
the Lord of the Spirits, the Before-Time, even before the creation
of the sun and the moon, before the creation of the stars, he was
given a name in the presence of the Lord of the Spirits. . . . He is
the light of the gentiles and he will become the hope of those who
are sick in their hearts. . . . He became the Chosen One; he was
concealed in the presence of the Lord of the Spirits prior to the
creation of the world, and for eternity. And he has revealed the
wisdom of the Lord of the Spirits to the righteous and the holy ones.
(48:2–7a)

Made manifest only at the end of time, this Son of Man would save
God's chosen people, pass judgment on the Gentile kingdoms, and
preside over the eschatological banquet in the new world.

Moreover, along with these otherworldly hopes there also arose, for
the first time in Judaism, the expectation of a resurrection of the dead
and personal survival in an afterlife.[15] Earlier predictions of "resurrection" in the writings of the prophets had been only figurative and

metaphoric. For example, in the preapocalyptic Book of Ezechiel, which dates from the time of the exile, God promises Israel, "I will open your graves and raise you from them" (37:12). But this promised "resurrection" was merely a symbol of Israel's eventual return from the Babylonian Exile to the very concrete and this-worldly land of Palestine, as the continuation of the passage shows: "You shall live, and I will place you in your own land" (37:14). However, in the apocalyptic Book of Daniel resurrection was promised not as a metaphor for future political restoration but quite literally as the otherworldly reward of the just at the end of time:

> And many of those who sleep in the dust of the earth shall awake, some to everlasting life, and some to shame and everlasting contempt. (Daniel 12:2)[16]

As we shall see, the elements of this stock apocalyptic scenario— the predicted period of eschatological woes, the cosmic collapse, the coming of the Son of Man, the divine judgment and reward—were known to Jesus. But strictly speaking, Jesus was not an apocalyptist at all. He was very restrained in his appeal to apocalyptic imagery and, when he used it, always adapted it to his very different message.

THE COMING SAVIOR

The historical event that most determined Judaism in the two centuries before Jesus was the successful Maccabean revolt (167–142 B.C.E.) against Syrian domination of Palestine. Outraged by the sacrileges of King Antiochus IV, the brothers Judas, Jonathan, and Simon Maccabee each in turn led the struggle against Seleucid tyranny, until Simon finally won freedom for Palestine. The result was a brief parenthesis of Jewish self-rule that lasted until the Roman conquest of the land in 63 B.C.E. What is more, the establishment of the new kingdom led to a radical shift in the Jewish concept of the promised Davidic messiah.

The triumph of the Maccabees was their undoing. While all Jews were happy to be a free people again, many of the more pious resented the fact that the new Hasmonean-Maccabean dynasty was not descended from King David. On religious grounds, therefore, this new regime could not be the kingdom promised by the prophets, and no Maccabee could be the true messiah. Not only that, but many found it intolerable that both Jonathan and Simon Maccabee had dared to make themselves high priests without being descended from the proper sacerdotal line of the ancient high priest Zadok (I Kings 1:26, II Samuel 8:17), whose family had held the office since the tenth century.[17] On two counts, therefore, Jonathan and Simon Maccabee were at fault. Neither Davidic nor Zadokite by descent, they seemed to be power-hungry interlopers in both the political and religious realms.

Opposition to the Maccabees ran high among their fellow Jews, and in particular the question of the proper bloodline of the high priesthood became the flashpoint of a religious revolt against the dynasty. One of the most important of the protesting groups was the devout lay sect of the Pharisees (Hebrew *perushim*, Aramaic *perishayya*, "Separated Ones"), who were later to figure so prominently in Jesus' ministry. They broke with the Hasmonean-Maccabean regime in 134 B.C.E. and proclaimed their hope for an ideal, non-Hasmonean king. This new messiah not only would be descended from David and therefore anointed as God's deputy but also—here was the radical shift—would have two new characteristics. First, he would be designated ruler of the *entire* world and not just of Israel; and second, he would arrive at the *imminent end of the world.* The messiah whom the Pharisees proclaimed was to be no longer a national king but a universal emperor, no longer a historical figure but an apocalyptic phenomenon.[18]

The absolute novelty of this idea of an eschatological emperor-messiah can be seen by contrasting it with earlier, more modest conceptions. Before the Babylonian Exile the term "messiah" ("anointed one") had none of the supernatural connotations that later generations of Jews and Christians would give it. Originally the word designated any Davidic king before the exile. He was a political and military leader, a man who lived in the flesh and was as mortal as any other human being. But Jews also believed that the king was the chosen agent of God's will on earth, and as a sign of that election he was anointed with oil either by a prophet or by a priest (I Samuel 10:1, 16:13; I Kings 1:39). When the ruler was anointed (and so became "messiah"), he was constituted the adopted "Son of God." We see this, for example, in Psalm 2:7, where Yahweh says to the king on coronation day, "You are my son, today I have begotten you." The title "Son of God" did not indicate that the king was ontologically divine but only that he was God's special agent on earth. Even during the difficult years surrounding the Babylonian Exile, when prophets projected an ideal future messiah-king and named him "Wonderful Counselor, Almighty God, Everlasting Father, Prince of Peace" (Isaiah 9:6), the reference was to a mortal human being, the national political leader in his unique theocratic role as God's worldly deputy.

The messiah of the Pharisees, for all his uniqueness as a universal and eschatological ruler, did in fact absorb and continue some of the national-historical traits of the traditional messiah. In the popular imagination the traditional national king now tended to become an idealized, even mythologized, ruler who, while certainly Davidic in descent, would be not just one more king in that line but the final and universal sovereign who would bring about God's definitive reign throughout the entire world. But conversely, for all these "transcendent" qualities, this eschatological world-emperor was still seen as a human and historical king and not as a supernatural being who would descend from heaven. In other words, as much as the new savior's *eschatological* features drew on the otherworldly spirit of apocalypse, his specifically *messianic* role anchored him squarely in the earthly order. The point is that his messiahship now had both universal political scope (since he would have dominion over all nations, not just Israel) and definitive religious significance (since he would appear at the end of time).

The Pharisees' new concept of the messiah was only one of the changes in Judaism that resulted from religious opposition to the Hasmonean-Maccabean dynasty. Another came from a group that was spiritually even more radical and in fact the first sect to break with the regime: the Essenes. Led by a charismatic Zadokite priest of Jerusalem who is known to us only as the Righteous Teacher, the Essenes were implacably set against the Hasmoneans' usurpation of the high priesthood. Around 142 B.C.E. they made a clean break with the Temple priesthood and trekked into the wilderness to found the monastic community of Qumran. This was the settlement whose eschatological doctrines and life-style came to light only in 1947 with the discovery of the Dead Sea Scrolls.[19]

Like the Pharisees, the Essenes were eschatologists, but rooted as they were in a sacerdotal tradition, they looked forward to a priestly rather than a political messiah. They maintained that their leader, the Righteous Teacher, was not the awaited messiah-priest but only a living sign that the world had entered upon its last days. They expressed their belief in the imminence of the eschaton not only by their cultic communism and (for some members) religious celibacy but also by the eschatological meal of bread and wine that they celebrated, almost like a pre-Christian Eucharist, in anticipation of the coming messianic banquet.

The death of the Righteous Teacher around 115 B.C.E. fed the Qumran community's hope for the end of the world and the appearance of a priestly savior who would be anointed by God. This hope was both increased and transformed around 110 B.C.E. when large numbers of Pharisees, who were fleeing persecution by the Hasmoneans, flocked to the desert community and brought with them their expectation of a cosmic *political* messiah. As a result, in the decades before Jesus the Qumran community came to expect *two* eschatological messiahs, one a high priest descended from Aaron and the other a world-emperor descended from David. Scriptural grounds for this dual messiahship were educed from an obscure passage in the prophet Zechariah which mentioned "two anointed ones who stand by the Lord of the whole earth" (4:14).

As if this syncretistic doctrine of a messiah-priest and a messiah-emperor were not enough, yet another expectation swept through Judaism at this time: the hope for an *eschatological prophet* who would appear shortly before the end of the world.[20] This popular idea grew up independent of Davidic messianism and took two distinct forms.

On the one hand there was the expectation of a nonnationalistic, nonmilitaristic messianic "prophet like Moses" who had been promised in the book of Deuteronomy. There Moses told the Israelites of a revelation he had had:

> The Lord said to me:
> "... I will raise up for them a prophet like you from among their brethren, and I will put my words in his mouth, and he shall speak to them all that I command him." (18:15)

On the other hand many Jews expected the return of the prophet Elijah, who had been swept up to heaven in a chariot eight centuries earlier (II Kings 2:11–12) and who, it was believed, would reappear toward the end of time to prepare Israel for God's judgment. A verse of the prophet Malachi, adapted to correspond to this hope, was often cited:

> Behold, I will send you Elijah the prophet before the great and terrible day of the Lord comes. And he will turn the hearts of fathers to their children and the hearts of children to their fathers, lest I come and smite the land with a curse. (4:5 = 3:23)

In short, the years before Jesus' birth witnessed an explosion of apocalyptic hopes for an imminent end of the world, and the popular religious imagination tended to multiply eschatological figures. (1) The traditional hope for a *national king* of the Davidic line who would restore the kingdom of Israel rubbed shoulders with (2) the new expectation of a *supranational Davidic savior*. But the latter in turn could be either political or sacerdotal, an imperial theocrat or a supreme high priest—or both ruling together. And before his coming there might arrive (3) a final, or *eschatological, prophet*—whether a Moses-like figure who would give a new Law or Elijah redivivus, who would prepare Israel for God's coming. Moreover, all of these figures tended to take on one another's traits and often to blur into one another in a complex spectrum of awaited saviors.

It was an apocalyptist's dream, frequently confusing but burning with hope and with heightened expectation that something momentous was soon to happen. What is clear is this: If a sensitive and deeply religious Jewish man felt called to be a reformer of Israel, a prophet who would galvanize his people with hope that God was coming soon to save his chosen faithful, and if *per impossible* he could have picked the place and time of his birth so as to facilitate his mission, he could hardly have chosen a better place than Palestine around the year 3755 of the Jewish calendar.

2

THE MAKING OF
A PROPHET

THE SCENE UNFOLDED near the mouth of the Jordan River late one afternoon two millennia ago. According to today's calendar the year was 28 or 29 C.E.; according to Jewish reckoning, it was the 3788th year since the creation of the world.[21]

The place is an inhospitable wilderness, its barrenness relieved only by the muddy river, winding its way south to the Dead Sea. A crowd of men and women, simple people, are listening intently to a strange figure, wiry and ascetic, dressed in rough animal skins and rumored to subsist on nothing but the wild honey and locusts he finds in the desert. His name is John, and he is a pious Hasidic Jew preaching the impending judgment of God.[22] He calls for conversion, and his message is fraught with urgency:

> Even now the axe is laid to the root of the trees. Every tree therefore
> that does not bear good fruit is cut down and thrown into the fire.
> (Matthew 3:10)

He practices a baptism of repentance for sin, as do the Essenes of nearby Qumran, with whom he may once have been associated. But whereas the Essenes invite their disciples to carry out their own ablutions, John himself performs the ritual washing on his followers and so earns the title "the Baptizer." His impact is tremendous. The Gospel says that multitudes went out into the desert to hear John's message and receive his baptism.

> And the people were in expectation, and all men questioned in their hearts concerning John, whether he might be the messiah. (Luke 3:15)

Imagine a young man, just over thirty years of age, who is walking by the river that afternoon. He was baptized by John some time before and is now a member of his inner circle. Perhaps he is even one of the assistants who help the Baptizer in his ritual. John notices him and points him out to two of his disciples, and these disciples, shyly but with deep interest, proceed to follow the young man at a distance.

> Jesus turned and saw them following, and he said to them, "What do you seek?" They said to him, "Rabbi, where do you dwell?" He said to them, "Come and see." They came and stayed with him that day, for it was about the tenth hour. (John 1:38–39)

"Rabbi, where do you dwell?"[23] It is impossible to know if this is exactly what happened that afternoon when the "Jesus-movement" is supposed to have been born out of that question. The scene sketched above is a composite, drawn from the four Gospels, each of which had a theological rather than a historical point to make about Jesus and John the Baptist. But historical or not, the story about the encounter of Jesus and his first disciples is true in its own way, for it contains *in nuce* the entire Christian experience: a mood of expectation, an earnest seeking, an exchange of questions to which no real answers are given, only the invitation to "come and see," indeed to see not who Jesus *is* so much as where and how he *dwells*.

The purpose of this chapter is not to produce a psychobiography of Jesus. The evidence for that is lacking. Rather, I am attempting, in part by means of an imaginative reconstruction, to relate the core of historical facts that contemporary scholars have managed to establish about the life of Jesus and, in what immediately follows, about his relation to John the Baptist. Many years after Jesus died, his Christian followers would attempt to resolve the rivalry between their sect and John's by interpreting the Baptist as a forerunner of Jesus. Indeed, Luke in his Gospel devised a family relation between the two and arranged their conceptions in such a way that even before they were born, John was a precursor of Jesus. Luke went so far as to have the prenatal Baptist "leap in the womb" at the presence of the unborn Jesus when their pregnant mothers met (1:36 and 44).

But that legend, like the inspiring but unhistorical story about the miraculous virginal conception of Jesus, is a theological interpretation created some decades after the death of Jesus to express Christianity's faith in his special status. In fact we know next to nothing about either John or Jesus before their meeting on the banks of the Jordan. But we can establish what they were about from then on, that is, in the scarce two years that both of them had left to live.

Where, then, did Jesus dwell? This question goes to the essence of his prophetic mission: what he taught, how he lived, who he thought he was. But Jesus' ideas, life-style, and self-understanding did not emerge from his consciousness ready-made. He developed them, as any human being does, in interaction with his environment and his contemporaries. To begin with, his encounter with John the Baptist had an important, if often overlooked, influence on Jesus' religious thinking, and so before taking up questions about his message (what he taught), his manner (how he lived), and the man himself (who he claimed to be), we shall begin by asking about his meeting with John at the Jordan.

Some might object that the following sketch of that meeting delves further into Jesus' psychology than the evidence will support—and that is true; others may claim that it does not portray Jesus for what he really was: an omniscient God who only "submitted" to John's teachings and baptism to set an example of how others should act— but that is not true. Whether his meeting with the Baptist planted the seed of Jesus' vocation as a prophet or whether he had already conceived his mission privately and merely came forward publicly with his baptism in the Jordan, we cannot know. But the best evidence shows that the encounter with John was a spiritual awakening for Jesus. How, then, did it come about and what effect did it have?

Jesus most likely was born not in the southern town of Bethlehem but in Nazareth, a village in the northern province of Galilee, the first child of a carpenter named Joseph and his young wife, Miriam or Maria. When his father had him circumcised at the local synagogue, he named him after Moses' successor, Joshua, in Hebrew Yehoshua ("Yahweh helps"), which in those days was usually shortened to Yeshua or even to Yeshu, which is how he was popularly known. When he grew up he followed his father's woodworking trade, as no doubt his younger brothers, James, Judas, Simon, and Joses, also did (Mark 6:3).[24]

But as the fame of the Baptizer spread even to his obscure village, the young man Jesus, after his father had died, left Nazareth for the Jordan valley. There, like many others, he was profoundly gripped by John's grim message of doom and his call for repentance.[25] It was not enough, Jesus heard, to be a child of Abraham, a son of the Covenant sealed with circumcision. It did not suffice to obey the Law and honor Yahweh with one's lips. The heart had to change. When the respected Pharisees and Sadducees, the pillars of Judaism, came to the Jordan to hear what the Baptist was preaching, Jesus was struck by how John railed at them for their smugness:

> You brood of vipers! Who has warned you to flee from the wrath to come? Bear fruit that befits repentance, and do not presume to say to yourselves, "We have Abraham for our father." For I tell you that God is able from these stones to raise up children to Abraham! (Matthew 3:7–9)

Jesus was also impressed by the fact that John, unlike the apocalyptic preachers so popular in those days, preached no messiah, proclaimed no end of the world, and promised no future aeon of bliss. He appealed to no signs of the alleged cataclysm to come and made none of the fantastic predictions that were the stock in trade of the apocalyptic writers. His message was simple and bare: The judgment is coming *now*, not in some distant future, and rather than being played out on the stage of world history with cosmic inevitability, it cuts to the inner core of the individual and demands personal decision.

To be sure, John often preached in eschatological terms. He spoke, for example, of "one who is coming" (he may have meant the "Son of Man," although he kept the reference vague), and he warned of eschatological fire.[26] But it was an eschatology without apocalyptic trappings, an existential crisis of imminent, definitive judgment with none of the wildly dramatic stage props of the apocalyptic scenario. The fire he spoke of was not a cosmic conflagration but a flame that sears to the heart of a person, enlivening the humble and damning the unrepentant:

> I baptize you with water for repentance, but he who is coming after me is mightier than I, and I am not worthy even to carry his sandals. He will baptize you with the Holy Spirit and with fire. His winnowing fork is in his hand, and he will clear his threshing floor and gather his wheat into the granary, but the chaff he will burn with unquenchable fire. (Matthew 3:11–12)

It was the message of a prophet, not an apocalyptist, and like the ancient prophets, John called for radical acts of justice and charity as the fruit of faith and repentance. When the people asked him what they must do to turn to God, John demanded not prayer or rituals but deeds. "He who has two coats, let him share with him who has none, and he who has food, let him do likewise." To the tax collectors who came for baptism he commanded, "Collect no more than is appointed you." And to soldiers, "No intimidation! No extortion! And be content with your pay" (Luke 3:10–14).

Jesus, we may imagine, was pierced to the heart. He repented and was baptized.

To accept John's message and enter his community meant to break in some degree with the prevailing religious orthodoxy. In John's day Judaism, like Christianity today, was in profound crisis, and the Baptist deepened the sense of uncertainty. By his time the brief parenthesis of freedom brought by the Maccabees (142–63 B.C.E.) had long since been closed, and Palestine was once again subject to foreign domination, this time under the Romans. So too the ancient form of faith in Yahweh was gone. In place of the old hopes for renewal within history there now stood apocalyptic expectations of an end of the world; and instead of attentiveness to the prophets' call for justice there prevailed scrupulous observance of the Law. The two went hand in hand: Apocalypse promised Israel salvation at the cosmic level, and adherence to the Law guaranteed that she would make it through the coming judgment unscathed.

All of this John called into question. First, the eschatological judgment he preached was directed against Israel, not her enemies. Whereas the apocalyptic writers foretold destruction of the Gentiles and vindication of the chosen people, John turned the knife against the very members of God's Covenant: the eschaton was as threatening to Jews as to pagans. Second, John declared that ritual observance and cultic sacrifice were no guarantee against the final judgment. God's fire burned through such externals; it demanded *metanoia*, "repentance" in the sense of a complete change in the way one lived. On both scores —hope for apocalyptic triumph and confidence in the Law—John cut the ground from under his own people.

What he did, in turn, was to deepen the crisis within Judaism. Instead of spinning out hopes for salvation in a new age, he pressed home the immediacy of God's judgment and the individual's responsibility to undergo conversion. And instead of encouraging the complacency of religious observance, he urged radical attention to the needs of one's neighbor. By this dual focus on the existential and the ethical, John demystified both eschatology and the Law and radically reinterpreted their meaning. Eschatology, when stripped of apocalyptic myths about Yahweh's defeat of the Gentiles, was about the personal immediacy of his judgment. And the Law, when freed from petty casuistry, was about being just in God's eyes by exercising concern for one's fellow man.

John's call to personal responsibility captured the religious core of eschatology by freeing Yahweh from the role of cosmic avenger of Israel and making him the Lord of those who repent. Likewise his insistence on inner conversion recovered the heart of the Law by liberating it from narrow and burdensome legalism. John's message, in short, reasserted the living kernel of Jewish faith—doing God's will by being just and merciful—and freed it from the elaborate but dead husks in which it was trapped.

And Jesus followed in John's footsteps. It is probable that when he left John's inner circle, Jesus stayed in the south of Palestine for a period of time and continued to preach and baptize in imitation of his mentor. After his baptism beyond the Jordan, the Fourth Gospel says, "Jesus and his disciples went into the land of Judea; there he remained with them and baptized" (3:22). For a while, then, it seems there were at least two prophetic baptizers in the area.

But there was a different tone to Jesus' message, and in the Fourth Gospel we read that "Jesus was making and baptizing more disciples than John" (4:1). Nonetheless, the preaching of Jesus, whatever its difference from John's, continued some of the major themes of the Baptist: the reduction of apocalypse to its existential core, the condemnation of those who locked man's relation to God inside the narrow confines of the Law, and the call for justice and charity as the enactment of fidelity to God. In fact, Jesus began to catch the attention of the ever-wary Pharisees, who had already disapproved of John's antiestablishment preaching. Prudently Jesus decided, as the Gospel says, to leave for his native Galilee. Most likely only after the Baptist's death did Jesus begin his own (and very brief) mission independent of John's.

Being a prophet in those days was dangerous business, and both John and Jesus were soon to pay the price. Besides the disapproving Pharisees and Sadducees, there were two political powers in the country, both within a few miles of the Jordan, who watched the movements of these eschatological eccentrics with considerable disapproval.

In the south, at Jerusalem, was the notoriously stern and arrogant Roman perfect Pontius Pilate, who had arrived in Palestine in the Roman year 779 (26 C.E.), just before John began his mission. Today he would probably, and correctly, be called an anti-Semite. His main jobs were to collect taxes and keep the public order as he put in his time in the provinces, awaiting a better assignment; but from the moment he arrived in the country he seemed never to miss a chance to offend pious Jews and in more than one instance to threaten and even murder them. Apocalyptic preachers, especially if they developed messianic delusions, were a threat to the empire and were better silenced. Jesus had no such pretensions, but when he met Pilate two years later, that would make no difference.

Pilate governed most of Palestine as a Roman province, but from ·the northern town of Tiberias on Lake Galilee Herod Antipas, a petty

Hasmonean prince and Roman vassal, controlled much of what was left, including Galilee and the trans-Jordan area where John often preached. Within a short while—either because he feared John's large following or because he was insulted by the prophet's criticism of his messy divorce and remarriage—Herod would have the Baptist imprisoned in the fortress of Machaerus east of the Dead Sea and soon thereafter murdered.

Luke's Gospel (23:1–25) says that when Jesus went on trial at the end of his brief career, both these rulers had the occasion to ask him who he was and where he dwelled. Like the two disciples who met Jesus late one afternoon at the Jordan, Pilate and Herod also got no answers, not even an invitation to "come and see." Herod laughed at him. The other one had him killed.[27]

3

THE KINGDOM
OF GOD

AFTER JOHN WAS IMPRISONED, Jesus came north to the towns around Lake Galilee to start his own mission, and his message exploded on the scene with a sense of overwhelming urgency: The eschatological future had already begun!

> The time is fulfilled,
> God's reign is at hand!
> Change your ways! (Mark 1:15)

Jesus' preaching was as riveting as John's, but different in tone and substance. Whereas John had emphasized the woes of impending judgment, Jesus preached the joy of God's immediate and liberating presence. A dirge had given way to a lyric.

The contrasting life-styles of the two prophets betrayed their very different messages, and the difference was not lost on the people. John scratched in the desert for locusts in order to remind his followers how bad things were and how few would be saved. But Jesus rarely passed up a good meal and a flask of wine, regardless of the company, as if to say that the eschatological banquet was now being served and everyone, including sinners, was invited. His reputation began to suffer because, in spreading the good news to all, he kept company even with prostitutes and tax collectors (Mark 2:16). No doubt some wags enjoyed playing one prophet off against the other—the lyrical Jesus against the railing Baptist—so as not to have to listen to either one. Jesus shot back at them:

> To what shall I compare this generation? It is like children sitting in the market places and calling to their playmates [and mimicking the two prophets],
> > "When we piped, you wouldn't dance,
> > When we wailed, you wouldn't mourn."
> For John came neither eating nor drinking, and they say, "He's possessed." I came eating and drinking, and they say, "Behold, a glutton and a drunkard, a friend of tax collectors and sinners." But wisdom is justified by her deeds. (Matthew 11:16–19)

Yet the generation was right about one thing: From John to Jesus the tune had indeed changed, in fact as much as it had changed earlier from the Jerusalem of the Pharisees and Sadducees to the Jordan of John the Baptist. In all three cases—the orthodoxy of the Jerusalem establishment, the protestantism of the Judean desert, and the Good News preached in Galilee—it was a question of invitation and response, of what was promised and what was demanded. The choices were clear. The reigning orthodoxy held out the promise of a future apocalyptic triumph in return for strict observance of the Law: the hard bread of obedience in this life, but an eschatological victory in the near future. The Baptist, on the other hand, preached a threatening judge who offered to save those who repented and changed: some existential anguish at first, but then the conviction that one was justified in God's sight. But Jesus proclaimed a loving Father who was *already arriving among his people,* bringing peace and freedom and joy. One simply had to let him in, for the kingdom of God had *begun.*

When we ask what Jesus' message offered and what it demanded— the invitation and the response—we find that Jesus took two important steps beyond his mentor. First, with regard to the offer, John the

Baptist had "existentialized" eschatology: He had demythologized the future apocalyptic catastrophe and proclaimed it to be God's present judgment on the individual. Jesus, however, went a step further and "personalized" John's existential eschatology: He interpreted it not as the harsh judgment of a terrifying God but as the intimate presence of a loving Father. Second, with regard to the demand, John had delegalized the Law by making it a matter of sincere piety and justice. But Jesus went further and relativized the Law by referring it to God as its beneficent author and to men and women as its immediate object.

To put it succinctly, in Jesus' message the offer was the presence of the Father, and the required response was mercy toward one's neighbor. These phrases may sound like tired slogans, and perhaps they are. But they contain the revolution that Jesus unleashed within Judaism: a radically personal eschatology that was fulfilled in a new interpersonal ethic.[28]

INVITATION:
THE FATHER'S PRESENCE

The heart of Jesus' message is summarized in the strikingly simple name with which he addressed the divine: "Abba," the Aramaic word for "papa" (Mark 14:36). This familial usage, which underlies all Jesus' references to "the Father," was a shock to the then current idea of God.[29] Late Judaism tended to see Yahweh as a distant and almost impersonal Sovereign whose presence to mankind required the mediation of angels, the Law, and the complexities of religious ritual. But with the simple and intimate word "Abba," Jesus signaled that God was immediately and intimately present, not as a harsh judge but as a loving and generous father. His presence was a pure and unearned gift, and one could relate to him without fear. "Be not afraid," Jesus told his followers. "Do not be anxious about your life," "Do not worry."

> Look at the birds of the air: they neither sow nor reap nor gather into barns, and yet your heavenly Father feeds them. Are you not of more value than they? (Matthew 6:25–30)

Nor did one have to earn this Father's favor or bargain for his grace by scrupulously observing the minutiae of the Law. One simply had to call on him.

> Ask and it will be given to you. . . . What man of you, if his son asks him for bread, will give him a stone? Or if he asks for a fish, will give him a serpent? If you, evil as you are, know how to give good things to your children, how much more will your Father who is in heaven give good things to those who ask him. (Matthew 7:7, 9–11)
>
> When you pray, say "Abba . . ." (Luke 11:2)

This immediate presence of God as a loving Father is what Jesus meant by the "kingdom."[30] The notion of the kingdom of God (or in Matthew's Gospel, the kingdom "of heaven") simply spells out Jesus' experience of the Father's loving presence that is captured in the word "Abba." As Jesus preached it, the kingdom of God had nothing to do with the fanciful geopolitics of the apocalyptists and messianists —a kingdom up above or up ahead—or with the juridical, hierarchical Church that Roman Catholics used to find in the phrase. Nor did the term primarily connote territory, spiritual or otherwise. Rather, it meant God's act of reigning, and this meant—here lay the revolutionary force of Jesus' message—that God, as God, had *identified himself without remainder with his people.* The reign of God meant the *incarnation* of God.[31]

This entirely human orientation of the Father—the loving, incarnate presence of a heretofore distant Sovereign—marked the radical newness of Jesus' message of God's reign. The kingdom was not something separate from God, like a spiritual welfare state that a benign heavenly monarch might set up for his faithful subjects. Nor was it any form of religion. The kingdom of God was the Father himself given over to his people. It was a new order of things in which God threw in his lot irrevocably with human beings and chose relatedness to them as the only definition of himself. From now on, God was one with mankind.

This utterly new doctrine is what gave revolutionary power to the "Beatitudes" that Jesus preached.[32] The kingdom he proclaimed—

God's presence among men and women—meant that from now on God's exercise of power was *entirely on behalf of mankind,* and especially the poor and needy. God's incarnation among them had already begun and would soon come to its fullness:

> Blessed are you poor,
>   for yours is the Kingdom of God.
> Blessed are you who hunger,
>   for you shall be satisfied.
> Blessed are you who weep,
>   for you shall laugh. (Luke 6:20–21)

The radicalness of Jesus' message consisted in its implied proclamation of the end of religion, taken as the bond between two separate and incommensurate entities called "God" and "man." That is, Jesus destroyed the notion of "God-in-himself" and put in its place the experience of "God-with-mankind." Henceforth, according to the prophet from Galilee, the Father was not to be found in a distant heaven but was entirely identified with the cause of men and women. Jesus' doctrine of the kingdom meant that God had become incarnate: He had poured himself out, had disappeared into mankind and could be found nowhere else but there. This incarnation was not a Hegelian "fall" of the divine into history, or Feuerbach's simplistic reduction of God to the human project of self-fulfillment. But neither did it mean the hypostatic union of two natures, the divine and the human, in a God-man called Jesus of Nazareth. The doctrine of the kingdom meant that henceforth and forever God was present only in and as one's neighbor. Jesus dissolved the fanciful speculations of apocalyptic eschatology into the call to justice and charity.

Jesus' message of the kingdom radically redefined the traditional notions of grace and salvation and made them mean nothing other than this event of God-with-man. Salvation was no longer to be understood as the forgiving of a debt or as the reward for being good. Nor was it a supernatural supplement added on to what human beings are, some kind of ontological elevation to a higher state. All such metaphysical doctrines are forms of religion, which Jesus brought to an end. His proclamation marked the death of religion and religion's God and heralded the beginning of the postreligious experience: the abdication of "God" in favor of his hidden presence among human beings. The Book of Revelation, written toward the end of the first century of Christianity, captured this idea dramatically and concretely, albeit apocalyptically, in a vision of the end of time.

> Then I saw a new heaven and a new earth, for the first heaven and the first earth had passed away, and the sea was no more. And I saw the holy city, new Jerusalem, coming down out of heaven from God, prepared as a bride adorned for her husband. And I heard a great voice from the throne saying:
> "Behold, the dwelling of God is with men and women. He will dwell with them, and they shall be his people, and God himself will be with them. He will wipe away every tear from their eyes, and death shall be no more, for the former things have passed away." (21:1–4)

RESPONSE: AN ETHICS OF MERCY

The morality Jesus prescribed followed from the kingdom he proclaimed. Unlike Greek philosophy, Jesus' ethical teachings were not based on a metaphysical concept of human nature and were not ordered to a eudaemonic theory of self-fulfillment. The moral ideal of classical Greek culture had been captured in Pindar's poetic phrase *Genoi' hoios essi,* "Become what you already are" (Pythian Odes, II, 72).[33] Ethics was the extension of ontology. The Greeks saw the good as a form of being, and they derived the ethical "ought" from the ontological "is," from the ineluctable structures of human nature. The moral person, therefore, was one who followed the finality of his or her essence, both spiritual and physical, instead of doing violence to it. In this view morality was grounded in free choice, but in the sense of an intelligent decision to obey the inner dictates of one's being. Insofar as it was rooted in ontology, Greek ethics was ultimately a matter of consciously conforming to an overriding necessity, and Pindar's protreptic to realize one's nature ended up as Nietzsche's counsel to love one's fate: *amor fati.*

In Jesus' message, however, ethics was not a matter of pursuing the fulfillment of one's nature within a framework of inevitability. Nor, as in the religious orthodoxy of the time, did it mean scrupulously obeying a Law imposed from without. Rather, it was a free response to a complete surprise: the unearned gift of God himself, who had suddenly arrived in one's midst. Here ethics was not an extension of ontology, not the exfoliation and realization of what is already, if inchoately, the case. Rather, it meant *metanoia,* conversion, or repentance: completely changing one's orientation and starting over afresh in response to something entirely new. "The kingdom of God is at hand. *Metanoiete:* Change your ways" (Mark 1:15).[34]

Moreover, God's presence in and as his people could not happen apart from this conversion: no *metanoia,* no kingdom. Although the kingdom was entirely God's gift and grounded in his initiative, the offer of God's presence turned into the challenge to let it happen; the invitation to the kingdom became the demand to live the dawning future—God's reign—in the present moment. Living the future in the present meant doing "violence" to the kingdom (Luke 16:16), not, however, by storming its walls with one's virtues or bribing one's way in with religious observance. The "violence" of living the future in the present was *metanoia,* "repentance." That did not mean self-flagellation for one's sins but "turning oneself around" and wholly changing one's life into an act of justice and mercy toward others. In Jesus' message, the invitation and the response were interdependent. The promised presence of God was the meaning of the demand for justice and charity, and yet only in such acts of mercy did the eschatological future become present.

This mutuality—eschatology as the ground of ethics, and ethics as the realization of eschatology—is what made Jesus' moral demands so radical. Those who accepted God's kingdom by doing God's will in the world already had as a gift what pious believers tried to earn through observance of the Law. Charity fulfills the Law—not because it *makes* God become present, but because it *is* his presence. And when God arrives on the scene, Jesus seemed to say, all go-betweens, including religion itself, are shattered. Who needs them? The Father is here!

In the concrete, this meant relativizing the Mosaic Law. Jesus, of course, was a pious Jew and therefore was far from intending to abrogate the Law, which he too saw as an expression of God's abundant love for his people.[35] But he was also a pious Jewish prophet, and specifically one who was convinced that the eschatological line separating the present from the future was already being crossed: History was entering its promised denouement. The eschatological nearness of the Father seared through all mediations and established a radically new order that demanded an equally radical response. Thus Jesus attacked not so much the specific rules of the Law as the legalistic attitude that blinded people to the fact that the Law, like its divine author, was entirely at the service of mankind. For example, when the Pharisees criticized Jesus' disciples for violating the sabbath by plucking and eating ears of corn as they walked through a field, the prophet retorted: "The sabbath was made for man, not man for the sabbath" (Mark 2:27). The Law, in short, was a gift from God, not a burden, and it should be bent in man's favor and even overridden when the need arose.[36]

Jesus did not engage directly in the then current dispute about whether the Law should be reduced to the simple Ten Commandments (the viewpoint of the Hellenistic Jews of the Diaspora) or should comprise the entire Torah and the commentaries of the scribes (as Palestinian Jewry generally held). Rather, with the authority of a prophet he cut through the theological complexities of that debate and pointed to the heart of what Judaism was about: revering God by loving one's neighbor.[37]

If the Father was henceforth identified with human beings—that is, if the kingdom of God was at hand—then strictly speaking there was no longer a God-up-above upon whom one could make religious claims by scrupulously observing the Law. In that sense, the demands of mercy that Jesus made were more rigorous than the stipulations of the Law. In calling for the commitment of the whole person to the immediate presence of the Father, Jesus necessarily pointed that commitment in the direction of one's fellow human beings, especially the socially powerless and disenfranchised. The ethics of the kingdom entailed always taking the side of the weaker or disadvantaged party and therefore the side of the poor and oppressed—including those whom the religious establishment declared to be outcasts. When the Pharisees criticized him for eating with such sinners, Jesus, citing God's words to the prophet Hosea, responded with a maxim that summed up not only the Jewish Law but his own eschatological ethics as well: "Go and learn what this means: 'I desire mercy, not sacrifice' " (Matthew 9:13).[38]

TIMING: THE PRESENT-FUTURE

If we ask about the timing of this eschatological event, that is, *when* God's kingdom was supposed to arrive, we are faced with an apparent contradiction. According to what Jesus preached, the reign-of-God-with-man at one and the same time had already arrived in the present and yet was still to come in the future. This paradox of the simultaneous presence and futurity of God's kingdom brings us to the core of Jesus' message: the eschatological present-future.[39]

On the one hand, it seems to be the case that Jesus, in conformity with the eschatological spirit of the times, did indeed preach that the kingdom lay in the immediate future but had not yet arrived. For example, he taught his disciples to pray: "Abba, may thy kingdom come!" But on the other hand, even if Jesus did expect an imminent and dramatic arrival of God among his people, he made no attempt to calculate the time of that coming, either in chronological or in apocalyptic terms. He refused to engage in predictions about its arrival, he never preached the dualism of "the age of darkness" followed by "the age to come," and he may not even have believed in a catastrophic end of the world. It seems that for Jesus the coming of God's kingdom was not measurable in such linear terms as "before" and "after," whether those be chronological or apocalyptic. Strictly speaking, it appears that for Jesus the future did not lie up ahead.

The uniqueness of Jesus' message lay in his conviction that in some way the future kingdom had already dawned and that the celebration could begin. The Baptist before him had preached an impending final judgment, but Jesus went him twice better: not judgment but a gift, in fact the gift of God himself; and not just impending but right here and now. God had already started to reign among men and women.

> The kingdom of God has come upon you. . . . Blessed are the eyes which see what you see. For I tell you that many prophets and kings

desired to see what you see, and did not see it, and to hear what you hear and did not hear it. (Luke 11:20, 10:23–24)

This paradoxical timing of the kingdom—the fact that it is both already present and yet still to come—tells us something essential about Jesus' vision of history. For him the past (mankind's sinful distance from God) was over, and the future (God's gracious identification with his people) had already begun. For Jesus, "past" and "future" were not points on a chronological or apocalyptic time-line: a bygone "no longer" and an upcoming "not yet." Rather, they were eschatological categories that had to be read in terms of the only thing that mattered to Jesus: the presence of God-with-man. The "past" was the reign of sin and Satan, the alienation of people from God, the weight of all that was impenetrable to the Father's gift of himself. And for Jesus all of that was gone or going. In its place came the "future," the presence of the Father himself among those who lived lives of justice and mercy. This unique, nonchronological sense of time explains why Jesus' message was so short on apocalyptic imagery. No such futuristic imagery was needed, for the eschatological line between the age of sin and the age of grace was already being crossed. God was now with his people.

The name Jesus used for this passing of the ages was "forgiveness" —but not in the usual religious sense of that term. The Father's forgiveness was not the canceling of an ontological debt, the undoing of some mythical sin that Adam had allegedly passed down through the generations. Nor was it God's benign overlooking of one's personal transgressions, an absolution for bad deeds done and good ones left undone. Forgiveness, as Jesus preached it, referred not primarily to sin at all but to the crossing of the eschatological line. What was "given" in the Father's for-giveness was the eschatological future—that is, God himself. Thus, forgiveness meant the arrival of God in the present, his superabundant gift of himself to his people, *his self-communicating incarnation.*

The Father's forgiveness meant a new beginning in the history of the ages, and for those who accepted his gift, the eschaton no longer lay up ahead but had arrived in the present. God was here in a new form of time, the existential present-future. Therefore, to believe in the arrival of God's kingdom and to be forgiven meant the same thing

—to be a prolepsis of God, to live the future now. It meant directing one's hopes toward the "future eschaton," that is, toward God himself, but then becoming in the present one's desire for that future which had already begun. "Set your hearts on the kingdom," Jesus said. "Store up treasures there, for where your treasure is, there is your heart" (cf. Matthew 6:33, 20f.).

In Jesus' preaching, the happening of this forgiveness, the coming of the kingdom, was entirely the initiative of God. And yet at the same time it was not an objective event that dropped out of the sky. God became present when people *allowed* that presence by actualizing it in lives of justice and charity. The promise of eschatology was converted into the demand for love and justice. "Be merciful, even as your Father is merciful" (Luke 6:36). Jesus extended this invitation to all who would hear it: "Convert, repent," that is, "Change the way you live, by accepting God's forgiveness." And accepting forgiveness meant enacting justice and mercy in the world, for the gift of God-with-men was a future that became present only in such a life of conversion.

And like a good rabbi, Jesus set the example. His followers had once asked him, "Master, where do you dwell?" and the answer was that Jesus dwelt beyond himself. He was an eschatologist in the literal sense of the term: an extremist. His own family thought he was "outside himself," the scribes thought he was "possessed," and others declared him "mad" (Mark 3:21–22, John 8:48). All of them were right: Jesus certainly was possessed, not, however, by Beelzebub, as the scribes thought, but by something that religious officialdom all too seldom understands: God's uncontrollable present-future, which Jesus felt had swept him up beyond himself. Jesus was what he was for, the presence of God among men. He lived his eschatological cathexis so intensely that he lost his identity to that present-future and became nothing but his hope for its realization. The kingdom was his madness. He celebrated it with anyone who would join him at table, declared everyone free in its name, broke all rules that stood in its way, and finally gave up his life for it—or rather, gave up his life to save the only thing he lived for.

Where did Jesus dwell? When he said he had nowhere to lay his head (Matthew 8:20), he was not referring simply to the obvious fact that he was an itinerant preacher. He was declaring that he lived beyond himself: He was giving his address as the presence of God among men. He claimed no family, no mother or brothers or sisters except those who lived with him there in God's present-future (12:48–50). He was no part-time prophet. The kingdom was his life, and "What would a man give in exchange for his life?" (17:26). The kingdom was like a pearl of immense value that Jesus had found and that he sold everything to buy (13:46).

This was the same call he held out to his followers: "If you wish to be perfect, go and sell what you own and give the money to the poor, and you will have treasure in heaven; then come, follow me" (Matthew 19:21). The vocation of Jesus and his followers was to live God's dawning presence—not up above in heaven or up ahead in an apocalyptic future, but there in their midst, at the edge of things where security unravels into risk, at the center of things where common sense is challenged by the wager that henceforth God is found only among men and women.

The presence of God among men which Jesus preached was not something new, not a gift that God had saved up for the end of time. Jesus merely proclaimed what had always been the case. He invited people to awaken to what God had already done from the very beginning of time. The eschaton that Jesus proclaimed was not a new coming of God but a realization on man's part that ever since the creation God had been there among his people. The "arrival" of the present-future was not God's return to the world after a long absence but the believer's reawakening to the fact that God had always and only been *there*. [40]

All Jesus did was bring to light in a fresh way what had always been the case but what had been forgotten or obscured by religion. His role was simply to end religion—that temporary governess who had turned into a tyrant—and restore the sense of the immediacy of God. Jesus, the first disciple of the kingdom of God, was "like a householder who brings out from his storeroom things both new and old" (Matthew 13:52). The newness of his message was the shock of something old and forgotten that was found again. Like the psalmist, Jesus could say:

I will open my mouth in parables,
I will utter dark sayings from of old,

Things that we have heard and known,
  That our fathers have told us.
We will not hide them from their children,
  but will tell them to the coming generation. (Psalm 78:2–4)

The "dark sayings from of old," the "things hidden since the foundation of the world" (Matthew 13:35), were the content of Jesus' message: The Father of the kingdom was the very same Father of the creation who had made all things good, had made man and woman good, who "saw everything that he had made, and it was very good" (Genesis 1:31).

To receive God's eschatological forgiveness was to realize that everything was already in God's graceful presence and that everyone was already saved—precisely because they did not need salvation: They had already been saved from the beginning. Jesus' proclamation of eschatological forgiveness was simply a reminder that everything had already been done, that grace (which means God) had already long since been abundantly bestowed, and that the only task left to do now was to live out that gift. Jesus' job as a prophet was to put himself out of business.

4

GOD'S WORD
AT WORK

JESUS DID NOT DEFINE the kingdom of God so much as he enacted it by the way he lived. In the previous section we considered the content of his message: The future becomes present, the Father becomes incarnate, wherever mercy and justice are done. We now take another look at that same message, but this time in terms of how it was inscribed in Jesus' style of living and preaching. We shall consider the manner in which Jesus concretely enacted the kingdom in the table fellowship that he shared with his followers, in the parables that he told them, and in the "signs and wonders" (Acts 2:22) that he worked among the people.

When we search the Gospels for clues to how Jesus lived, we get the impression that, in the scarce two years of his mission, he spent an inordinate amount of time at the dinner table and not always in the best of company. Jesus admitted as much: "I came eating and drinking," he said (Matthew 11:19). And on these occasions, in turn, he frequently preached about the kingdom of God in terms of a great meal, as if to say that the eschatological presence of the Father was like a banquet, as generous as the one at which he and his outcast friends reclined, with invitations showered on those who seemed the least deserving.

> The kingdom of heaven may be compared to a king who gave a marriage feast for his son, and sent his servants to call those who were invited to the marriage feast; but they would not come. ... Then he said to his servants, "The wedding is ready, but those invited were not worthy. Go therefore to the thoroughfares, and invite to the marriage feast as many as you find." (Matthew 22:2–3, 8–9)

The meals of fellowship that Jesus shared with his followers were an enactment of the reign of God, a sacrament of the Father's incarnate presence. They were not just a model of, but, more important, an anticipatory realization of, the dawning presence of God—the first course, we might say, in the eschatological banquet. And on the invitations to these dinners was printed "Whores and tax collectors first!" (cf. Matthew 21:31). Jesus' meals were typified by their inclusion of such pariahs and by the prophet's proclamation that the Father's gift in these end-times was universal forgiveness.

When a prostitute, on her off hours, joined Jesus at table at a Pharisee's house and even washed his feet, Jesus told his shocked host, "Her sins, which are many, are forgiven, for she loved much; but he who is forgiven little, loves little" (Luke 7:47). And when the pillars of the religious establishment questioned his practice of eating with the hated tax collectors—an act that violated the Law—Jesus responded, "Those who are in good health have no need of a physician, but rather those who are sick; I came to call not the righteous, but sinners" (Mark 2:17).

There is no evidence that Jesus himself forgave sinners in his own name.[41] Rather, in keeping with his proclamation of the dawning of God's reign, he announced that it was the Father who was bestowing the eschatological gift of forgiveness in Jesus' presence. However, in retrospect the Church found in Jesus' prophetic authority and in his liberating words and actions the grounds for attributing to him the eschatological power of having absolved the repentant of their sins during his lifetime. What is clear is that his followers perceived in Jesus' table fellowship the direct presence of the Father, whose love encompassed the rejected of society. The disciples saw in Jesus' eschatological etiquette a preview of who would be on the guest list at the Father's final banquet: "When you give a feast, invite the poor, the maimed, the lame, the blind . . ." (Luke 14:13).

After Jesus had died, his followers continued that memory in their own communal repasts and even in the Eucharistic feast. These later meals, which may have included the washing of feet in imitation of Jesus (cf. John 13:5), at one and the same time recalled Jesus' meals of liberatory fellowship and anticipated the definitive eschatological banquet when, reunited with Jesus, they would "drink of the fruit of the vine anew" and "eat bread in the kingdom of God" (cf. Mark 14:25 and Luke 14:15).

The parables that Jesus recounted, many of them at table, continued the theme of abundant eschatological forgiveness and spelled out the response of radical change that the Father's invitation required.[42] Palestine at that time was a culture of storytelling, and Jesus was a master of the art. His stories were not moral or intellectual allegories that required exegetical deciphering, but straightforward and concrete descriptions that drew his listeners into the drama and called for decision on their part. Rarely if ever did Jesus' parables speak of God or were they set in a religious context. Rather, they described God's reign in terms of everyday life situations, as if to say that the kingdom had to do not with a heavenly Beyond but with concrete possibilities in this world.

The themes of the kingdom were simple—for example, the excitement of discovering something present but hidden:

> The kingdom of heaven is like a treasure hidden in a field, which a man found and covered up; then in his joy he goes and sells all that he has and buys that field. (Matthew 13:44)

Or the joy of finding something precious that had been lost:

> What woman, having ten silver coins, if she loses one coin, does not light a lamp and sweep the house and seek diligently until she finds

it? And when she has found it, she calls together her friends and neighbors, saying, "Rejoice with me, for I have found the coin which I had lost." Just so, I tell you, there is joy before the angels of God over one sinner who repents. (Luke 15:8–10)

Jesus also told parables about the reversal in attitude that the dawning of the kingdom demanded. At the end of a day (representing the eschatological judgment), the owner of a vineyard pays grape pickers who worked only one hour the same wages as those who worked from dawn to dusk, for "the last will be first, and the first last" (Matthew 20:16). Or God justifies a sinful tax collector who repents, rather than a law-abiding Pharisee who prides himself on his strict religious observance, because "everyone who exalts himself will be humbled, but he who humbles himself will be exalted" (Luke 18:14). Jesus' eschatological theme of startling reversal, of the overturning of all seemingly reasonable values, runs from the story of the Prodigal Son through the tale of the Good Samaritan to the depiction of the Last Day, when the ruler gives his kingdom to those who had simply fed the hungry and clothed the naked because "as you did it to one of the least of these my brethren, you did it to me" (Matthew 25:40). Even in those parables that the later Church rewrote to fit her own situation, the core still shines through: Jesus the prophet was the master of novelty and surprise as he challenged traditional religious values in the name of the utterly new eschatological event of God-with-man.

The "signs and wonders" (Acts 2:22) that Jesus is reported to have worked have long been the subject of scholarly dispute, and it is fair to say that throughout much of Christian history their meaning has been misunderstood.[43] Generally these "miracles" have been interpreted apologetically as proofs that Jesus was divine and that his mission originated in heaven. This approach, which has been dominant in Christian teaching from Quadratus' "Apology to Hadrian" (ca. 125 C.E.)[44] to early in the present century, is attended by a number of intrinsic difficulties. For one thing, Saint Paul's epistles, which were written before the Gospels, mention no miracles at all. For another, exegetes have established that one of the earliest sources underlying the

Gospels reports only two such "wonders" worked by Jesus: a cure and an exorcism (Luke 7:1–10 and 11:14).[45]

But in the decades after Jesus' death Christian legends began to inflate both the quality and the number of the miracles. For example, in Mark's Gospel, written around 70, we find the ruler of a synagogue begging Jesus to lay his hands on his daughter, who "is at the point of death" (5:23), whereas in Matthew's Gospel, written some fifteen years later, the same man changes and heightens the diagnosis: "My daughter has just died" (9:18). Likewise, the number of cures increases. Mark's Gospel has Jesus simply "casting out demons" (1:39), whereas the parallel text in Matthew has him "healing every disease and every infirmity among the people" (4:23).

Eventually accounts of "nature miracles" began to appear: Jesus arranges the catch of an extraordinary number of fish, makes a fig tree dry up, walks on water, stills a storm, raises people from the dead, multiples loaves and fishes to feed four thousand or even five thousand people, and apparently even makes a shekel appear in the mouth of a fish. These nature miracles are simply legends which arose among early Christians and which were projected backward, under the impact of faith, into the life of the historical Jesus. The motive may have been to make him appear at least the equal of the numerous miracle workers widely reported in the rabbinical and Hellenistic religious literature of the times.[46]

Another problem with the traditional approach to Jesus' "miracles" is that it misses the eschatological, and specifically the apocalyptic, context within which the stories of his signs and wonders grew up. Beginning some centuries before Jesus, popular Jewish apocalyptic literature elaborated tales about the fall of the sinful angels from heaven before the creation of the world and their subsequent conflict with human beings. These evil spirits were understood to have taken possession of some people, rendering them deaf and dumb and afflicting them with a variety of diseases. But believers saw in Jesus' eschatological words and deeds the definitive defeat of these cosmic powers of darkness. In the words of the Epistle to the Colossians, Jesus "disarmed the principalities and powers and made a public example of them, triumphing over them" (2:15).[47]

Jesus himself was a child of this apocalyptic picture of the world, and he saw his own work in that context. For example, when speaking of his and his disciples' mission, he said, "I saw Satan fall like lightning from heaven" (Luke 10:18). There is no doubt that he gained a reputation in his lifetime as an exorcist and that he caused wonderment among the simple people around the northern shore of the Sea of Galilee. Regardless of the possible medical and psychosomatic explanations that can be given for the cures he is said to have effected, early Christian preaching preserved this memory: "He went about doing good and healing all that were oppressed by the devil, for God was with him" (Acts 10:38). Jesus, they remembered, "did all things well" (Mark 7:37).

But the framework within which he gained this reputation was not that of the traditional Christian understanding of "miracles" as sovereignly divine interruptions of the laws of nature. The Bible depicts the universe not as a closed system of laws, the way modern science does, but as the arena in which God was enacting his will. Therefore, even phenomena such as cures by exorcism, which might well be explained by empirical causes, were seen by Jesus' contemporaries as signs of God's power.

Jesus' "miracles," whatever they might have been, get their sense from the apocalyptic belief that the end of time had arrived. There were plenty of exorcists in Palestine at the time of Jesus—perhaps including some of his own followers—and Jesus himself predicted more to come (Mark 13:22). But the point was not that these exorcists, or Jesus himself, were divine (in fact, some of them were considered to be working for the devil) but rather that the divine Father himself was making his eschatological appearance in Jesus' words and deeds and was conquering the powers of evil for the good of mankind. The focus was not on Jesus as a worker of "miracles" but on the arrival of God-for-man. "If it is by the Spirit of God that I cast out demons, then the kingdom of God has come upon you" (Matthew 12:28).

However many or few exorcisms Jesus may have performed in his few months as a prophet, it is clear that he inspired in his followers the belief that the Father's eschatological reign had already begun. The wonders he worked were not appeals for faith in himself, regardless of how closely he identified himself with God's cause, but only for faith in the coming climax of history. His works were not proofs of his own divinity or messiahship—claims he never made—but rather, like his meals and parables, were signs of the dawning of God's reign. If there was anything miraculous about Jesus, it all lay in the coming of the kingdom in which he and eventually his followers so earnestly believed. For all the prophetic authority with which he spoke and for all his conviction that his words and works were the instrument of God's final breakthrough in the Jewish community, Jesus remained only the locus, and never the focus, of the eschatological event.

5

REJECTION AND DEATH

SINCE WE HAVE no privileged access to Jesus' psychology, we must divine what he thought about himself from his public words and deeds. And there we find a man so totally absorbed in and identified with the cause of God-with-man that it would be true to say he was nothing other than that cause: Jesus *was* what he preached. Traditional Christianity, to be sure, goes further and claims that Jesus understood himself to be the very content of his own message, the kingdom of God incarnate; but that is an extrapolation from Jesus' life that Jesus' followers made in the years after he died.

We have seen how Jesus enacted the kingdom of God in his table fellowship, his parables, and his miracles. We now turn to the question of how he faced, and perhaps accepted, the disappointments of the last months of his mission, and even his death. We shall look as well at the question of how Jesus may have understood himself and his work as he approached the end of his days.

Jesus' mission in Galilee, independent of that of John the Baptist, lasted only a few months and initially met with enormous success. He drew great crowds and inspired amazement—"We never saw anything like this!" the people exclaimed (Mark 2:12). But his relatives thought he was out of his mind and tried to drag him home (3:21).[48]

But it was not long before his popularity peaked, and enthusiasm for this extraordinary but eccentric man began to drop off in the north country. The Gospels give a clear impression that Jesus began to be rejected not only by the authorities of the religious establishment but by the common people as well. All four Gospels record Jesus' complaint that he felt spurned by his own people, and two Gospels hint that his wondrous powers waned in his own hometown.

> They [his townspeople] took offense at him. And Jesus said to them, "A prophet is honored everywhere except in his own country, and among his own kin, and in his own house." And he could do no mighty work there, except that he laid his hands upon a few sick people and healed them. And he marveled because of their unbelief. (Mark 6:3–6; cf. Matthew 13:57f.)

In a later elaboration Luke says that the same people were so incensed at Jesus that they almost killed him.

> And when they heard this, all in the synagogue were filled with wrath. And they rose up and put him out of the city, and led him to the brow of the hill on which their city was built, that they might throw him down headlong. But passing through the midst of them, he went away. (4:28–30)

As things turned out badly for his eschatological mission, Jesus vented some apocalyptic anger against the northern lake towns where he had preached:

> Then he began to upbraid the cities where most of his mighty works had been done, because they did not repent. "Woe to you, Chorazin! woe to you, Bethsaida! for if the mighty works done in you had been done in Tyre and Sidon, they would have repented long ago in sackcloth and ashes. But I tell you, it shall be more tolerable on the day of judgment for Tyre and Sidon than for you. And you, Capernaum, will you be exalted to heaven? You shall be brought down to Hades!" (Matthew 11:20–23)

Even his closest disciples were not spared his anger and disappointment.

> Do you not yet perceive or understand? Are your hearts hardened? Having eyes, do you not see, and having ears do you not hear? (Mark 8:17–18; also 6:52)

It was bad enough that the simple people of Galilee, Jesus' natural constituency, misunderstood and rejected him, but the real threat to his mission came from the established political and religious authorities. Always shadowing Jesus as his fame spread through the area was the chilling memory of the fate that John the Baptist had suffered at the hands of Herod Antipas for preaching a message not unlike his own. The word was out that Jesus would be the next to go. "The Pharisees left and immediately held counsel with the Herodians against Jesus, how to destroy him" (Mark 3:6). Luke's story may not be far from the truth:

> Now Herod the tetrarch heard of all that was done, and he was perplexed, because it was said by some that John had been raised from the dead, by some that Elijah had appeared, and by others that one of the old prophets had risen. Herod said, "John I beheaded. But who is this about whom I hear such things?" And he sought to see him. (9:7–9; cf. Mark 6:14–16)

Apparently Jesus was not so eager to see Herod. With the rumor circulating that Jesus was the Baptist come back to life, Herod's interest had a smell of murder about it that was not lost on the prophet from Nazareth. Luke writes:

> At that very hour some Pharisees came, and said to him, "Get away from here, for Herod wants to kill you." And he said to them, "Go and tell that fox, 'Behold, I cast out demons and perform cures today and tomorrow, and the third day I finish my course. But for today, tomorrow and the next day I must go on, since it would not be right that a prophet should die outside Jerusalem.' " (13:31–33)

Then there were the Pharisees, or at least some of them, who took offense at Jesus' sovereignly highhanded attitude toward the Law:

eating with legally unclean people (Mark 2:16), bending the sabbath tradition by healing on the day of rest (3:1–5), allowing his disciples to eat without first washing their hands (7:2ff.). Sometimes Jesus simply turned his back on them and went away (8:11), but at least once he lashed out at them:

> Well did Isaiah prophesy of you hypocrites, as it is written,
> "This people honors me with their lips,
> but their heart is far from me;
> in vain do they worship me,
> teaching as doctrines the precepts of men."
> You leave the commandment of God, and hold fast the tradition of men. (7:6–8)

According to a text in Matthew's Gospel, which reflects the anti-Pharisee polemics of later Christians but which is grounded in Jesus' jeremiads against legalistic religion, the prophet goes even further:

> Woe to you, scribes and Pharisees, hypocrites! because you shut the kingdom of heaven against men; for you neither enter yourselves, nor allow those who would enter to go in. . . . Woe to you, scribes and Pharisees, hypocrites! for you are like whitewashed tombs, which outwardly appear beautiful, but within they are full of dead men's bones. (23:13,27)

By such attacks on the religious establishment Jesus put himself beyond the pale of acceptable protest and reform. The prophet from Galilee had become a dangerous man.

Faced with rejection by both the common people and their religious leaders, Jesus apparently decided that his last chance lay in taking his failing mission to the heart of Israel, to the city of Jerusalem itself. In the spring of the Jewish year 3790, after his disciples had completed a missionary tour in the north in what may have been a last-ditch effort to rally faith in the kingdom, Jesus gathered an inner circle of friends and set off on his last pilgrimage to the Holy City for the Passover feast.

Perhaps at this point too he began to have presentiments of the fate that awaited him. Matthew writes: "From that time Jesus began to show his disciples that he must go to Jerusalem and suffer many things from the elders and chief priests and scribes, and be killed" (16:21). For whatever the later Church may have added to this verse, it is not unlikely that Jesus was aware, to some degree, of what lay in store for him. He would have to be blind not to see that his reputation as a radical prophet had already preceded him. The congeries of political apprehension on the part of Herod and religious outrage on the part of the scribes and Pharisees spelled trouble for anyone announcing the eschatological "kingdom of God," especially at Passover in Roman-occupied Jerusalem. Jesus' predictions of his coming death, which are multiplied in the Gospels at this point, may well have a historical basis in his own words. It is possible that Jesus became convinced that "it would not be right for a prophet to die outside Jerusalem" (Luke 13:33).

Jesus never made his own status a special theme of his preaching, and he never turned himself into a second topic alongside the reign of God-with-men. Nonetheless, it is not unlikely that as his mission fell on hard days and as he sensed his death approaching, he became more reflective about his role in the coming of God's rule and even about his own personal status. Who did he think himself to be?[49]

In the tinderbox of occupied Palestine, it would have been sheer madness for Jesus to declare himself a Davidic "messiah," with the overtones of political liberation that this title bore; and in fact he never did. In any case, in the Jewish Scriptures the title "messiah" ("anointed one") does not refer to a divine person (even when he is called "Son of God") or to a spiritual redeemer who would expiate sins (even when, as with the expected Davidic messiah, he was called "savior").[50] Rather, the term designated a political and military king who would reestablish a theocratic nation-state at some point in history. In the century and a half before Jesus, this future king came to be seen in broader eschatological terms as the ruler of all nations (not just of Israel), whom God would appoint at the end of time. Nonetheless, the title "messiah" still kept its political overtones, and Jesus vehemently rejected any such designation as a provocation from Satan (Mark 8:33).

It is true that he counted at least one Zealot (anti-Roman revolutionary) among his closest followers, and it is possible that this man and others once nurtured the futile hope that Jesus might prove to be a national liberator. Jesus not only rejected that role but also never designated himself as a "spiritual" messiah, an anointed prophet without political intentions, although it is quite possible that some of his followers saw him that way.

Nor did Jesus ever identify himself with the apocalyptic Son of Man who, according to the Book of Daniel, was to appear "on the clouds of heaven" at the last day. When Jesus used the phrase "son of man," *bar nasha,* with regard to himself (for example, "The son of man has nowhere to lay his head," Matthew 8:20), he was not referring to the awaited apocalyptic figure but was simply employing a common Palestinian-Aramaic circumlocution for the indexical pronoun "I," as if to say "I have no place to sleep." However (this is a matter of great dispute), he may have seen his own mission against the backdrop of the future apparition of this figure.[51]

What we can say with considerable certainty is that before he died, Jesus may have had intimations of being the long-awaited "eschatological prophet," God's definitive mouthpiece who was to arrive just before the coming of God himself. It is clear that Jesus saw himself as a prophet, and he certainly conceived his ministry in eschatological terms. But never did he actually declare himself to be the eschatological prophet, whether in the form of Elijah redivivus or as a new Moses.[52] Nonetheless, the title of (nonnationalistic-messianic) eschatological prophet was to be the first that his followers would bestow on Jesus after he had died. And given the authority with which he acted and taught, it is very likely that even during Jesus' lifetime his disciples thought he was this final prophet. Jesus enhanced that expectation when, at the end of his pilgrimage to Jerusalem, he triumphantly entered the city to the acclaim of the people and (whether on this final trip to Jerusalem or, as is possible, on an earlier one) drove the sellers and money changers from the Temple precinct.[53]

But Jesus' days as a prophet were numbered, and we may presume that he not only knew it but also prepared his disciples for the eventuality. The farewell dinner, or Last Supper, that he shared with them in

Jerusalem before he died crystallized Jesus' awareness of his approaching death and offered his closest followers the promise of continuing fellowship regardless of what was to come.

The actual date of the meal (see chart) is the subject of some dispute.[54] All the Gospels agree that it took place, by current reckoning, on a Thursday evening some twenty hours before his death or, according to the Jewish way of reckoning days from dusk to dusk, on the same day he died. The Synoptics date it on the fifteenth day of the month of Nisan, that is, sometime after sundown on the first day of the Passover festival. However, John's Gospel places the Last Supper after sundown on the fourteenth of Nisan, the day before the feast, and dates Jesus' crucifixion to the day before the Passover feast, that is, the day when the paschal lambs were ritually slaughtered in the Temple (19:14). In any case, John's dating gave rise to a rich theology of Jesus' death as a sacrifice for sins and a Passover to new life. There is also disagreement about whether the meal was a Passover feast (as the Synoptic Gospels maintain) or not (John's position), and even about whether Jesus instituted a new liturgy, the Eucharist of sacred bread and wine, at the dinner.[54]

But what is clear is that Jesus took the occasion of this farewell meal, whenever and however it took place, to express to his disciples his vivid awareness that he was about to die: "I shall not drink again of the fruit of the vine" (Mark 14:25). He assured them as well that despite rejection and failure, he remained unshaken in his confidence that the Father would vindicate his mission. Although the Gospels record no historical words of Jesus that show him conceiving of his death as a propitiatory sacrifice to save mankind from its sins, we are not amiss in seeing the Last Supper as Jesus' final interpretation of his life and imminent death in terms of the kingdom he had preached and the life-for-others he had led.

It is possible that Jesus had come to see his coming death as the inevitable price to be paid for living according to God's eschatological will. Other prophets had been rejected before him, and now it was his turn. His death, therefore, would be his final identification with the cause of the kingdom of God. This identification once again took the form of a meal of fellowship in which he invited his disciples to share the offer of salvation that was not merely promised in the future but

HOLY WEEK CHRONOLOGY FOR 30 C.E.

According to John:

	Thursday, April 6		Friday, April 7		Saturday, April 8		Sunday, April 9	
	Night	Day	Night	Day	Night	Day	Night	Day
			PREPARATION DAY FOR PASSOVER		SABBATH AND PASSOVER FEAST IN ONE			FIRST DAY OF THE WEEK
				Lambs are slaughtered in the Temple.	The Jewish community celebrates the Passover meal.			
			Jesus celebrates a non-Passover meal.	Jesus is crucified, dies, and is buried.				
	13 Nisan		14 Nisan		15 Nisan		16 Nisan	

According to the Synoptics:

	Thursday, April 6		Friday, April 7		Saturday, April 8		Sunday, April 9	
	Night	Day	Night	Day	Night	Day	Night	Day
		PREPARATION DAY FOR PASSOVER	PASSOVER FEAST			SABBATH		FIRST DAY OF THE WEEK
		Lambs are slaughtered in the Temple.	The Jewish community celebrates the Passover meal.	Jesus is crucified, dies, and is buried.				
			Jesus celebrates a Passover meal.					
		14 Nisan	15 Nisan		16 Nisan		17 Nisan	

concretely offered in Jesus' own words and deeds, including his death. He shared with them—for the last time "until the kingdom of God comes" (Luke 22:18)—a cup of wine. In drinking it together they sealed their fellowship, as if to say that the reign of God was linked inextricably with what they had lived through with him, right up to the end. The kingdom of God-with-men was stronger than death.[55]

Later that night, as he prayed in the olive grove of Gethsemane just east of the city, Jesus was arrested by a delegation from the Sanhedrin, the supreme council of the religious establishment. What happened between then and his crucifixion is a matter of dispute. The Roman historian Tacitus, writing around 114 C.E., reports simply that Jesus "was put to death by the Procurator [in fact, Prefect] Pontius Pilate during the reign of Tiberius."[56] The Gospels, which at this point are particularly interlaced with anti-Jewish polemics, disagree among themselves on such matters as the nature and number of trials that Jesus underwent before his crucifixion, as well as the charges leveled against him and the responses Jesus gave to them. We are left with rough approximations of what happened.

The night on which he was arrested, Jesus either (1) was brought first to the former high priest Annas, who was the father-in-law of the current high priest, Caiaphas, and then to Caiaphas himself (John's Gospel); or (2) was brought to Caiaphas alone (Luke); or (3) was taken before the assembled Sanhedrin (Mark and Matthew). The Synoptic Gospels agree that whether or not Jesus underwent an official trial that night, he did undergo an interrogation by the Sanhedrin sometime the next morning before he was led off to Pontius Pilate. The Sanhedrin was composed of some seventy members, including the current and former high priests as well as laymen, scribes and lawyers. In Jesus' time it was dominated by the Sadducees rather than the Pharisees (in fact, the Pharisees tend to drop out of the picture as Jesus' death approaches), and it had juridical power over religious questions, probably backed up by the legal right to execute grave offenders by stoning.[57]

Whatever its specific form, legal or otherwise, Jesus' hearing before the Sanhedrin was not a show trial but a serious investigation into what he was saying and doing. It seems that the Sanhedrin was split over the question of whether Jesus' prophetic mission had gone too far, and this disagreement may have been the reason for a second hearing in the morning. Within the Sanhedrin, the liberal Hillel school of the Pharisees, which may have included Joseph of Arimathea (Luke 23:50), probably sympathized with some aspects of the prophet's attitude toward the Law, but his radical relativization of the Torah in the name of an immediate relation with God was too much even for them.

Did Jesus deserve death under Jewish law for what he was doing? Did he, for example, commit blasphemy in the eyes of the Sanhedrin by making divine or messianic claims? Declaring himself the messiah would not have been a capital crime as far as the Sanhedrin was concerned: There were many messianic pretenders in Palestine in those years, and the Sanhedrin did not condemn one of them to death. And in any case, the words the Gospels put into Jesus' mouth at his hearing (for example, his claim to being the messiah: Mark 14:62) are later theological interpolations on the part of the early church and cannot be credited as historical sayings.[58]

Rather, what seems to have happened is that Jesus refused to respond to the questions that the Sanhedrin put to him about his authority and status and that he thereby incurred the serious charge of contempt of authority. The Book of Deuteronomy says: "The man who acts presumptuously, by not obeying the priest who stands to minister there before the Lord your God, or the judge, that man shall die" (17:12). This law, even though it was applied rigorously only after 70 C.E., may be the one Jesus was condemned for violating. In keeping with his sense of his authority as eschatological prophet, he simply refused to submit his teaching to the judgment of the high priests and the religious establishment.

If the members of the Sanhedrin condemned Jesus to death on these grounds, it is not clear why they did not execute the order on their own authority but instead chose to bring the case before the Roman prefect. John's Gospel claims that the Sanhedrin did not have the legal right to carry out capital punishment (18:31), although a few years after Jesus' death the council reportedly did execute Stephen, a follower of Jesus (Acts 7:58). As a putative reason for why the Sanhedrin itself did not execute Jesus, Luke says that the Sanhedrin presented *political* rather than religious charges against the prophet when they brought him before Pontius Pilate: "We found this man perverting our nation, and forbidding us to give tribute to Caesar, and saying that he himself is

Christ a king" (23:2). In any case, whatever Pilate's reasons for deciding to have Jesus put to death, it is not true that the Jewish crowds shouted out that Jesus should be crucified (Mark 15:12ff.) or that they took his blood upon themselves and their children (Matthew 27:25). Nor did the high priests tell the prefect "We have no king but Caesar" (John 19:15). These sentences, which were later written into the accounts of Jesus' passion, are the products of a bitter polemic between early Christianity and Judaism and have helped to cause the horrors of two millennia of anti-Semitism.[59]

Under Roman jurisdiction Jesus was scourged with leather straps fitted with pieces of sharp metal and bone—a punishment commonly administered to those condemned to crucifixion.[60] He was then forced to carry a crossbeam, or *patibulum,* weighing some eighty or ninety pounds, to the place of execution outside the city. He was affixed to the beam and to an upright pole with ropes and nails, and over his head was placed the *titulum* that gave the reason for his punishment: "Jesus of Nazareth, King of the Jews." Quite apart from the intentions of the Sanhedrin, the Romans had found their own reasons for putting Jesus to death: He was being executed as a messianic pretender.

Death usually came in ten or twelve hours, although the Jewish historian Josephus records that some crucifixion victims held on for days.[61] The end came slowly, by exposure, loss of blood, and gradual asphyxiation. The pain and degradation were augmented by blocked circulation and the torment of flies and insects. It is doubtful that any of his closest followers were present at Jesus' final agony.

The date was probably Friday, April 7, in the 30th year of the current reckoning, the 783rd year since the founding of the city of Rome and the 16th since Tiberius Augustus had been declared Caesar Augustus. By the reckoning of the religious establishment, it was the 3,790th year since the creation of the world. Jesus, the carpenter turned prophet, had expected the kingdom of God to come in its fullness very soon, perhaps within his own lifetime. He may have clung to that hope during his final agony. He was crucified around midday. He was dead before dusk.

TWO

HOW JESUS WAS RAISED FROM THE DEAD

SOON AFTER JESUS DIED, something dramatic happened to his reputation: His followers came to believe that he had been raised from the dead and was alive with his heavenly Father. This enhancement of Jesus' reputation is a historical fact, observable by anyone who studies the relevant documents.

But according to Christians, something dramatic happened not just to Jesus' reputation but above all to Jesus himself. They believe he actually *was* raised from the dead, was taken into heaven, and is now reigning there as the equal of God the Father. These, however, are not observable historical facts but claims of faith.

The purpose of this central part of our study is to distinguish between the facts of history and the claims of faith, between what certainly happened to Jesus' reputation after he died and what allegedly happened to Jesus himself. There is no doubt that Christianity formally began with the disciples' claim that Jesus had been rescued from death. Our question, however, is what that claim meant in the early church and what historical experiences lay behind it. (When speaking of resurrection, the New Testament writers generally use the passive construction "Jesus was raised [by God]"—in Greek *ēgerthē* or *egēgertai* —rather than the active-voice "Jesus rose" [*anestē*]. In what follows I use the word "resurrection" in the New Testament's passive sense: Jesus' "being-raised" by God.[1])

Here, in the search for the historical origins of Christian faith in the resurrected Jesus, what I said in the Introduction holds especially true: I rely upon the scientifically controllable results of contemporary Christian exegesis of the New Testament texts that bear upon the resurrection. However, I also go beyond that exegesis by using its results as data for my own interpretation.

The last event in Jesus' life was his death, but even in death his fame began to grow. We now study the first stirrings of the movement that transformed Jesus, in the eyes of his followers, from the crucified prophet into the ruling Son of God. First, under the rubric of "Simon's Experience," we investigate the scriptural claim that Jesus appeared to Simon Peter after the crucifixion. Second, in "The Empty Tomb," we study the story in Mark's Gospel that Jesus' tomb was found empty on Easter Sunday morning.

SIMON'S EXPERIENCE

1

THE MYTH OF
EASTER

POPULAR CHRISTIAN PIETY holds that Jesus' existence on earth extended beyond his death on Good Friday and spilled over into a miraculous six-week period that stretched from his physical emergence from the tomb on Easter Sunday morning, April 9, 30 C.E., to his bodily ascension into heaven forty days later, on Thursday, May 17, 30 C.E.[2]

To judge from the Gospels, it would seem that the activities of the risen Jesus during the forty days after he died included: one breakfast; one and a half dinners; one brief meeting in a cemetery (in fact with his clothes off: John 20:6, 14);[3] two walks through the countryside; at least seven conversations (including two separate instructions on how to forgive sins and baptize converts)—all of this climaxing in his physical ascension into heaven from a small hill just outside Jerusalem. Impossible though the task is, if we were to try to synthesize the gospel stories into a consistent chronology of what Jesus did during those hectic six weeks between his resurrection from the dead and his ascension into heaven, the agenda would look something like this:

MORNING

1. Jesus rises from the dead early in the morning (Mark 16:9). Mary Magdalene, alone or with other women, discovers the open tomb. *Either* she informs Peter and another disciple, who visit the tomb and find it empty (John 20:1–10); *or* she and the others meet one or two angels inside, who announce the resurrection (Mark 16:5–6; Luke 24:4–6); or she flees, saying nothing.

2. Later, outside the tomb, Jesus appears to Mary Magdalene alone, who at first mistakes him for a gardener. He tells her to inform the disciples that he is ascending at that moment to his Father (John 20:17; Mark 16:9).

3. Jesus also appears to Mary Magdalene and *another* Mary, who grasp his feet and worship. Jesus tells them to send the brethren to Galilee, where they will see him (Matthew 28:10).

4. Sometime during the day Jesus appears to Simon Peter (Luke 24:34).

AFTERNOON AND EARLY EVENING

5. Jesus walks incognito through the countryside for almost seven miles with two disciples. He starts to eat dinner with them in Emmaus but disappears as soon as they recognize who he is (Luke 24:13–31; Mark 16:12–13).

EVENING

6. Back in Jerusalem, Jesus appears to the disciples in a room even though the doors are locked. He tries to overcome their doubts by showing them his wounds and by eating broiled fish and honeycomb. He either gives them the Holy Spirit and the power to forgive sins (John) or does not (Luke), and either sends them out into the whole world (Mark) or tells them to stay in Jerusalem for a while (Luke). The disciple Thomas either is present (Luke and Mark, by implication) or is not (John). (Luke 24:36–49; John 20:19–23; Mark 16:14–18).

7. Jesus ascends into heaven that night from Bethany (Luke 24:51; Mark 16:19).

SUNDAY, APRIL 16, 30 C.E.: STILL IN JERUSALEM

8. Jesus appears again to the disciples behind locked doors, and invites Thomas, who now is present, to put his fingers and hands into the wounds (John 20:26–29).

OVER THE NEXT WEEKS

9. Jesus offers the disciples many other proofs and signs, not all of which are recorded in the Gospels (John 20:30).

LATE APRIL OR EARLY MAY, 30 C.E.: GALILEE

10. Early one morning Jesus makes his "third appearance" (*sic*, John 21:14), this time to Simon and six others on the shore of Lake Galilee. He miraculously arranges for them to catch 153 large fish and invites them ashore for a breakfast of broiled fish and bread, which he has prepared. Jesus instructs Simon, "Feed my lambs, feed my sheep," and discusses how Simon and the Beloved Disciple will die (John 21:1–23).

11. Jesus appears to the eleven disciples on a mountain, but some still doubt. He commissions them to baptize all nations and assures them, "I am with you always, to the close of the age." He does not ascend into heaven (Matthew 28:16–20).

THURSDAY, MAY 17, 30 C.E.: BACK IN THE JERUSALEM AREA

12. Jesus appears again and tells the disciples to wait in Jerusalem until they receive the Holy Spirit (even though, according to John, they had already received the Spirit on April 9: John 20:22). Then he ascends into heaven from Mount Olivet, just west of Jerusalem (Acts 1:1–12).

SUNDAY, MAY 27, 30 C.E.: JERUSALEM

13. God sends the Holy Spirit upon the twelve disciples, Mary the mother of Jesus, and about 107 other people (Acts 2:1–4; cf. 1:13–15, 26).

It is clear that the scriptural stories about this six-week period contradict one another egregiously with regard to the number and places of Jesus' appearances, the people who were on hand for such events, and even the date and the location of the ascension into heaven. Despite our best efforts above, the gospel accounts of Jesus' *post mortem* activities in fact cannot be harmonized into a consistent "Easter chronology." Nor need we bother to ask if the miraculous events of this Easter period could have been observed or recorded by cameras or tape recorders, had such devices been available. The reasons for both the patent inconsistencies and the physical unrecordability of these miraculous "events" come down to one thing: The gospel stories about Easter are not historical accounts but religious myths.[4]

I say this not at all out of disrespect for Christian faith or for the doctrines that it holds. Rather, I mean to indicate the general literary form of the Easter accounts. They are myths and legends; and it is absurd to take them literally and to create a chronology of preternatural events that supposedly occurred in Jerusalem and Galilee during the weeks after Jesus had died. My purpose here is not to undo the meaning of Easter but precisely to reconstruct it by interpreting the myths that have been used to express that meaning.

In anticipation of what we shall see later, it is worth noting at this point that the New Testament does not in fact assert that Jesus came back to life on earth, or that he physically left his grave after he had died, or that faith in him is based on an empty tomb. What is more, almost forty years would pass after Jesus' death before the Christian Scriptures so much as mentioned an empty tomb (Mark 16:6, written around 70 C.E.), and it would take yet another fifteen years after that (ca. 85 C.E.) before the Gospels of Matthew and Luke would claim that Jesus' followers had seen and touched his risen body. I hope to show that (1) even though Jesus' tomb was probably found empty after his death, that fact says nothing about a possible resurrection; and (2) the stories about Jesus showing his disciples his crucified-and-risen body are relatively late-arriving legends in the Christian Scriptures and in the final analysis are not essential to Christian faith.

But if Christianity stands or falls with the resurrection, may we ask "when" Jesus was raised from the dead? The Scriptures make no attempt to date the resurrection to Easter Sunday morning, nor do they claim that anyone saw it happen.[5] They do not even assert that the resurrection took place at Jesus' tomb. In fact, catechetical popularizations aside, the church does not claim that the resurrection was a historical event, a happening in space and time.

Nonetheless, about 150 years after Jesus' death the so-called Gospel of Peter (an apocryphal work which the church does not accept as authentic Scripture) did offer what purports to be an eyewitness account of what happened at Jesus' grave on the first Easter. The narrative has had considerable influence on Christian iconography, but all that notwithstanding, the story remains pure legend.[6]

According to the Gospel of Peter the resurrection took place during the Saturday night after the crucifixion. As the legend tells it, the drama started with a loud voice that rang out from heaven and startled the soldiers who were guarding Jesus' tomb. Then the extraordinary action began:

> They [the soldiers] saw the heavens open and two men [angels] come down from there in a great brightness and draw nigh to the sepulcher. The stone that had been laid against the entrance to the sepulcher began to roll by itself and gave way to the side. The sepulcher was opened, and both the young men entered in. (8:36–37)

The soldiers, understandably taken aback by all of this, awaken the Jewish elders who are also guarding the grave, and the group witnesses a spectacular procession featuring a giant-sized Jesus and two only slightly shorter attendants.

> And they saw three men come out of the sepulcher, two of them [the angels] sustaining the other [Jesus], while a cross followed them, the heads of the two reaching to heaven, but the head of [Jesus, whom] they were leading by the hand overpassing the heavens.
> And they heard a voice out of the heavens crying, "Thou hast preached to them that sleep." And from the cross was heard the answer, "Yes." (8:39–42)

The tale continues in an equally fanciful vein, but the point is clear: This eyewitness account of the resurrection is a myth. Nonetheless, the fiction is correct in at least one matter: If any witnesses *had* observed such a bizarre scene, it would have convinced them of absolutely nothing relevant to Christian faith. According to the Gospel of Peter, the Roman soldiers and Jewish elders who allegedly saw the resurrection did not thereby become believers but rather ran off in confusion and reported the scene to Pilate. In other words, whatever religious intentions moved the author of the apocryphal book to concoct this graphic description of the resurrection, the text itself shows that physically witnessing Jesus' alleged emergence from the tomb on Easter Sunday morning would not have moved anyone to believe. As we shall see later, the Gospels of Mark and John show that the sighting of an empty tomb by women on Easter Sunday morning neither provided them with evidence of a resurrection nor motivated them to believe in it. But the Gospel of Peter shows that even viewing the resurrection (if that were possible) would not of itself elicit Christian faith.[7]

Quite apart from the apocryphal Gospel of Peter, the accepted scriptural accounts of Easter are themselves riddled with contradictions, as we saw above—proof, according to the village atheist, that the Gospels are frauds, and evidence, according to the fundamentalist believer, that God is indeed mysterious. But the naïve historical positivism that characterizes both camps is simply a category mistake—like looking up "poetry" in the dictionary and expecting to find rhyming verse, or searching for mathematics in the phone book because it is full of numbers. Both sides miss the point of the apocalyptic literary forms in which the writers of the New Testament couched early Christian faith—a matter to which we shall return.

Granted that the gospel accounts of Easter are myths rather than historical accounts, what actually did happen after the crucifixion? Bereft as we are of historical access to the "resurrection," we find ourselves thrown back on the claims of Simon Peter and other early believers that they had certain supernatural experiences ("appearances") which convinced them that Jesus was alive after his death. The first recorded claim of such appearances (I Corinthians 15:5–8) was not written down until some twenty-five years after the crucifixion; we shall turn to that text in a moment. First, however, let us attempt to reconstruct the historical events that actually took place in the days and weeks after Jesus died.

2

THE BIRTH OF CHRISTIANITY

T HE LAST HISTORICAL EVENT in the life of Jesus of Nazareth was
his death on April 7, 30 C.E., following the torture of crucifixion.
No coroner was present to record the medical facts, but the Scriptures
and the Christian creed put the matter simply and directly: He died
and was buried.

Jesus had not fainted. He was dead. And in the spirit of the New
Testament we may add: He never came back to life.[8]

As a deterrent to crime the Roman authorities usually left the bodies
of the crucified hanging on the cross until they had decomposed, but
in Palestine this practice was suspended out of respect for a Jewish law
that mandated the burial of a hanged man on the day of his death.[9]
As criminals, the victims of crucifixion were usually buried in a
common grave rather than in individual tombs, and Jesus' corpse may
have suffered that fate. This possibility is increased by the fact that the
Jewish law considered hanged or crucified men to be accursed by God
(Deuteronomy 21:23; cf. Galatians 3:13).[10] In fact, one scripture text
indicates that Jesus was buried not by his disciples but by his enemies,
the very ones who had arranged for his death ("those who live in
Jerusalem and their rulers," Acts 13:27, 29). This rough burial would

thus have constituted the final rejection of the prophet by those to whom he had preached.

On the other hand, there may well be historical truth to the gospel stories that before evening fell and the Passover began, Joseph of Arimathea, a member of the Sanhedrin, removed the body from the cross with Pilate's permission, wrapped it in linen cloths, and sealed it in a tomb hewn out of rock.[11] (Matthew's story that the high priests set guards the next day at Jesus' tomb is a later legend, as we shall show below.)

The Passover festival of 30 C.E. came and went, and life returned to normal. Caiaphas and the Sanhedrin, no doubt with some remorse over the brutal turn of events, went back to their religious duties. Pilate and the Roman garrison breathed more easily as the pilgrims poured out of Jerusalem and the city resumed the routine of everyday life.[12] Across Palestine farmers began the spring planting, workers pursued their trades, Zealots continued to hatch their revolutionary plots against the Roman Empire.

Jesus' closest disciples probably knew of the prophet's death only by hearsay. Most likely they had not been present at the crucifixion and did not know where he was buried. Having abandoned Jesus when he was arrested, they had fled in fear and disgrace, probably immediately to Bethany, where they had been living with Jesus in the previous days, and then a few days later to their homes in Galilee. There, grieving at their loss and struggling to pick up the scattered bits of their lives, they faced the crushing scandal of those last days in Jerusalem.[13]

The scandal was not that God's eschatological prophet had been condemned to die on the cross. Traumatic as it was for the disciples, the murder of Jesus was not entirely a surprise; indeed, it seemed to be almost inevitable. Death was the price that prophets had long paid (John the Baptist was only the most recent case) for threatening the tidy, cherished world of the religious establishment and the vaunted omnipotence of empire. Jesus had known what was in store for him, and he accepted it with courage. By proclaiming the revolution of God-with-man to people who preferred the security of religion and power, he had sealed his fate.

But he had also secured his reward. By trusting himself entirely to the present-future, by giving himself without reserve to the cause of God-with-man—that is, by living the kingdom and becoming what he lived—Jesus proclaimed that not even the grave could cancel God's presence. "You will not abandon my soul to hell, you will not let your holy one see corruption" (Psalm 15:10; Acts 2:27). This is what Jesus finally meant by "Abba": that everything, even death, was in the hands of his loving Father, with whom he was as one.

Thus, as Jesus prepared the disciples for his inevitable fate, they came to believe, even before the crucifixion, in a higher inevitability: No matter what happened, God would *have* to awaken his servant from the sleep of the tomb and take him into heavenly glory (Mark 8:31; Luke 24:26).

No, the scandal of those last days in Jerusalem was not that the prophet was crucified, but that the disciples lost faith in what he had proclaimed. Jesus' every word had been a promise of life, but they fled when threatened with death. He had trusted utterly in God; but they feared men. On the night before Passover, they abandoned the prophet to his enemies, just after sharing with him the cup of a fellowship that was supposed to be stronger than death.

We may imagine the disciple Simon, later to be called Cephas or Peter —a fisherman perhaps thirty years of age—now returned to Capernaum, his village on the Sea of Galilee.[14] He thinks of the prophet, his friend, whose body is rotting in a grave outside Jerusalem. He recalls their last meal together.

> Simon declared to Jesus, "Though they all fall away because of you, I will never fall away!" Jesus said to him, "Truly, I say to you, this very night, before the cock crows, you will deny me three times." Simon said to him: "Even if I must die with you, I will not deny you." (Matthew 26:33–35)

Simon remembers the darkness of Gethsemane that same night as Jesus went ahead into the grove to pray. Suddenly the arrival of armed men, the torchlight red on sweaty faces, a kiss of betrayal. Then the cowardly flight through the olive grove and away into the night.

> But Simon followed Jesus at a distance, as far as the courtyard of the high priest, and going inside, he sat with the guards to see the end.

And a maid came up to him and said, "You also were with Jesus the Galilean." But he denied it before them all: "I do not know the man."

When he went out to the gateway, another maid saw him and said to the bystanders, "This man was with Jesus of Nazareth." And again he denied it with an oath, "I do not know the man!"

After a while the bystanders came up and said to Simon, "Certainly you are one of them, for your accent betrays you." Then he began to invoke a curse on himself and to swear, "I do not know the man!"

And immediately the cock crowed, and Simon remembered the saying of Jesus, "Before the cock crows, you will deny me three times." And he went out and wept bitterly. (Matthew 26:58, 69–75)

Jesus had said, "If the light inside you is darkness, what darkness that will be!" (Matthew 6:23). There in Capernaum Simon, the young fisherman, felt that inner darkness: It was like being storm-tossed on the night sea, when the savage waves lash your face and you watch helplessly as the sail tears loose from the mast and the rudder breaks free of your grasp. You are lost and there is nothing to do.[15]

Then Jesus, followed by his disciples, got into the boat, and without warning a storm broke over the lake, so violent that the waves were crashing right over the boat. But Jesus was asleep. So they ran to him and shook him awake, saying, "Save us, Lord, we're going under!" (Matthew 8:23–26; cf. 14:28–33)

In those dark days after Jesus' death, Simon had an insight, a "revelatory experience" that he took as a message from God's eschatological future.[16]

We cannot know exactly how the insight dawned on him. But we do know that the spirit of apocalypse was in the air and that Simon had breathed it deeply. He was convinced that these were the final days before the end, and he knew that God had promised:

In the last days
   I will pour out my Spirit on all flesh,

And your sons and daughters shall prophesy,
      and your young men shall see visions. (Joel 2:28)

In the apocalyptic spirit of the times, pious Jews felt at home with a broad spectrum of ecstatic visions and eschatological manifestations: theophanies (Acts 7:55), angelophanies (Luke 1:11), revelations (Galatians 1:12), epiphanies of returning prophets (Mark 8:28), and stories about how Gentiles had converted to Judaism after having visions of blinding light (the way Saint Paul turned to the Jesus-movement: cf. Acts 9:3). It was this lexicon of apocalyptic revelations that Simon spontaneously drew upon when he first tried to put into words the "Easter experience" that he had undergone there in Capernaum.[17]

Simon hastened to share his experience with Jesus' closest followers. He gathered them together at his house, to reflect on what they had earnestly hoped for and to renew their faith. They spoke of their master, recalled his extraordinary message, and prayed his eschatological words: "Abba, thy kingdom come!"

Simon told them his Easter experience: In his despair, when he felt like a drowning man pulled to the bottom of the sea, the Father's forgiveness, that gift of the future which was God himself, had swept him up again and undone his doubts. Simon "saw"—God revealed it to him in an ecstatic vision—that the Father had *taken his prophet into the eschatological future and had appointed him the Son of Man.* Jesus was soon to return in glory to usher in God's kingdom!

And having "turned again" under the power of God's grace, Simon "strengthened the brethren" (Luke 22:32). Jesus' disciples began to call him "Simon *Kepha,*" the rock of faith. They clung to that rock, and they too sensed the gift of God's future undoing their lack of faith. They too "saw" God's revelation and had the Easter experience.[18]

There in Capernaum—without having laid eyes on Jesus since the moment he was dragged off to his trial, without seeing Jesus' tomb in Jerusalem or hearing that it was supposedly empty[19]—Simon and the other disciples experienced Easter. We cannot know with certainty the psychological genesis of that experience, but we do know its result. They believed that Jesus had been designated the coming Son of Man. God's reign would soon be realized.

The Jesus-movement was born—or rather, reborn—and it came forth proclaiming the message of the prophet in the same synagogues of Capernaum, Chorazin, and Bethsaida where he himself had preached it. "Repent!" they exhorted the people. "The kingdom of God is at hand!"[20]

How did Simon (and the other disciples) put the Easter experience into words?[21] We should not conclude too hastily that Simon proclaimed that Jesus had been physically raised from the dead. The "resurrection" was not a historical event but only one possible way, among many others, in which Simon could interpret the divine vindication of Jesus that he claimed to have experienced.[22] In fact, "resurrection" was probably not the first term that he used to express what he had "seen." Probably the earliest way that Simon put into words his renewed faith in God's kingdom was to say that God had "glorified" his servant (Acts 3:13), that he had "exalted" him to his right hand (2:33), that he had assumed him into heaven and "designated" him the agent of the coming eschaton (3:20)—without any mention of a physical resurrection. Later believers would say merely that Jesus had "entered heaven" and "appeared before God" (Hebrews 9:24) or simply that he was "alive" (Acts 1:3). Simon and the disciples probably used all these ways to express their Easter experience, the revelation that Jesus had been rescued from death and appointed God's eschatological deputy.[23]

Of course, the language of resurrection was also available, but in the apocalyptic context of the times a resurrection did not necessarily mean that a dead person came back to life and physically left his grave. Some rabbis, to be sure, did promise a dramatically physical resurrection at the end of time, when bodies would return with the same physique that they formerly had (including blemishes) and even with the same clothes. But these fanciful hopes were only one part of the broad spectrum of eschatological hopes, which included as well the promise of resurrections that entailed no vacating of the grave.[24]

The Gospels, for example, say that Herod Antipas thought Jesus was really John the Baptist raised from the dead (cf. Mark 6:16). Today we might suggest that the tetrarch could have allayed his fears by making a trip to the Dead Sea and having John the Baptist's body exhumed. But that thought probably did not even occur to Herod, any more than it occurred to Simon to go down to Jerusalem from Galilee to check whether Jesus' bones were still in the tomb. In first-century Palestine, belief in a resurrection did not depend on cemetery records and could not be shaken by exhumations or autopsies. Resurrection was an imaginative, apocalyptic way of saying that God saved the faithful person *as a whole,* however that wholeness be defined (see, for example, I Corinthians 15:35ff.). Resurrection did not mean having one's molecules reassembled and then exiting from a tomb.

Regardless of whether Simon used the apocalyptic language of exaltation or of resurrection to express his identification of Jesus with God's coming kingdom, neither of these symbolic terms committed Simon to believing that Jesus went on existing or appearing on earth after his death. Affirmations of resurrection or even appearances are not statements about the *post mortem* history of Jesus but religious interpretations (in fact, secondary ones) of Simon's Easter experience. And for Christianity, Simon's experience is the first relevant historical event after the death and burial of Jesus.[25]

In other words, according to the popular and mythical "Easter chronologies" that some Christians try to establish from the Gospels, the *putative* order of events after the crucifixion is as follows:

THE EASTER EVENT	POST-EASTER EVENTS	
The Resurrection ⟶	The Appearance ⟶	The Result
Jesus is raised	Jesus appears to Simon	Simon's faith in Jesus
(April 9, 30 C.E.)	*(later that day)*	*(soon thereafter)*

However, the *actual* sequence of events after the death of Jesus seems to be quite different, and on our hypothesis would look like the following:

THE EASTER EXPERIENCE	A SECONDARY FORMULATION OF THE EASTER EXPERIENCE
Simon, in what he took to be an eschatological revelation or appearance, "saw" that God had 1. taken Jesus into the coming future and 2. appointed him the Son of Man	⟶ "God raised Jesus from the dead"

Some remarks are in order about this second—and, I maintain, correct—hypothesis concerning the sequence of "Easter events."[26]

THE EASTER EXPERIENCE. Something happened to Simon and the other disciples in the order of space and time, perhaps even over a period of time—an experience that could have been as dramatic as an ecstatic vision, or as ordinary as reflecting on the meaning of Jesus. In any case it was an experience to which no one else, whether believer or non-believer, could have direct, unmediated access. In fact, not even Simon could claim unmediated access to the experience he underwent: He knew it only by interpreting it. Eventually Simon and/or the others would speak of his experience in one of the many apocalyptic symbols that were at hand: "Jesus has appeared to Simon." As we shall see below, such an appearance need not have been a physical–ocular manifestation of Jesus. Simon understood his experience as an eschatological revelation that Jesus had been appointed the coming Son of Man. Simon now believed that God had taken his prophet into the eschatological future and would send him at the imminent end of time to usher in the kingdom.

A SECONDARY FORMULATION OF THE EASTER EXPERIENCE. The rescue of Jesus from death and his exaltation to the status of Son of Man soon came to be codified in yet another of the available apocalyptic formulae: "God has raised Jesus from the dead." Eventually "resurrection" became the dominant and even normative term for expressing what Simon and the disciples believed had happened to Jesus.[27]

But even then, for the early believers to speak of Jesus' resurrection from the dead did not mean that they looked back to a historical event that supposedly happened on Sunday, April 9, 30 C.E. The "event" of the resurrection is like the "event" of creation: No human being was present, no one could or did see it, because neither "event" ever happened. Both creation and the resurrection are *not events but interpretations* of what some people take to be divine actions toward the world. Thus, all attempts to "prove the resurrection" by adducing physical appearances or the emptiness of a tomb entirely miss the point. They confuse an apocalyptic symbol with the meaning it is trying to express. For Simon and the others, "resurrection" was simply one way of articulating their conviction that God had vindicated Jesus and was coming soon to dwell among his people. And this interpretation would have held true for the early believers even if an exhumation of Jesus' grave had discovered his rotting flesh and bones.[28]

In short, the grounds for Simon's Easter faith were neither the discovery of an empty tomb (Simon most likely did not know where the prophet was buried) nor the physical sighting of Jesus' risen body (this is not what an eschatological appearance is about). Easter happened when Simon had what he thought was an eschatological revelation, which overrode his doubts and led him to identify Jesus with the coming Son of Man.[29]

What I have stated thus far is obviously a hypothesis, and the question now is whether the Scriptures support such an interpretation or whether it too is only a fanciful reconstruction with no more basis than the mythical "Easter chronologies." To test the hypothesis, we must turn to the New Testament texts. As we noted earlier, the first recorded mention of Simon's experience was written down twenty-five years after the fact. The claim is found in an epistle of Paul, an itinerant Jewish evangelist who had converted to the Jesus-movement a few years after the crucifixion. Let us turn now to Paul's text in order to see how he interpreted Simon's experience.

3

AN
EARLY FORMULA
OF FAITH

WITHIN A FEW YEARS of Jesus' death a kerygma (a proclamation of faith in Jesus) began to circulate in certain synagogues of Palestine and Syria. It declared that Jesus, having died and been buried, had been raised up on the third day and—here was the first mention of it—had appeared to his followers. Paul himself learned the formula soon after he joined the Jesus-movement around 32–34 C.E., and he both recorded and expanded it in his First Letter to the Corinthians, which he dictated some twenty years later, around 55 C.E.[30]

In its expanded form, Paul's kerygma went beyond the mere statement *that* Jesus had appeared. It went on to *list* those who had experienced an appearance of Jesus. Stated in direct discourse, the expanded kerygma that Paul recorded in First Corinthians declared that Jesus

    died for our sins
        in accordance with the Scriptures,
    and was buried.

And he was raised on the third day
    in accordance with the Scriptures,
and appeared to Cephas
    and then to the Twelve.

Afterward he appeared to more than five hundred brethren, most of
    whom are still alive, though some have fallen asleep.

Afterward he appeared to James,
    and then to all the missionaries.

Last of all, as to one untimely born,
    he appeared also to me. (I Corinthians 15:3–8)

This formula, which is among the earliest written statements of Christian faith, is striking for one thing that it does not say: It neither mentions nor presumes the discovery of an empty tomb on Easter Sunday morning. The kerygma says merely that Jesus "was raised"— that is, was taken up (in whatever fashion) into God's eschatological future—but not that he physically came out of his grave. Paul does not mention the empty tomb in any of his writings, and it is far from clear that he even knew of it. It is clear that an early Christian evangelist could preach the triumph of Jesus, his entry into God's eschatological presence, without mentioning the alleged emptiness of Jesus' grave.[31]

In this section we shall put two questions to this early kerygma. First, we must ask whether the Pauline kerygma, insofar as it is cast as a sequence of events, intends to provide an "Easter chronology" of historical happenings running from Good Friday through Easter Sunday and beyond. That is, our first question is whether Paul's kerygma necessarily commits believers to some chronological progression like the following:

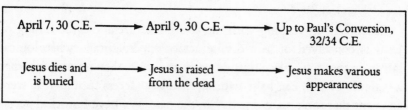

April 7, 30 C.E. ——→	April 9, 30 C.E. ——→	Up to Paul's Conversion, 32/34 C.E.
Jesus dies and is buried ——→	Jesus is raised from the dead ——→	Jesus makes various appearances

Second, given the emphasis that the formula puts on the appearances to Simon and the other disciples, we shall ask what this text can tell us about the way or ways in which Jesus allegedly appeared to his followers after he died. Specifically, we shall ask whether Paul's kerygma in First Corinthians is committed to physical, visible manifestations of the risen Jesus.

AN EASTER CHRONOLOGY?

The kerygmatic formula recorded in First Corinthians almost gives the impression of an inchoate Easter chronology, a mythical sequence of events in which first Jesus died and was buried, then he was raised from the dead, and afterward he appeared to Simon and the other disciples. But such is not the case. Consider the following points:

First: Paul's formula makes no statement about either the time or the place of Jesus' being raised. As regards the "time" of the resurrection, the phrase "on the third day" is *not a chronological designation but an apocalyptic symbol* for God's eschatological saving act, which strictly speaking has no date in history. Thus the "third day" does not refer to Sunday, April 9, 30 C.E., or to any other moment in time.[32] And as regards the "place" where the resurrection occurred, the formula in First Corinthians does not assert that Jesus was raised from the tomb, as if the raising were a physical and therefore temporal resuscitation. Without being committed to any preternatural physics of resurrection, the phrase "he was raised on the third day" simply expresses the belief that Jesus was rescued from the fate of utter absence from God (death) and was admitted to the saving presence of God (the eschatological future). The raising of Jesus has nothing to do with a spatio-temporal resuscitation, a coming-back-to-life in Jerusalem on Easter Sunday morning. "Resurrection" is an apocalyptic term for "being definitively saved by God."[33]

Second: If, in keeping with the above interpretation, the raising of Jesus is conceived of as a divine act of supernatural, eschatological salvation that took place outside space and time, then no one, whether a believer or not, can have natural, historical access to it as if it were an event that took place one day in the past. We have historical access not to such a supposed event but only to certain faith-claims, made first of all by Simon and then by other of the disciples, that God saved Jesus from the dead. What is more, neither Simon nor any other of the original believers had any natural, historical access to the raising of Jesus. In fact, no scriptural text describes the resurrection and no one claims to have witnessed it. Simon, the original believer, came to hold that the kingdom which Jesus had preached was soon to be fulfilled —indeed, that Jesus was now living in God's future—on the grounds of an experience that Simon interpreted as an eschatological revelation. The experience and Simon's first interpretation of it constitute his "Easter experience." But that interpretation does not, and on its own terms could not, commit Simon to a date in time when an alleged raising of Jesus—a nonhistorical, eschatological act of salvation by God —would have taken place. As we suggested earlier, this "raising" was not an event at all but a secondary apocalyptic *interpretation* of what Simon had experienced about Jesus.

Third, therefore: In searching out the origins of Christianity, the furthest back we can go in history is not the "resurrection of Jesus," not even the alleged appearance of Jesus to Simon, but only Simon's interpretative *claim* to have received a revelation that the words and works of Jesus were definitively vindicated by God. Earlier than Simon's "Easter experience" the only relevant event to which we have historical access is the death and burial of Jesus.[34] The text in First Corinthians gives us no warrant to postulate a historical event called "resurrection" which occurred between Jesus' death and Simon's experience, and the text gives us no grounds for saying that Jesus' alleged resurrection took place chronologically *before* his alleged appearance to Simon.

The terms "resurrection" and "appearances" do not indicate temporal happenings at all. They express faith-interpretations rather than historical events, and they point to apocalyptic eschatology rather than to natural history. Moreover, these two apocalyptic interpretations can be neither separated one from the other nor dated relative to each other. Paul and the other believers of his time could not credibly assert that Jesus had been taken up into God's future without also claiming that Jesus had been made manifest from there (how else would they have known that Jesus had been raised?). Nor could they claim that Jesus had appeared from the eschatological future without likewise asserting that he had been assumed into it (otherwise they could not claim that Jesus had been revealed *as risen*). But this interconnectedness of resurrection and appearance does not entail a temporal sequence ("first he was raised, then he appeared") or even a causal one ("because he was raised he therefore appeared").

Thus Paul's text says nothing about earthly activities of Jesus after his crucifixion and gives us no grounds for constructing an Easter chronology in which the resurrection would be a historical event that happened before yet another historical event called the appearance to Simon. Indeed, if both the resurrection and the appearance of Jesus are only derived apocalyptic interpretations of what Simon "saw" in Galilee and what other believers "saw" after him, then as regards the origins of Christianity the only relevant historical event following Jesus's death was Simon's experience. If Paul's kerygma points us backward at all to any "Easter events" in the historical past, it leads us not to a resurrection in Jerusalem one Sunday morning, not even to subsequent appearances of Jesus to Simon and others, but only to the disciples' interpretative claims that they experienced the triumphant Jesus. The text points us to hermeneutics rather than to history.

Even though Paul's text is, in fact, innocent of a mythical "Easter chronology" of the risen Jesus, it nonetheless seems to record the church's first halting step in that misguided direction. As we shall see in the next chapter, the codified interpretation "Jesus was raised on the third day" would eventually be taken as a datable, historical event that took place once at a specific point in time at Jesus' tomb in Jerusalem. And the formula "Jesus appeared to Cephas" would quickly develop into the elaborate gospel stories of Jesus' postresurrection apparitions throughout Palestine.

HOW DID JESUS APPEAR?

According to Paul's list, Simon was the first person to experience an eschatological manifestation of Jesus; and in asking now about the way or ways in which Jesus showed himself after he died, we shall focus entirely on that appearance to Simon. (When I speak about "appearances" in what follows, I am of course referring to alleged appearances —experiences that Simon and the others claimed to have had—without passing judgment on whether or how those "appearances" actually happened.)[35]

In mentioning Jesus' appearances to Simon and the others, Paul in I Corinthians does not relate how or where these manifestations took place. To be sure, elaborate narratives about such appearances would eventually make their literary debut in the Gospels of Matthew and Luke (ca. 85 C.E.), but that would not be until some thirty years after Paul's First Epistle to the Corinthians and at least fifty years after the events these stories purport to recount. By contrast, in this earliest mention of Jesus' appearances, written around 55 C.E., Paul does not provide narratives of such appearances but only bare formulaic statements stripped down to a personal subject (Jesus), a descriptive verb ("appeared"), and a personal object or dative (the people who had the experience).[36]

The verb "he appeared" is the most important element in the formula. Paul uses the Greek word *ōphthē*, which is the third person singular, passive voice, of the aorist (past) tense of the irregular verb *horaō*, "I see." *Ōphthē* can mean equally that someone "made himself seen," "showed himself," or, when used with the dative, as it is here, "was seen by" or "appeared to." Scholars point out that in the Septuagint (the Greek translation of the Jewish Scriptures), *ōphthē* renders the *niph'al* (simple passive) of the Hebrew verb *ra'ah*, "see," which, when used with *le*, means "appear." The Jewish Scriptures frequently use this Hebrew verb and its Greek translation to describe manifestations of God or angels, and the verb always puts emphasis on the divine initiative underlying the appearance rather than on the psychological or physiological processes by which the recipient experienced the manifestation.[37]

In Exodus 6:3, for example, Yahweh says to Moses, "I am the Lord, I appeared [*ōphthēn*] to Abraham, to Isaac, and to Jacob, as God Almighty." The finite verb here does not describe how God appeared to the patriarchs, whether by means of dreams or physical visions or spiritual insight. In fact, Genesis implies that God first "appeared" to Abraham as a voice: "Now the Lord *said* to Abram, 'Go from your country . . .'" (12:1). In short, in these Old Testament contexts the verb *horaō* and its aorist form *ōphthē* indicate simply that God actively reveals something that was heretofore hidden. The verb leaves open the question of *how* (that is, by what physical or psychological processes) the recipients experienced the manifestation.[38]

The same holds true in the text from First Corinthians. In the context of the passage, the verb *ōphthē* does not necessarily indicate the visual sighting of a physical object. For example, Paul lists himself as the last person to receive an appearance of Jesus. He is referring to his experience on the road to Damascus, which, for all its differences from Simon's experience, is here described with the same verb (*ōphthē kamoi*, "he appeared also to me," I Corinthians 15:8). However, in Luke's three accounts of that scene, Paul hears a voice but *sees nothing*. In fact he is rendered temporarily blind by "a light from heaven, brighter than the sun" (Acts 26:13; cf. 9:3, 22:6). Even more important, when Paul himself described this experience some fifteen years after it happened, he called it not a "vision" but more neutrally an apocalyptic "revelation" (*apokalypsis*, Galatians 1:12). "He who had set me apart before I was born, and had called me through his grace, was pleased to reveal his son *in* me [*apokalypsai . . . en emoi*]" (1:16).

What is more, the usage here of the verb *ōphthē* has a particularly eschatological sense to it that forces us to rethink the "temporality" of the appearances. The revelations or appearances to Simon and the others were not understood by them as proofs of a past event (a physical resurrection three days after Jesus' death). Nor, strictly speaking, did these revelations point to an eternal present in heaven from which Jesus had manifested himself. For Simon, the Jesus in whom he believed had "future" written all over him: The "raising" of Jesus meant that he was already living in the final state of things that was soon to dawn on earth. As far as Simon was concerned, Jesus had appeared *from that future,* from God's coming eschatological kingdom; and he was calling them into that future and into the apostolic mission of preaching its imminent arrival. Not to see that eschatological future meant not having seen the risen Jesus at all.[39]

I stress this last point in order to bring out the difference between, on the one hand, Paul's bare formulaic statement "Jesus appeared to Simon" and, on the other hand, the elaborate and mythological apparition-narratives that emerge in the Gospels of Matthew, Luke, and John some fifty to seventy years later. These later legends, which are the basis of so much Christian art and popular mythology, would almost have the reader believe that at a certain point in time Jesus "came back to life" in a preternatural body that could walk, talk, eat, be touched, and even levitate—with the effect that for six weeks Jesus was able to drop in on his disciples at any time or place (in a graveyard or along a country road or in the middle of a Sunday dinner) and disappear just as quickly.

For Simon, on the contrary, Jesus did not wander through Palestine in a resurrected body for forty days after his death. As far as Simon was concerned, the "appearance" he claimed to have had came from the eschatological future into which Jesus had already been assumed. Simon understood his "Easter experience" as a prolepsis of that future, an anticipation of the kingdom which was soon to arrive in its fullness. That is why neither Simon nor any of the other early believers claimed to see Jesus ascend physically into heaven, and why three of the four gospel writers do not even mention such an ascension. Such a journey was unnecessary, for the early believers held that God's rescue (or "raising") of Jesus from the dead meant that the prophet had thereby been taken into his Father's eschatological future.

In conclusion: The text from First Corinthians—the first recorded mention of Jesus' "appearances"—does not tell us how Jesus manifested himself after his death. The verb *ōphthē* simply expresses the Christian claim that Jesus "was revealed" from the coming eschaton in an entirely unspecified way. The manner in which he was made manifest is not mentioned and is not important. The text does not assert that Jesus appeared in any kind of body (be it natural or preternatural) that the disciples could see or touch, nor does it say that Jesus spoke to the disciples. In fact, since Paul makes no claims here about "visions," with their physical and ocular connotations, it would be more accurate to speak not of "appearances" of Jesus but more neutrally of eschatological "manifestations" or "revelations."[40]

To judge from Paul's early formulation of faith, then, the raising of Jesus from the dead has no chronological date or geographical location ascribed to it and no connection with an empty tomb. In fact, the raising of Jesus seems to be no event at all, but only an expression of what Simon had experienced in Galilee. And as regards the appearance to Simon, the text in First Corinthians, upon closer examination, calls into question the notions (1) that such an appearance was an "event" that occurred after Jesus had physically left his tomb and (2) that Jesus was made manifest to Simon in any visible or tangible way. Jesus' "appearance" to Simon refers to the eschatological revelation that Simon claimed to have had in Capernaum. It names what we have been calling Simon's Easter experience.

In other words, when we search for the origins of Christianity, we find not an event that happened to Jesus after he died ("resurrection"), or supernatural actions he allegedly performed ("appearances"), but only apocalyptic interpretations of an experience of Jesus that Simon and others claimed to have had. And the original interpretation underlying these later interpretations seems to have been that God had rescued Jesus from death and appointed him the coming Son of Man. Simon was not theologically equipped to devise an elaborate theology of what had happened to Jesus; rather, he was content to say that God still stood behind what the prophet had preached and would soon send him again. In that sense, the Father had "glorified" Jesus and had let him be "seen" as such.

The text in First Corinthians does not take us very far toward *positively* interpreting the meaning of Easter, but it does ward off some of the more extreme notions of popular Christianity concerning what happened to Jesus after he died. Now we take the next step. We have seen that Paul's text incorporates a formula of faith that probably goes back to at least 32–34 C.E., that is, to within two to four years of the crucifixion. But we must try to burrow even further back than that. We shall continue to probe Simon's experience, but now we try to capture him in the last few hours before the crucifixion, on the night when Jesus was arrested and when Simon last laid eyes on the prophet.

4

THE DENIAL
OF JESUS

We ARE TRYING to return to the very birth of Christianity, to the event that began the enhancement of Jesus' reputation from eschatological prophet to divine cosmocrator. We have no illusions that we can return to supposed historical events called the "resurrection" or the "appearances" of Jesus. The furthest back we can go in history is Simon's assertion of his belief that God had vindicated Jesus and that the kingdom was soon to come—an assertion which took the form of various apocalyptic statements, such as "Jesus appeared [from the eschatological future]" and "Jesus was raised from the dead."

Behind Simon's assertion of his renewed faith in the kingdom there presumably lay an as yet undetermined experience that could have extended over some period of time and could have been as simple as Simon's reflection on the life and message of the dead prophet. Whatever the experience was, we have no access to it in an uninterpreted state; we cannot discover the raw psychological processes that Simon went through "before" he understood them in terms of Jesus and the kingdom of God. Such an interpreted experience is unavailable not just to us but to Simon as well, and in fact it is a contradiction in terms.

Human experience—that is, history—is not an "objective" succession of happenings in the world. Such happenings, whatever they might be, become history—that is, experience—only when they enter the sphere of human interpretation, which we call "language" in the broad sense (Greek *logos*). We know only what we interpret, and there is no way out of this predicament, this "hermeneutical circle," for human beings essentially *are* the act of making sense (= *logos* or *hermēneia*). We cannot peek over the edge of our interpretations to see things or happenings "in the raw," any more than we can step outside of our *logos* and see the world as it is without us.

Therefore, our effort to discover the birth of Christianity within Simon's original Easter experience remains ineluctably caught in a hermeneutical web. As we look back to the origins of Christianity we see not pristine, untouched events but only interpretations: human experiences articulated in human language. Caught as we are within interpretations, our task is, first, to uncover Simon's primordial interpretation of Jesus both before and after the prophet died, and then to interpret that interpretation. At the birth of Christianity we find—whether as believers or as nonbelievers—not happenings observable in the raw but a hermeneutical task.

What, then, was the original content of Simon's Easter experience? To answer that question we must enter into the dynamics of Simon's denial of Jesus on the night of the Last Supper. The matter is of paramount importance, for with Simon's sin and eventual repentance we come to the innermost secret of the original Easter experience and thus to the birth of Christianity.[41]

The Gospels retrospectively put in Jesus' mouth a prediction that Simon's faith would falter when Jesus was arrested—but that he would "turn again" after Jesus had died. Luke, for example, has Jesus say,

> Simon, Simon, behold, Satan demanded to have you that he might sift you like wheat, but I have prayed for you that your faith may not fail. And when you have turned again, strengthen your brethren. (Luke 22:31–32)

The text does not suggest that Simon's failure would be an apostasy or loss of faith. Perhaps it was more a loss of nerve, a fall into doubt that severely tested his faith but did not entirely undo it. Simon's movement from faith to doubt and his turning again to faith begin to reveal to us the content—that is, the primordial interpretation—of Simon's eschatological Easter experience.

What, then, was Simon's failure? Was it that, after protesting his loyalty so loudly at the Last Supper, he abandoned Jesus in the Garden of Gethsemane when the guards from the Sanhedrin came to arrest him? No, the flight from the garden had certainly been the wisest course, for how could a handful of perhaps tipsy and certainly sleepy men have fended off a band of armed soldiers? All things considered, the wisest course was not to mount a futile show of strength but to flee and save oneself for the future.

Or did Simon's failure lie in the fact that later that night, when he was questioned in the high priest's courtyard, he denied that he knew Jesus? No, that too was a prudent decision. The bystanders in the courtyard had no right to know who Simon was or whom he was with. Had they known, they might have seized him too, perhaps even had him crucified. No doubt Simon felt degraded by the incident, but it would be wrong to blame him for what was, after all, an expedient subterfuge. He might be faulted, perhaps, for not organizing a guerrilla band to storm the Sanhedrin and rescue Jesus (even though that would have been entirely contrary to the prophet's wishes); but he should not be condemned for saving his life instead of needlessly throwing it away.

The Gospel says that after Simon had denied Jesus in the courtyard,

> the Lord turned and looked straight at Simon, and Simon remembered the word of the Lord, "Before the cock crows today, you will deny me three times." And he went out and wept bitterly. (Luke 22:61–62)

Much has been made of this wordless encounter between the guilty Simon and his captive master. It would seem that with that silent gaze Jesus was confronting Simon with his sin of abandoning Jesus. Is that indeed the case?

What was in that gaze of Jesus'? Was it anger at Simon for doing what Simon had to do? Was it sadness that Simon had denied knowing him? It is difficult to imagine that Jesus could have been so foolish and resentful—or that he so badly wanted a fellow martyr—that he would expect Simon to stand up in the courtyard of the Sanhedrin and declare, "I'm with him! Take me too!" If Jesus' gaze was meant to confront Simon with his sin, that sin could not be the petty lie of denying that he knew Jesus.

Or did Simon's sin consist in his not being at the foot of Jesus' cross the next day? Perhaps Simon did feel regret at not assisting at Jesus' final agony, but what difference would it have made if Simon had been there? His presence might have been a gesture of solidarity, a last act of friendship, perhaps even a chance for the disciple to purge himself of his grief. But as far as the history of salvation goes, it would have been an indifferent act.

Such attempts to identify Simon's failure by sentimentalizing his sense of guilt—as, for example, Bach does in the *Saint Matthew Passion* —lead nowhere. Whatever remorse Simon may have felt for those acts, his failure was not that he abandoned Jesus or denied that he knew him. These acts in no way touch on Simon's real flight and his denial of Jesus. To know how Simon sinned, we must see what he sinned against.

Simon had learned one major lesson from the preaching of Jesus: The apocalyptic line had been crossed, the dead past was over, God's future had already begun. As we have seen, the name for the crossing of that apocalyptic line was "forgiveness": the gift of God himself to his people, his arrival among them. Therefore, the entire point of the kingdom was to live God's future *now*. But this did not mean looking up ahead toward the future in an effort to glimpse the imminent arrival of God, for he was no longer up ahead in time, any more than he was up above in heaven. He was with his people, in their very midst: "The kingdom of God is among you." In that sense there was no more waiting, for forgiveness meant that the future—God himself—was becoming present among those who opened a space for him. Crossing the line into the future meant no longer searching for God in the great Beyond, but living the present-future with one simple rule: "Be merciful as your Father is merciful" (Luke 6:36).

Simon's sin, his denial of Jesus, consisted in fleeing from and forgetting what he and all Jesus' followers had become: the place where the future becomes present. His sin lay not in abandoning Jesus but in abandoning himself. If anything, he did not deny Jesus enough.

Simon's sin was to have momentarily forgotten where Jesus dwelled, in fact where Simon himself had dwelled. Simon put his hopes on Jesus rather than on what Jesus was about. "Follow me," the prophet had said, and he meant ". . . into God's present-future." But Simon was a literalist. As the soldiers dragged his master away, he got up his courage and "followed at a distance" (Luke 22:54). In so doing he began walking back into the past. The Gospel records Jesus as saying: "No one who puts his hand to the plow and then looks back is fit for the kingdom of God" (Luke 9:62). Ironically, Simon was doing just that—looking back toward the dead past—when he followed Jesus from the Garden of Gethsemane through the dark streets of Jerusalem.

Simon's sin did not lie in abandoning Jesus in Gethsemane or in denying him a few hours later but in following Jesus to the courtyard of the Sanhedrin. His fault was not that he denied Jesus but that he affirmed him too much and feared that if Jesus died, God's kingdom would come undone. Simon had focused his attention so intensely on Jesus that he ended up *taking Jesus for the kingdom* and thereby mistaking the kingdom itself. In his desperate effort not to lose Jesus, Simon lost himself and his grip on the presence of God.

Once, when Jesus had told his disciples that his death was inevitable, Simon took him aside and tried to argue him out of it. But Jesus rebuked him: "Get behind me, Satan! You are on the side of men, not the side of God" (Mark 8:33). The point was clear: The only way to save Jesus was to let him die, and then to go on living the kind of life that Jesus had led, a life set entirely on the present-future, on God-with-man. For the rest, "Leave the dead to bury their dead" (Matthew 8:22).

This, I believe, was the real denial: Simon forgot that the kingdom of God-with-man was not any one person, no matter how extraordinary that person might be, that the kingdom could not be incarnated in any hero, not even in Jesus. By following his master to the courtyard of the Sanhedrin, Simon was setting his heart on Jesus rather than on the kingdom. He was turning Jesus into the last thing the prophet wanted to be: a hero and an idol, an obstacle to God-with-man. Simon failed to see that the future had been given unconditionally and could not collapse with the death of one man—because the kingdom was not Jesus but God.

Simon's threefold "denial" of Jesus in the courtyard of the Sanhedrin was a morally neutral and even a prudent act. The real denial of Jesus lay in holding on to Jesus and thereby forgetting what Jesus was about. Simon erred not in abandoning Jesus but in not abandoning him enough. The right way to acknowledge Jesus would have been to forget him, to let him go, to let him die, without regret. Simon had missed the point: Jesus "was" the kingdom only because he lived his hope so intensely that he became that hope, became the very thing he lived for. And having made his point as well as he could, Jesus had the good sense and courage to die and get out of the way.

After his failure, Simon "turned again." He did see Jesus again—but only in the sense of remembering, re-seeing, the present-future that Jesus, by living out his hope, had once become. This was not a vision but a re-vision, Simon's renewal of his former insight into the kingdom. This re-vision *was* the Easter experience, the rebirth of what Jesus had preached, just as what Jesus preached was a renewal of what had always been the case since the beginning of the world. This re-vision gave Simon his vocation to preach the same message as his master: The sinful past is over; God's future becomes present wherever men and women live in justice and mercy. While Jesus was alive, he had become what he preached. Now that he was dead, his words were reborn in Simon's proclamation.

The content of Simon's eschatological experience was summarized in the simple message that he proclaimed, the same invitation and response that Jesus had preached. The offer was captured in the sentence "The kingdom of God is at hand," and the demand was even simpler: "Repent" (Mark 1:15). These two parts of the message are reducible to each other, just as all later Christian doctrines are reducible to them. The message that "the kingdom is at hand" meant that God was with his people; but God *was* with mankind only if they "repented," that is, changed the way they lived, and enacted the kingdom *now*.

What Simon experienced—both before and after Jesus' death—was not a "vision" but an insight into how to live. The question that gave birth to Christian faith was: "Master, where do you dwell?" (John 1:38). Following Jesus did not mean having a vision of the future but rather realizing that God's future was already present wherever justice and mercy were enacted. Faith was not a matter of possessing the kingdom, but of *living* the kingdom by enacting one's hope in charity. The kingdom could not be verified by any kind of "proof" except the proof of how one lived. The proof was all in the doing. In Jesus' preaching, eschatology had been removed from the mythical context of apocalypse and had become a simple but radical appeal to be as merciful as the Father was. Therefore, for Jesus' disciples to preach the nearness of the kingdom did not mean to pass on information about an imminent end of the world, but to live an exemplary life "worthy of God, who calls you into his own kingdom" (I Thessalonians 2:12). It meant dissolving eschatology into ethics.

But something else came of Simon's insight. The core of his revision had been that the present-future was still a reality after the crucifixion, that Jesus' word—the way he lived the kingdom of God-with-man—was true. But the manner in which Simon and the first believers articulated that insight came to be focused not on Jesus' way of living but on Jesus himself. They announced that his word had been vindicated; and they expressed that vindication by saying that Jesus had been rescued, that is, taken into the eschatological future, and was living there now with God.

This reinterpretation of the kingdom was the first momentous step toward personifying the present-future and turning God-with-mankind into a single individual. In that sense, Simon continued his denial of Jesus by creating Christianity. He reified Jesus' word, his way of living, into the man himself, and then identified the man with a kingdom that was not present but still to come. Simon gave God back his future by personifying that future as Jesus, who was soon to return. Henceforth, preaching the kingdom of God-with-man meant preaching Jesus as the one to come.

Here the prophet's original message of God-with-man began edging toward the later Christian doctrine of God-with-one-particular-man. It was not yet a full-blown "ontological christology," a doctrine of the nature of Jesus as divine (although that would come soon enough). At this point Simon and the others were interested in Jesus only for the role he would play in ushering in God's eschaton. For the earliest believers the name "Jesus" became a code word for the imminence of that eschaton. This was a portentous shift of focus. Now, alongside the prayer Jesus had taught the disciples—"Father, may thy kingdom come!" (Luke 11:2)—there stood another one: *"Maranatha:* Come, Lord Jesus!" (cf. I Corinthians 16:22, and Revelation 22:20).

This first step toward founding Christianity was a retreat from Jesus' original message: It reinserted his *trans*-apocalyptic preaching into the apocalyptic expectations of the age. There is no doubt that Jesus himself was a child of his times and that his message was clothed in some apocalyptic imagery. But that garment fit loosely and not well. Jesus' preaching transcended its own language: Its true meaning lay more in the way he lived than in what he said. After Jesus' death Simon had an opportunity to rescue the core of that message—a unique way of living—from the symbols in which it was couched. But Simon, even more than Jesus, was a child of the age, and ultimately he missed his chance insofar as he interpreted his renewed insight in the apocalyptic terms of a future kingdom, perhaps an "appearance" and even a "resurrection." He reified the future, sent it up ahead again in time, and identified that future with the Jesus who he believed was soon to return. The prophet's message of urgency and immediacy—"Live the presence of God's future!"—fell back into an apocalyptical eschatology, the awaiting of a future kingdom. Christianity is built on that mistake.

With Simon's experience we are present at the turning point: the end of Jesus and the beginning of Christianity. That topic will concern us in a later chapter, but for now we must remain a while longer with the question of the resurrection, the "event" that Christianity proclaims as the basis for the dramatic change in Jesus' reputation.

There is a text in Saint Mark's Gospel that seems to overcome the hermeneutical distance that separates us from Jesus' "resurrection" and that may allow us to discover an uninterpreted "Easter event." That text, to which we now turn, recounts the story of how Jesus' tomb was found empty on the Sunday after he died.

THE
EMPTY TOMB

THE APPEARANCE OF Saint Mark's Gospel, around 70 C.E., brought something radically new into the Scriptures: the first legends about what happened on the Sunday morning after Jesus had died. This event is of paramount importance, for it marks the first literary appearance of what was to develop into the "Easter chronologies" of Jesus' postresurrection activities.

Mark's Gospel was the first of the four to be written; the Gospels of Matthew and Luke would follow about fifteen years later (ca. 85 C.E.), and the Gospel of John would be written toward the end of the century. The only Christian Scriptures predating Mark's Gospel are the epistles of Saint Paul, his ad hoc letters written during the fifties to bolster the faith of his converts. Whereas Paul's writings hardly mention the life of Jesus except for his crucifixion, Mark's Gospel presents the putative words and deeds of Jesus from his baptism in the Jordan to his death and burial. Strictly speaking, however, it is not a historical record of Jesus' ministry but a faith-charged theological treatise that reflects the beliefs and concerns of later Christians, mostly Greek-speaking Jewish converts in the Mediterranean Diaspora.

Our concern here is with Mark's last chapter, his narrative of what happened at Jesus' tomb on the Sunday after his death. Before this Gospel appeared, scriptural proclamations of Jesus' resurrection were limited to brief and simple formulaic sentences, such as "God raised him from the dead" (I Thessalonians 1:10). Mark continued the tradition of kerygmatic brevity with regard to the resurrection itself, but he also launched the new biblical genre of narrating stories about what took place immediately *after* the resurrection.[42] A close look at the final chapter of Mark's Gospel and at other material in the New Testament may lead us to what actually happened at the tomb on April 9, 30 C.E.

1

EASTER
ACCORDING
TO MARK

THE EASTER STORY that appears in the last chapter of Mark's Gospel is brief, bare, and deeply disturbing. Besides failing to mention most of the events that traditional Christian piety associates with the first Easter morning, the gospel story ends without the disciples believing that Jesus had been raised from the dead. It concludes instead with the confusion and disbelief of the women who had gone to visit his grave: "They said nothing to anyone, for they were afraid" (Mark 16:8). Given their reaction, we might find ourselves, as we reach the last word of the Gospel, wondering how faith in the risen Jesus came about at all.

It was precisely this question that moved a later, anonymous Christian writer to flesh out Mark's concluding chapter (16:1–8, the "first ending") with eleven more verses (16:9–20, the "second ending") that bring it into line with the elaborate appearance stories in the later Gospels of Matthew, Luke, and John.[43] However, the original Easter story in Mark—the one we shall focus on in this chapter—is about the confusion and fear that overcame the three women who visited Jesus' tomb on Sunday morning with the intention of giving him a proper burial. The "first ending" runs as follows:

MARK 16:1–8

I. SATURDAY NIGHT (VERSE 1)

And when the sabbath was past, Mary Magdalene and Mary the mother of James, and Salome, bought spices, so that they might go and anoint him.

II. SUNDAY MORNING (VERSE 2)

And very early on the first day of the week they went to the tomb when the sun had risen.

III. THE STONE (VERSES 3–4)

And they were saying to one another, "Who will roll away the stone for us from the door of the tomb?" And looking up, they saw that the stone was rolled back; for it was very large.

IV. THE ANGEL'S TWOFOLD MESSAGE

A. The resurrection (verses 5–6)
And entering the tomb, they saw a young man [= an angel] sitting on the right side, dressed in a white robe; and they were amazed. And he said to them:
"Do not be amazed.
You seek Jesus of Nazareth, the crucified.
He has been raised.
He is not here. See the place where they laid him."

B. A future appearance (verse 7)
"But go, tell his disciples and [especially] Peter that he goes before you to Galilee; there you will see him, as he told you."

V. THE REACTION (VERSE 8)

And they went out and fled from the tomb; for trembling and astonishment had come upon them. And they said nothing to anyone. For they were afraid.

There is no more to the earliest recorded account of Easter Sunday morning, and no more to the written Gospel. Mark's narrative ends there, abruptly. The events at the tomb provoke confusion and fear rather than joy and proclamation, and the women retreat into a hermetic silence. With no report of the birth of Easter faith, Mark's account seems to leave Christianity stillborn at Jesus' grave.

Moreover, when we compare Mark's final chapter with the Easter accounts of the later Gospels and above all with the popular legends about Easter that have grown up over the centuries, the account strikes us as stark and minimalistic. There are no guards at the tomb, no emergence of Jesus from the grave, no burial shroud left behind to prove that the prophet had risen from the dead. Notice what Mark's Gospel fails to say:

First, Mark's final chapter does not describe Jesus' resurrection. As we have already seen, it was well over a century after Jesus' death before the apocryphal Gospel of Peter (which the Church does not, in fact, accept as authentic Scripture) attempted to describe Jesus' emergence from the tomb. There is no text in the New Testament that describes the resurrection of Jesus or that claims there were any witnesses to it. For if it indeed was an eschatological event, there would have been quite literally nothing to see. Mark stays within that tradition when he has the angel say simply, "He has been raised."[44]

Second, Mark's Easter story is characterized by a stunning absence: The risen Jesus does not appear at all. Indeed, according to this Gospel, once he was sealed in his tomb, Jesus was never seen again. It is true that the angel in the story does *allude* to a future appearance in Galilee ("there you will see him, as he told you"), but this may well refer to Jesus' universal appearance at the end of time.[45] In any case, Mark's Gospel gives no description of such an appearance and has nothing more to say about it. Nor, to be precise, does the angel tell Jesus' followers to go to Galilee; and judging from the account of the women's reaction, we get the impression that no one went. In fact, within the rhetorical structure of the narrative, the prediction of the future appearance seems to be tacked on as an afterthought to the centerpiece of the story: the announcement that whereas, yes, Jesus has been raised, he is in fact absent and unavailable to visitors. "He has been raised; he is not here."

Third, we are struck by the effect that the angel's message has on the women—or perhaps better, the lack of effect. As far as Mark's story goes, the women do not believe the angel's message about the resurrection, and they ignore his order to pass on the word to the disciples. They tell absolutely no one what they have seen and heard (*oudeni ouden eipon*, verse 8). This passage is the earliest account we have of the events of the first Easter morning; and if it were the only account, we might be left wondering how faith in the resurrection of Jesus originated among his disciples. In any case, Mark is clearly saying that

Jesus' empty tomb is *not* the origin of that faith, and that if some women did discover such a tomb on Easter Sunday morning, the event led to confusion rather than to faith.[46]

Thus the earliest gospel account of Easter Sunday provides no description of the resurrection, only an announcement that it had happened; no description of a resurrection appearance, but at best only a prediction of one to come; and no indication that the scene at the tomb (if such a scene ever really took place) gave rise to Easter faith.

Nonetheless, for all these apparent defects, the genius of Mark's story is precisely that it raises more questions than it answers. Mark's story casts Easter in the interrogative mode, and yet his account may say more about Christian faith than the more mythological accounts that the later Gospels provide. According to the majority of exegetes, *all* the gospel accounts of the first Easter morning are legends, with or without an original historical base. It is unfortunate, however, that the church has usually preferred to read the later legends, and not this barer and more evocative one, at the annual celebration of Easter.

2

AN EARLIER LEGEND

MARK'S ACCOUNT OF Easter morning occupies a vantage point midway between the elaborate Easter stories that are found in the later Gospels and the even starker *oral* narrative that exegetes generally agree preceded Mark's own Gospel. For a moment let us stand at that middle point and look both forward and backward in time.

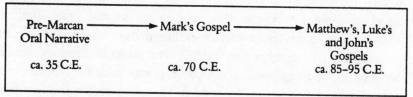

Looking forward in time from Saint Mark (70 C.E.), we find that the Gospels of Matthew, Luke, and John (written fifteen to thirty years later) make a qualitative leap in the way they treat Easter, in that they offer *the first descriptions of Jesus' postresurrection appearances.* Those later Gospels give at least eight accounts of such apparitions, characterized by increasingly concrete physical details of Jesus' apparitions (ingestion of food, showing of wounds, ascension into heaven, and so forth). But while these legendary additions to Mark are noteworthy, even more important is what the later Gospels omit, namely, Mark's story about the women's scandalous disbelief and their frightened flight into silence.[47]

For example, fifteen years after Mark's Gospel, Luke dropped the women's disbelief altogether and changed their confused flight from the tomb into a simple "return" to Jerusalem in order to inform the apostles (24:9). Matthew, writing at about the same time as Luke, chose to have it both ways: the women are filled with both fear *and* "great joy," and even though they still run from the tomb, it is to tell the disciples what they have seen (28:8). It is as if Mark's stark account of the women's fear and incredulity was too troubling for later generations of believers and therefore had to be changed.

Those later revisions of Mark unquestionably resulted in beautiful and moving stories—for example, Saint John's sublime account of the meeting of Jesus and Mary Magdalene on Easter Sunday morning (20:13–18). But for all their mythological richness, these later Easter stories still leave us wondering about Mark's startling claim that the first proclamation of the resurrection (by an angel, no less), along with the discovery of the empty tomb, failed to instill faith in the women. Where did Mark's story come from, and what does it say about the resurrection? To answer those questions we must look backward in time from Mark's Easter account to the oral story that preceded it.[48]

Whereas the final chapter of Saint Mark's Gospel is the earliest *written* narrative of Easter morning, the tale about the women, the angel, and the empty tomb did not originate with him. Biblical scholars, using form- and redaction-criticism, have managed to sift out of Mark's narrative what they believe is *an earlier oral version*, which he drew on and expanded, a legend that dates back to the primitive community of believers who lived in Jerusalem during the first few years after the crucifixion. The process whereby exegetes have arrived at this hypothetical earlier version is largely a matter of subtracting the editorial elements that Mark appears to have added to an earlier narrative. The process is complex, and here we shall only allude to some aspects of it, while keeping the details for later. For example, as we shall see below, minor details of the gospel version—such as the women's purchase of spices with the intention of anointing the body (verse 1) and their discussion about the stone as they walk to the tomb (verses 3–4)—seem to be later (and generally incongruent) additions that Mark edited into an earlier and simpler narrative that he inherited. And most important, the striking contrast in Mark 16 between the angel's prediction of a future appearance of Jesus ("But go, tell his disciples . . . that he goes before you to Galilee; there you will see him," verse 7) and the conclusion of the narrative ("And they went out and fled from the tomb . . . and said nothing to anyone," verse 8) seems to indicate that the promise of a future appearance of Jesus is a Marcan addition to an earlier story that neither narrated nor alluded to any appearances at all. When these presumably later elements are subtracted from the last chapter of Mark's Gospel, the original oral legend that the evangelist drew upon looks like this:

THE EARLIER, PRE-MARCAN ORAL VERSION

I. SUNDAY MORNING (= MARK 16:2, 4)

Very early on the first day of the week Mary Magdalene [and perhaps some other women] went to the tomb when the sun had risen. They saw that the stone was rolled back.

II. A SIMPLER MESSAGE: ONLY RESURRECTION (= VERSES 5–6)

Entering the tomb, they saw a young man [= an angel] sitting on the right side, dressed in a white robe; and they were amazed. He said to them:
    "Do not be amazed.
    You seek Jesus of Nazareth, the crucified.
    He has been raised.
    He is not here. See the place where they laid him."

III. THE SAME REACTION (= VERSE 8)

They went out and fled from the tomb, for trembling and astonishment had come upon them. They said nothing to any one. For they were afraid.

This story is even starker than the one found in Mark's final chapter, for the women flee from the tomb not only without faith in the resurrection but also without Mark's promise of a future appearance that might eventually lead them and others to believe that Jesus had been raised.

Have we, with this earlier version, arrived at "what really happened" on the first Easter morning? We must remember that this hypothetical oral tale is still a *religious legend* that makes no claim to giving a historical account of what actually transpired at the tomb on

Easter morning. As regards the origin of this pre-Marcan tomb narrative, some exegetes have made the plausible case that the original occasion for the telling of this story was a liturgical celebration held at least annually at Jesus' tomb. Within that liturgy, the story functioned as an "etiological legend," a narrative that justified the religious service by explaining its alleged origins.[49]

In the first decades after Jesus' death, the theory claims, believers made pilgrimages to Jesus' grave "very early in the morning on the first day of the week," presumably on what we now call Easter, but perhaps even more frequently. At the tomb they would hear a story about women who came there after the crucifixion, found the tomb open, and encountered an apocalyptic messenger, who announced that Jesus had been assumed into God's eschatological future. The pilgrimage reached its climax when the liturgical storyteller proclaimed, "He has been raised," and then pointed to the tomb: "He is not here; see the place where they laid him." The pilgrims' trip to the tomb to "seek Jesus of Nazareth, who was crucified" was meant to end with the insight that the journey in a sense had been fruitless—for why should they seek the living among the dead?

Before delving into this earlier narrative, we would do well to pause for a moment and consider the various stages in the evolution of the Easter story over the sixty years between the death of Jesus and the writing of the last Gospel. (See the accompanying chart.)

It would seem that, whatever may have happened in the days and weeks after Jesus died, the narratives that purport to relate the Easter period developed incrementally from

(1) a pre-Marcan story in which an apocalyptic angel *announces that Jesus has been raised,* but does not mention any appearances at all, to

(2) Mark's story, in which the angel, after announcing the resurrection, also *alludes to a future appearance* in Galilee (which is never described), to

(3) the later evangelists' *narrations of a variety of appearances* that allegedly take place in Jerusalem and Galilee.[50]

The increment between Stage One and Stage Two is relatively modest, whereas the leap to Stage Three—that is, from the *allusion* to an

First Stage: An oral story is invented by the community in
Jerusalem (ca. 35 C.E.?).

The pre-Marcan narrative (perhaps an etiological legend):
  The resurrection is proclaimed.
  No appearances are mentioned.
    1. A young man (or angel) tells women that Jesus is risen.
    2. The women flee in fear and tell no one.

Second Stage: The oral story is expanded and written
down by Mark (ca. 70 C.E.).

The Marcan narrative (16:1–8):
  The resurrection is proclaimed.
  An appearance is alluded to but not narrated.
    1. A young man (or angel) tells the women that Jesus is risen.
    2. He announces that Jesus will be seen in Galilee.
    3. The women flee in fear and tell no one.

Third Stage: The story grows; elaborate appearance–narratives
are added in the Gospels of Matthew, Luke and
John (85–100 C.E.). ~

For the first time appearances are narrated, in the Gospels of Matthew, Luke
and John and in the appendix to Mark (16:9–20).
  Details and physical concretion increase.
  Appearances are multiplied; they occur in both Jerusalem and Galilee.
    1. An earthquake occurs; an angel descends, rolls back the stone, and sits
    on it (Matthew). Or two angels appear (Luke and John).
    2. The angelic dialogue expands into a recollection that Jesus had
    predicted his death and resurrection (Luke).
    3. The women inform the disciples about the empty tomb, with the
    result that Peter visits the tomb (Luke) and with another disciple sees the
    burial clothes (John).
    4. Narrations of appearances of Jesus
    In Jerusalem
      On Easter Sunday:
      a. To one or more women (Matthew, Mark-appendix, John)
      b. To Simon (not narrated, Luke)
      c. To two disciples at Emmaus (Luke)
      d. To ten disciples (John), or to eleven disciples, followed by his
      ascension (Luke, Mark-appendix)
      A week later:
      a. To eleven disciples (John)
      Forty days later:
      a. Ascension into heaven (Acts of the Apostles)
    In Galilee (time unspecified):
      a. To eleven disciples on a mountain (Matthew)
      b. To Simon and six others at the Sea of Galilee (John)

appearance (which, in fact, may refer to the parousia) to the concrete *description* of multiple appearances in Palestine—is quite dramatic. The years between 70 and 85 C.E. seem to have been the period when the elaborate "Easter chronology" of popular Christian piety was born.

Our first step back behind Mark's Gospel has provided us not with a historical record of what "really happened" on the first Easter Sunday but only with another, if earlier, religious story. Whether or not we believe the story's message, it is necessary, if we hope to understand its point, that we stay *within* its rhetorical boundaries, at least initially, rather than try to look over its edges for an underlying historical event. In other words, we must perform a "phenomenological epoche," a provisional suspension of concern about the historical realities that may lie behind the tale. Our purpose in performing this suspension of concern is to find out first of all what the legend is saying, before we look into the question of where it came from and whether it is true. Let us begin, then, with some general remarks about the way this early, pre-Marcan legend works.

Like any story (but unlike a historical report), this narrative has a double focus, one explicit and the other implicit. Its explicit or "thematic" focus is set on certain narrative events, specifically the visit of some women to Jesus' tomb on the Sunday after he died. But it also has an implicit and unthematic focus, which is directed not upon the narrated events but upon the person who is listening to them. We may call this the "rhetorical focus," not only to call attention to the story's forms and styles of narration but also to emphasize the effect those forms and styles are meant to have on the person who is listening to the tale.

Whereas the original, pre-Marcan Easter story is thematically focused on the women's visit to Jesus' tomb on the first Easter Sunday, it is rhetorically geared to building up faith in the listener. That is, the narrative's final purpose is precisely not to refer the listeners to an event that supposedly happened in time past but rather to confront them with their own faith-decision in the present moment. To be sure, it is quite legitimate to seek out whatever historical events may lie behind the narrative; but such an enterprise requires that the inquirer, at least provisionally, step outside the story and, to that degree, miss its point. However, the rhetorical structure of this narrative is calculated to hold the reader within the tale and, from within the tale, to confront the reader with the possibility of believing in the resurrection. The narrative effects that purpose in part by allowing the listener to understand more than the subjects of the story do. Whoever follows the story line —peeking over the characters' shoulders, as it were, and overhearing the dialogue—is expected to get the point, even if the protagonists do not.

What, then, is this early oral story attempting to say?

You, the listener, are the story's rhetorical focus, its reason for being told. The narrative is directed entirely to you. It confronts you with a question as you too accompany the women on their visit to the tomb. You listen, and whether or not you share the storyteller's faith, simply by listening you are drawn into the movement of the narrative and are invited to get its point. And no doubt you do. You realize that the story is urging you to believe that "Jesus, the crucified one whom you seek, has been raised" (cf. Mark 16:6). But you also notice—this is equally the point of the story—that the women who are the narrative's thematic focus do not understand the message. Instead of believing, they run away in fear and tell no one what they have seen. It would seem, then, that the story is confronting you with a decision and inviting you to do precisely what the women did not do: to believe that Jesus has been raised rather than to flee in confusion.

But is it as simple as that? It is true that the listener is faced with a straightforward decision to believe or not to believe in the resurrection—but he or she is also faced with a puzzling question: What about those who came looking for Jesus and, despite an angel's assurance, fled without believing he was raised? How did such a scandalous story of disbelief find its way into a narrative that ultimately seeks to inspire people to an act of faith in the resurrection? The question about the women's disbelief is not peripheral to the story but is an essential element of its rhetorical appeal for faith. That is, the question arises from within the story's rhetorical boundaries and, if it is to have meaning for faith, must ultimately be answered from within those boundaries.

We could, of course, deal with the question of the women's disbelief by stepping outside the rhetorical confines of the original oral narrative —either by historical *de*construction or by literary *re*construction.

The first option would be to attempt to go back behind the story: to demythologize or deconstruct the narrative and search for the historical events that gave rise to it in the first place. For example, as a first step we might postulate that the women who actually came to the tomb on the first Easter morning did in fact find it empty— without, of course, seeing an angel or hearing him announce the resurrection—and that their response was to flee in confusion. Then we might surmise that this historical fact was so well known in the early Jerusalem church that the author of the original oral legend could not ignore it. And finally we might propose that in the interest of Christian belief the author invented the angel and the angel's announcement of the resurrection in order to provide a faith-explanation for the emptiness of the tomb. Such a historical-"deconstructive" interpretation does have the advantage of helping to clarify how the element of the women's incredulity found its way into the original legend. However, it fails to explain the rhetorical function of that incredulity within the story.

The second way to deal with the women's faithless flight from the tomb is the method chosen by the four evangelists. It too entails stepping outside the original legend, but this time not in the backward direction of the historical past but rather in the forward direction of the literary future. This option consists of changing future versions of the story so as to play down the element of disbelief. Utilizing this option, Mark, of all the evangelists, stays the closest to the original legend. He does retain the (arguably historical) element of the women's confusion and flight, but he also minimizes the starkness of it, at least somewhat, by adding the promise of a future appearance (Mark 16:7). Unlike Mark, however, the other evangelists either omit the women's disbelief altogether (Luke) or dispel it by rewriting the story so as to have Jesus appear to the women soon after they leave the tomb (Matthew).[51] These later revisionist myths may have the advantage of edifying the faithful by covering over the element of doubt and confusion; but they do not help us at all to understand the narrative structure either of Mark's Easter story or of the pre-Marcan oral legend.

Whatever their advantages, both of these options overstep the boundaries of the original legend and therefore cast no light on the *rhetorical function* of the women's confusion in the original story. Therefore, I propose a third option: Rather than stepping outside the pre-Marcan narrative, let us remain within it for a moment and allow it to speak to us in the way it spoke to the proto-Christian community in Jerusalem. Since the question of the women's disbelief arises within the story, let us see whether the story itself provides an answer to that question.

The original legend clearly implies that the emptiness of the tomb does not of itself inspire faith. Presumably the women in the story accept the angel's invitation to "see the place where they laid him." They look, and yet the sight of the empty tomb does not move them to believe that God raised Jesus from the dead. At this point in the narrative the rhetorical sequence is of utmost importance. Notice that the angel's proclamation "Jesus has been raised" (verse 6a) comes *before* he draws the women's attention, for the first time, to the fact that the tomb is empty: "He is not here; see the place where they laid him" (verse 6b). In a strict sense the emptiness of the tomb is not discovered by the women; it is pointed out to them by the angel, in fact *after* his proclamation of the resurrection.[52] This matter is very important, and some conclusions may be drawn from it.

First: *The empty tomb is not a proof of the resurrection.* The angel does not say that the tomb is empty and therefore Jesus has been raised, but that Jesus has been raised and therefore the tomb is empty. It is the resurrection that explains the tomb, not vice versa. Of itself the empty tomb leads to confusion rather than faith.

Second: Not just the empty tomb but *even the angel's announcement that Jesus has been raised does not bring about faith.* Having heard the proclamation and seen the empty tomb, the women simply flee without believing that Jesus has been raised. As listeners, we are expected to understand that if the angel's kerygma did not bring the women to believe, neither will it instill faith in us. That is, if one does not have faith already, neither the pronouncements of angels nor the emptiness of tombs can provide it. The source of Easter faith must lie elsewhere.

Third: The listener is therefore meant to understand that *the women's confused flight and subsequent silence is in fact the appropriate response to the scene at the tomb.* It is rhetorically understandable that the women tell no one what they have heard and seen, for the point of the story is that angels' words do not effect faith (they did not for the women in the legend, and they will not for the listeners) and that empty graves of themselves say nothing about a resurrection. The women's flight in disbelief is not an embarrassment to Christian faith but rather is the very point of the story: Those who go looking for Jesus in a tomb (be it empty or occupied) are left in the dark.

Therefore, what may have seemed at first to be an improper ending for a Christian Gospel turns out to be appropriate and illuminating: It shows that one approach to the resurrection is a dead end. The legend refers the listener not to the empty tomb or the angel's message but primarily to his or her own faith—or lack of it. Upon reflection we see that the women *could not* believe the angel and that optimally the listener *does not need to.* The story is narrated not in order to effect faith in the listeners but in order to strengthen the faith that they are presumed to have already. And if one does not have that faith, the angel's pronouncement is useless.

The legend does not say what the source of that faith might be, but since this is an eschatological story, we may deduce that that source of Easter faith is God's "future" (that is, God himself) insofar as it is becoming present. It is clear that the narrative does indeed point beyond itself—not, however, to an alleged happening in the past, since the story's purpose is precisely to show that such past "events" do not bring about faith. The point of the story is that it is *nothing but a pointer;* and the listener gets the message by following that pointer, that is, by looking not into the tomb but into God's present-future.

The pre-Marcan oral legend about Easter is a gem of storytelling which brilliantly subverts its own apparent theme. Far from being a deficient skeleton that needs to be fleshed out with the promise of appearances (as in Mark) or even with appearance stories (as in the other three evangelists) in order to communicate its message, this stark oral narrative is one of the richest parables about the kingdom of God-with-man to be found in the Christian repertoire. Like all parables, it confronts the listener with a question and a decision, and its narration of thematic "events" is solely for the sake of leading the listener to insight and commitment. Like many of the parables, it hinges on surprise and the reversal of expectations. Here the parable destroys the hope that seeing an empty grave could lead one to believe that Jesus has been raised from the dead. It subverts the theme of a pious visit to Jesus' tomb in order to deliver a very different message: that something other than an empty sepulcher is required to motivate Easter faith.

The emptiness of the tomb does have a positive function in the legend, but it is not an apologetic one. The sentence "See the place where they laid him" was not an invitation to look outside the parable and into the tomb for a historical "proof" that Jesus had been raised. The listeners were expected to see that the absence of a corpse does not prove the resurrection any more than the presence of one disproves it. The narrative invited them to believe in the victory of Jesus *regardless* of the empty tomb.

If the story presumes that its listeners already believe in the resurrection before the angel's announcement and apart from the empty tomb, where does that belief come from? The genius of the pre-Marcan parable was that it did not answer the question, either for the women who appear in the narrative or for anyone who listens to it. The community that originally recounted the oral story was content to leave the question unanswered. That is, their legend says nothing about appearances of Jesus that might lead people to believe that he had been raised from the dead.

Even Mark's later revision of the legend did not answer the question of how Easter faith came about. His Gospel does have the angel allude to a future appearance of Jesus (". . . go to Galilee; there you will see him," verse 7), but Mark describes no such appearance, and in fact the angel's allusion may well refer to Jesus' hoped-for second coming at the end of time.[53] We have, in that verse, the mere hint of an answer to the question of how Easter faith arose. Mark points to Galilee, the place where Jesus had preached the kingdom and where Simon had his Easter experience of Jesus' role in the eschatological future. Mark may be suggesting that all faith in the resurrection goes back to a single source, which is not an "event" that happened to Jesus three days after he died. The source of Easter faith, both for Simon and for all believers since, is not the historical past but the eschatological present-future.

However, just as hearing the angel's announcement did not move the women to believe, so neither will hearing the news about Simon's eschatological experience lead anyone else to faith. Such proclamations might set the stage for belief, or reinforce an already existing faith, but each new believer must undergo the experience for himself. Jesus must be revealed-and-believed to have been raised into God's future, or otherwise everything is beside the point—angels' messages, empty tombs, and apostolic proclamations included. This was already the unspoken point of the original Easter legend, and Mark's reference in verse 7 to the experience in Galilee merely drew out the implication. He made no attempt to *describe* the revelation, for it can only be experienced. Therefore, he simply pointed into the eschatological future where Jesus "goes before you."

3

WHAT REALLY
HAPPENED

W E HAVE ALREADY taken one step behind the first written account of Easter to a hypothetical earlier version. Can we now
take another step, even further back, and arrive at the original historical
event that happened at the tomb on Easter Sunday morning?

The primitive pre-Marcan narrative that we have just discussed
offers little help in taking such a step back. Although we can establish
the story's relative antiquity, it is the antiquity of a *legend*, not a
historical record.[54] It is quite possible that the pre-Marcan Easter
narrative is based on some historical memory of what actually happened at the tomb on the first Easter, but that recollection has been
so totally assimilated into the legend that it is difficult to distinguish
the authentically historical elements. Moreover, if the legend did indeed function as an etiological justification of a liturgical visit to the
tomb, then the possible historicity of the recollection is even further
blurred. The symbiotic relation of the liturgy and the etiological
legend tends toward a closed circle: The legend exists to explain and
justify the liturgical cult, and the cultic practice codetermines the form
and content of the legend that explains it. Using the original legend

to establish facts about the first Easter morning is somewhat, if imperfectly, analogous to using the Genesis legend to reconstruct the creation of the universe. Both legends—that which describes the creation of the world and that which describes the "new creation" effected by Jesus' resurrection—exist not to recount events that took place in the past but to inspire faith in God in the present.

However, even though all the gospel accounts of the first Easter morning are legends, some recalcitrant historical factors still push through the surface of those narratives.

First, the women. All the Gospels give the names of certain women who first came to the tomb; and even though the lists of names differ from and even contradict one another from Gospel to Gospel, one name, that of Mary Magdalene, appears in every account. Could this fact reflect an accurate historical recollection of at least one person who came to the tomb on the first Easter morning?[55]

Second, the tomb. The existence of the pre-Marcan etiological account, with its phrase "See the place where they laid him," would seem to argue that the Jerusalem community claimed to know the location of Jesus' tomb—or at least the location of a tomb which they venerated as that of Jesus. But was the venerated tomb the same one in which Jesus had actually been buried? We must note at least three things.

First, if the Acts of the Apostles is correct in stating that the religious authorities, not the disciples, buried Jesus, then it is very possible that those buriers disposed of the corpse in a common grave. In that case, it is not likely that the tomb that the Jerusalem community venerated (which presumably was not a common grave) was the one in which Jesus had been buried. Second, it is also possible, as all the Gospels assert, that Jesus was buried in a private grave by a sympathetic (or at least law-abiding) member of the Sanhedrin, Joseph of Arimathea. In that case, given the possible haste of the burial and the desire not to contaminate other already interred bodies with the corpse of a criminal, it could well be true that the tomb in which Jesus was buried was a new one, "where no one had ever been laid," as John asserts (19:41). Thus the chances would be increased that the Jerusalem community would know the tomb in which Jesus was buried.[56] Third, regardless of whether Jesus was buried in a common grave or a private tomb, it seems that the women disciples did not help with his burial and that they may not, in fact, have witnessed it. But Mark does assert that "Mary Magdalene and Mary the mother of Joses [or Joset] saw *where* he was laid" (15:47), even if they did not see him *being* laid there. The Gospels of Matthew and Luke, which draw upon Mark's, follow him on this matter; John's Gospel stands alone in not mentioning it.[57] It seems plausible, therefore, that *if* Jesus was buried in a private tomb rather than a common grave, the early church did know where that tomb was and did venerate the site.

Finally, the date. It was the custom in Palestinian Judaism to visit the graves of relatives and friends for some time after burial to ensure that the deceased had not been entombed alive.[58] Some scholars believe that mourning reached its height on the third day, when, at least according to certain rabbis, the soul was thought to leave the body definitively. A visit to the tomb on the Sunday after the crucifixion would correspond to contemporary custom and thus may reflect a historical fact.[59]

It is possible, therefore, that the Easter story preserves a historical memory of at least the "who," the "where," and the "when" of an original event. That is, (1) Mary Magdalene (2) went to a certain tomb (3) on the Sunday after Jesus' death. However, other elements of the legends, both in the gospel accounts and in the early oral version, seem to be historically questionable. Let us look at some of those.

THE ANOINTING

The motive Mark gives for the visit to the tomb—to anoint Jesus' body—is of dubious historicity.[60] In the first place, it is not certain that the anointing of bodies was customary in Palestine at the time of Jesus; and even if it was, we may presume that the women knew that, given the warm Palestinian climate, Jesus' body would already be in an advanced state of decomposition by Sunday morning. Secondly, in the days of Jesus, even the crucified were carefully buried in accordance with Jewish law, and Mark's account gives no indication that Joseph of Arimathea neglected any of the Jewish customs in burying Jesus.[61] Thirdly, the Gospels do not agree about the anointing. Matthew, who was familiar with Mark's Easter narrative, omits mention of the anointing altogether; in his telling, the women go to the tomb simply to *see* it (28:1). Luke retains the anointing as the women's motive for visiting the grave, but he has them prepare the spices late Friday afternoon (Luke 23:56), rather than on Saturday after sunset, as in Mark (16:1). Although John does not mention Mary Magdalene's reason for going to the tomb, it certainly was not to anoint the body, for according to John's Gospel (19:39), Joseph of Arimathea and Nicodemus had already given Jesus what amounted to a royal burial on Friday, using "a mixture of myrrh and aloes, about a hundred pounds [!] in weight." All of these elements cast into doubt the historicity of the anointing as the women's motive for going to the tomb.[62]

THE GUARDS

Matthew is the only one of the four evangelists who claims that the religious authorities set a guard at Jesus' tomb, and virtually all modern exegetes consider this story to be a relatively late apologetic legend.[63]

According to Matthew's story, on the day after Good Friday the chief priests and Pharisees—at the risk of violating the Passover Sabbath—went to Pilate and told him:

> Sir, we remember how that imposter said while he was still alive, "After three days I will rise again." Therefore order the sepulchre to be made secure until the third day, lest his disciples go and steal him away and tell the people, "He has risen from the dead," and the last fraud will be worse than the first. (27:63–64)

Pilate tells them to use their own guard (presumably Roman soldiers detached to the high priests) to secure the tomb. "So they went and made the sepulchre secure by sealing the stone [presumably this too would have violated the Sabbath] and setting a guard" (27:66).

The next day, according to Matthew's story, an earthquake struck as the women approached the tomb, and an angel descended from heaven, rolled away the stone, and sat on it. "And for fear of him the guards trembled and became like dead men" (28:4). The guards remain unconscious during the angel's message to the women ("He is not here, for he has risen as he said")—but afterward "some of the guard went into the city and told the chief priests all that had taken place." The religious authorities then bribe the guards to keep quiet about the event:

> Tell the people, "His disciples came by night and stole him away while we were asleep." And if this comes to the governor's ears, we will satisfy him and keep you out of trouble. (28:13–14)

The story is rich in apocalyptic imagery (the earthquake, the angel, the fainting of the soldiers) and equally full of questionable elements: How did the priests know about Jesus' prediction? Would they have violated the Passover Sabbath as they did, first by visiting Pilate and then by sealing the tomb? Did Roman soldiers actually witness the appearance of an apocalyptic angel? How could they have reported "all that had taken place" if, as the Gospel says, they "became like dead men"?

Matthew's purpose in devising this legend is revealed at the end of the story: "So [the guards] took the money and did as they were directed; and this story has been spread among the Jews to this day" (verse 15). Matthew's tale was created in order to answer the widespread Jewish charge that the resurrection of Jesus was a hoax. Among other things, Matthew wanted to claim that the religious authorities admitted the emptiness of the tomb but explained it away by saying the disciples stole the body.[64]

THE STONE

The stone at Jesus' tomb raises a number of questions that bring us to the heart of what happened on the first Easter morning. All the gospel accounts of Easter use the stone as a prominent stage prop, almost as a character in the drama. However, its role is negative. Like the leader of a Greek chorus (in this case, a silent choragus) or like Socrates' daimon, the stone acts as a negative "voice of conscience," not telling us what is going on but warning us *away* from erroneous interpretations. It casts its shadow over the entire scene and leads to some questions about what might have happened.

Let us grant the historicity of the claim that after the burial on Friday afternoon, a stone was rolled in front of Jesus' tomb.[65] But at that point the problems begin. In the first place, if indeed the stone was "very large" (*megas sphodra*, Mark 16:4), its size throws doubt on Mark's story about the women's intention to anoint the body of Jesus. If, as Mark relates, Mary Magdalene had already seen Jesus' tomb on Friday (15:47), it is highly unlikely that she and other women would set off to anoint Jesus and only along the way begin to wonder "Who will roll away the stone for us from the door of the tomb?" (16:3). This incongruity between the women's intention to anoint the body and their initial oblivion to the problem of moving the stone may explain why the later Gospels change Mark's story. It could be the reason why Luke, although (for whatever reason) retaining the motif of anointing, omits the query about the stone, and why Matthew and John entirely drop the women's intention to anoint the body of Jesus.

Second, the stone compels us to make some distinctions about the resurrection. Granted the likelihood that there originally *was* a stone in front of Jesus' tomb, does it matter for the resurrection of Jesus whether or not the stone was rolled away? No, not at all. For surely a resurrected Jesus would not require that the exit be cleared in order for him to leave the tomb. If his body was still such a prisoner of space that he would have been trapped inside the tomb unless the stone had been removed, then either he did not have a risen body or he was in for some bedeviling problems in the days and weeks ahead.

Whether the stone was found rolled away or in place says nothing one way or the other about a resurrection. If the tomb was still sealed, at most the women would have been unable to discover whether or not the tomb was empty—that and nothing more. They probably would have spent some moments mourning outside the tomb (cf. John 20:11) and then gone home. But as they wept outside the tomb, with the entrance blocked, the tomb could have been empty *because* Jesus had been raised; or the corpse could have been inside *without* Jesus having been raised; or the corpse could have been inside *even though* Jesus had been raised; or, if someone had rolled the stone back in place after rolling it away, the body could be gone (for example, it could have been stolen) without any "resurrection" at all.

Third, *if* the stone was in fact rolled away, how did that come about? Was it by divine or human intervention? (Of course, it could have been moved by a natural occurrence—an earthquake—but the results would have been the same as those discussed below.)

Regarding divine intervention, we have seen that Jesus himself, if risen, would not have required a way out of the tomb. In fact, if we take Matthew's Gospel (even with its apocalyptic trappings) as a clue, the stone was rolled away *after* Jesus was raised from the dead (Matthew 28:2). Nor can we seriously imagine that God arranged for the stone to be removed so that it would serve as a sign for the women (or the guards) that Jesus had been raised from the dead, for in neither case did it work to that end. Apparently, then, there was no reason or need for God to intervene and roll the stone away. A risen Jesus would not have required it and the women would not have understood it.

Therefore, if we postulate that the stone was in fact rolled away, and if we ask how that was done, we are left with the answer: It was moved by human hands. Here a number of possibilities present themselves.

First, the stone might have been moved by a still living and unresurrected Jesus, with or without the help of others (the trance theory or, in a more spectacular form, the "passover plot"). According to such theories, Jesus was not actually dead but only in a faint when he was put in the tomb. When he regained consciousness and got back his strength, he, either by himself or with the help of people outside, removed the stone so that he could get out. Then he left the tomb and died elsewhere. Later, when the grave was found empty, it was said that Jesus was risen from the dead.[66]

Second, the stone could have been moved by Jesus' followers sometime after Jesus' death and burial (the stolen-body theory). To be sure, there was an acute problem of grave-robbing in Jesus' time, but who would want to steal an entire corpse? The answer: only the disciples, who imagined that the absence of Jesus' body might convince some people that he had been raised from the dead. In fact, some members of the religious establishment did accuse the early disciples of precisely this hoax, and Matthew's legend of the guards at the tomb was devised as a response to this accusation.[67]

Finally, the stone might have been moved by Joseph of Arimathea or others (the double-tomb theory). Perhaps after the crucifixion Jesus' dead body was hastily buried in a makeshift grave and then, over the weekend, was moved to a different tomb, without his followers being told. On Sunday morning the women found the first grave empty and proclaimed a resurrection.[68]

In short, the stone at the sepulcher plays an important role in the Easter drama and lets us draw the following conclusions about the original historical event. First, the fact that there once was a stone in front of Jesus' tomb casts doubt on the anointing motif. Second, whether or not the stone was moved says nothing one way or the other about a "resurrection." And finally, *if* it was removed, it seems probable it was done, for whatever reasons, by human beings.[69]

At the end of this attempt to step out of the legend and back into the underlying events, we see how little has been gained. If we had any expectations of finding historical evidence that Jesus was raised from the dead, those hopes have been thoroughly dashed. Perhaps a historical residue can be found in the story, but it is very meager: Mary Magdalen and possibly some other women may have visited Jesus' tomb on the Sunday after he died, found the stone removed from the entrance, perhaps even found that the corpse was gone, then fled in confusion and told no one. That much and no more may be the historical fact underlying the Easter legend.[70] But we cannot establish historically whether the tomb was indeed open and empty; and if it was, we cannot say why. All we can establish—with a very high degree of historical probability—is that to those who may originally have seen it, the empty tomb did not signify that Jesus had been raised from the dead. If indeed the tomb was found empty three days after the crucifixion, its emptiness originally had no "Easter meaning."[71]

Has this attempt to step out of the pre-Marcan *legend* of Easter and to arrive at the historical *fact* of Easter been worthwhile? Yes, very much so, at least insofar as the failure of the effort has blocked yet another attempt to escape from hermeneutics and to seek refuge in pristine "Easter events." Just as Paul's First Letter to the Corinthians opened no passageway back to such events, so neither does the Easter legend, even in its reconstructed original form. When we look behind the legend for historical events, we find not the resurrection but, at most, an unexplained empty tomb that provoked confusion and silence rather than faith that Jesus had been raised.

The original Christian community in Jerusalem was deeply troubled by that deathly silence of the tomb, that utter absence of Jesus. They began to speak into the dark cavity of the tomb and give it a meaning born of their disappointment and their hope. The women had fled into a silence that corresponded to the absence of Jesus; but the Jerusalem community began to fill that silence with words. *They invented a story of an angel who appeared inside the empty tomb.* Notice the probable steps in the creation of that marvelous legend:

First, the community of people who had followed Jesus during his lifetime heard about an apocalyptic revelation ("appearance") that Simon had after Jesus' death (cf. the formula, "The Lord has been raised indeed, and has appeared to Simon," Luke 24:34). They too came to believe, quite apart from seeing an allegedly empty tomb, that God had vindicated his prophet, had taken him into the eschatological future, from which some day soon this Jesus would reappear as the apocalyptic judge.

Gradually, they and others began to use one particular apocalyptic formula (among the many available) in order to express their eschatological conviction. They said: "Jesus has been raised from the dead."

Finally, they concretized that apocalyptic formula by connecting it with the site of the empty grave: They invented the story of an apocalyptic angel who was made to recite the resurrection formula to the women who had originally found the tomb empty. Only at that point did the otherwise confusing phenomenon of Jesus' grave—if indeed it was found empty—first assume, at least for believers, an eschatological meaning: The tomb was empty *because* Jesus had been raised from the dead and taken into God's future. Jesus was indeed absent, but he could be found: He was present with God in heaven.[72]

4

AN
APOCALYPTIC
MESSENGER

IT IS NOT VERY LIKELY that anyone who went to the grave on the first Easter Sunday met an angel who announced that Jesus had been raised from the dead. Modern exegetes are unanimous in interpreting the angel as a legendary figure, drawn from apocalyptic literature and used as a mouthpiece for the faith of the early church. The angel was born of the same disappointing conclusion that we reached in our step back into history, namely, that the empty tomb says nothing about a victory of Jesus over death. The early believers in Jerusalem realized that fact, and they invented the angel and his proclamation in order to turn the puzzling story about the emptiness of the tomb into a vehicle for their faith that Jesus had been taken by God into heaven.[73]

But mythical though he is, the angel is the centerpiece of the story, and if we interpret his role properly we will have answered many of the historical and theological questions that cluster around Jesus' tomb. In contrast to the stone at the tomb, which functions in the Easter drama like a silent Greek choragus who warns us how *not* to interpret the scene, the angel has a speaking part and he directs us *positively* to what the Jerusalem church thought was the significance of Jesus' grave. The angel was invented to act as a role model for the listener, and he speaks forth what the community thought was the proper response to the empty tomb, namely the affirmation "Jesus has been raised."

Who, then, is this angel? I propose that we take him for what he really is: not a supernatural being who actually appeared in a tomb one Sunday morning, but a *dramatis persona* who was invented to play a role in an early Christian legend. Later readers of the legend who mistake him for a real angel who appeared to some women on the morning of April 9, 30 C.E., misunderstand the literary form, and therefore the point, of Mark's Gospel.

The Easter narrative, both in its pre-Marcan oral form and in the gospel version, is a legend, not a historical account. It is structured in the form of a drama, a religious play, and therefore could be mistaken for a piece of history. However, in order to grasp the story according to its proper literary form (and therefore according to the way it was originally meant to be understood), I propose to treat the text of Mark 16:1–8 explicitly as a drama, which I shall call "Easter at the Tomb." If we look at the Easter legend as a religious play, the "angel" who appears at the tomb is, in fact, an actor who recites dramatic lines that were created for him, first by the early Jerusalem community (in Aramaic) and then by the evangelist Mark (in Greek). This approach may be strained at points, but it does help to clarify how the Easter legend developed from the early oral version to Mark's written account and beyond.

To begin with, the actor who appears inside the tomb is not called an "angel" in either the oral or the written version of "Easter at the Tomb." However, we may presume that no one in the original audience was confused about his identity. The early Jewish Christians had seen him on stage, as it were, many times before in intertestamental apocalyptic works such as *Tobit* or *The Testament of Abraham*, and he always had the same role. He was a stock character playing a stock part. He was the Apocalyptic Messenger, always disguised as a young man, always dressed in white robes, and he usually frightened those to whom he appeared. There was no misunderstanding in the original audience's mind when they saw this character appear on stage in "Easter at the

Tomb": He was playing a messenger from the eschatological future, and they knew that once he began to speak, they were in for an apocalyptic pronouncement from God.

Like any good actor, he read only the lines that were written for him. In the early Aramaic version of "Easter at the Tomb," which appeared in Jerusalem some decades after Jesus had died, his role was not only to proclaim the community's faith in the resurrection, but also to add some local color to that faith. The community set his role within the context of their own *cultic veneration of Jesus' tomb,* and they had him say a word or two that went beyond the usual and rather bare formula of resurrection faith ("Jesus has been raised"). They had him point to the empty tomb and say, "He is not here. See the place where they laid him."

In other words, this Apocalyptic Messenger was employed not simply to proclaim a resurrection (the community did not need him for that) but also to make that proclamation in such a way that it would shed light on the emptiness of the tomb and give it an eschatological meaning. But in the original Aramaic version of "Easter at the Tomb," the actor's role ended there. Even though the Jerusalem community probably knew of another, coequal formulation of faith ("Jesus has appeared to Simon"), it chose not to add that formula to the script —perhaps because that formula arose in Galilee, whereas the play was set in Jerusalem. In short, the resurrection formula ("He has been raised") plus the added local color ("He is not here. See the place where they laid him") were enough to express the Jerusalem community's faith in the victory of Jesus.

But in Saint Mark's Greek revival of this Aramaic "play" (in Antioch or Rome, around 70 C.E.), the evangelist created *another* line for the Apocalyptic Messenger in order to express the evangelist's own theological viewpoint and the religious concerns of his Hellenistic audience. Mark and his community were interested in Jesus' *appearance* after he died (whether that appearance was Jesus' revelation to Simon in Galilee or his expected return on the last day), and the gospel writer felt he should at least allude to such an appearance. Therefore, while retaining the original lines written for the Apocalyptic Messenger, Mark also added another verse. After the "angel" proclaims the resurrection and points to the empty tomb, Mark has him continue:

But go, tell his disciples and [especially] Peter that he goes before you to Galilee; there you will see him, as he told you. (16:7)

And this is the version of the story that stuck. Mark's "play" had a wider audience and a much longer run than the original Jerusalem version, and, as so often happens when particular interpretations of a role become well established, the script was revised—in this case fleshed out with the allusion to a future appearance—and became the accepted text.

We may draw some conclusions from this development of the Easter drama. First of all, at least *two distinct interpretations* of the Easter experience (of Simon and the other believers) circulated in primitive Christianity, and they took the form of brief kerygmatic sentences: "Jesus appeared" and "Jesus has been raised." Where and how they originated we cannot say precisely, but it is probable that the appearance formula is earlier than the resurrection one. In any case, the two interpretations were equivalent ways of putting the eschatological experience into apocalyptic language. Neither formula, of course, was a substitute for the experience itself; that, the church insisted, was what made someone a Christian: the "Easter experience," which Simon was the first to undergo.

The second conclusion that we can draw is that the drama of the empty tomb was merely a *local* illustration of *one* interpretation of that eschatological experience. As we saw, the members of the Jerusalem community gave the angel a script that combined the general resurrection formula with more specific elements relating to their veneration of Jesus' tomb. In this way they localized the resurrection interpretation by associating it with a particular place (the tomb) and quasi-historicized it by connecting it with a specific moment in time (the Sunday after the crucifixion). Whether or not the community thought Jesus had actually been raised at that place and on that day (later Christians would certainly think he was) is irrelevant. The point is that this pseudo-localization and -historicization of the resurrection made sense only within the Jerusalem community that venerated the tomb. The legend originally had no function outside of Jerusalem and had no binding power over the rest of the Jesus-movement. Simon in Galilee came to believe in the vindication of Jesus without even knowing about the grave of Jesus, and Paul never mentioned the empty tomb in his proclamation of the resurrection.[74]

The third conclusion is that when Mark absorbed the Jerusalem legend into his Gospel, he linked it with the *other* widespread tradition: the "appearance" of Jesus. To be sure, Mark did not effect a complete synthesis of the two traditions, since the apocalyptic angel in his Gospel merely alludes to a future appearance in Galilee. Nonetheless, by synthesizing these two very different formulae—the tomb scene and the appearance—in one and the same text, Mark launched the idiosyncratic local legend of the Easter angel (who would soon become two angels: Luke 24:4) on a much broader literary career, one that would eventually make that legend the normative way to proclaim the Christian faith. It seems that as late as 70 C.E., when Mark wrote his Gospel, an "appearance" still meant a "revelation from God's eschaton," and it did not necessarily have to have physical or visual connotations. As far as we can tell, no written descriptions of apparitions of Jesus were available at that time, only simple formulae such as "Jesus appeared." However, by connecting the Jerusalem community's localized and historicized interpretation of the resurrection-from-the-tomb with an appearance formula ("you will see him in Galilee"), Mark licensed the later evangelists to go a step further and create the elaborate mythical stories of how Jesus "physically" appeared to his disciples after he (and his body) had left his grave.

Fourth, by synthesizing three originally separate interpretations— a resurrection formula, an appearance formula, and a local tradition about the empty tomb—Mark's Gospel helped *reduce the plurality* of interpretations of the eschatological experience to a single normative one and helped transform that increasingly normative *interpretation* into an *"event"* that had happened one Sunday morning in the past. Thus the final chapter of Mark's Gospel opened the door to the creation of a narratable Easter chronology: "First Jesus rose, then he appeared, and then he ascended into heaven."

Finally, Mark's Easter account contributed significantly to the growing tendency to force Jesus' eschatological message back into the Procrustean bed of apocalypticism which Jesus, to a large degree, had managed to avoid. We shall take this matter up in the next chapter, but for now we may simply point out three stages in the reapocalyptizing of Jesus' message.

(1) JESUS' MESSAGE: GOD AS THE DAWNING ESCHATOLOGICAL KINGDOM. Jesus' preaching, like the Jewish tradition of which it was a part, was entirely about God—but not God as a nationalistic deity who intervened in history on Israel's behalf, nor as the somewhat legal-minded divinity of the Pharisees, nor as some apocalyptic avenger who would soon destroy the world. Jesus preached God as a loving Father who was already reigning among his people. It was an eschatological message with a minimum of apocalyptic baggage.

(2) SIMON'S REVISION: THE KINGDOM BECOMES APOCALYPTIC. By identifying Jesus with the coming Son of Man, Simon and the early believers reinserted Jesus' transapocalyptic message of God's presence into the myth of an apocalyptic future. Jesus, the proclaimer of God's now-dawning kingdom, became identified with the apocalyptic judge who was to come at the end of time. The grammar and syntax of this new belief was apocalyptism, and it found expression in a number of coequal formulae, among them: Jesus is the coming judge, Jesus has appeared from the future, and Jesus was raised from the dead.

(3) CHRISTIANITY'S DOCTRINE: THE APOCALYPTIC BECOMES HISTORICAL. Later believers narrowed that reapocalyptized vision even further by turning the resurrection into a historical event. They eventually took one local apocalyptic legend—a resurrection from a tomb—and made it a normative formulation of faith. They forced the message of God's presence among men into the narrow framework of a local myth. Notice the levels of devolution:

A proposal of how to live
("Be as merciful as your Father")

which was originally expressed in

an eschatological symbol
("The kingdom of God is among you")

was revised into

an apocalyptic belief
("Jesus will be the Son of Man")

which was further narrowed to

one apocalyptic formula
("Jesus has been raised from the dead")

which was concretized in

a very local legend
(the empty tomb).

That legend eventually became the "thing itself." Christianity took a local and idiosyncratic myth about what allegedly happened one morning in a tiny corner of Palestine, and turned it into a supernatural event that supposedly transformed the ontological structure of the world.

Jesus' message, which had started as an invitation to live God's future in the present, devolved into a dogma about what had happened in the past. What began as a challenge to work God's mercy in the world was reduced to an apocalyptic myth. A movement that should have accepted the fact that Jesus was dead, and then gone on from there, ended up trying to hope him out of the grave.

Christianity has never pretended to be easy. It demands a difficult choice in the face of a stark either/or: Either Christ was physically raised from the tomb on Easter Sunday morning, or your faith—which means your life—is in vain (cf. I Corinthians 15:14). Christianity proposes, as an object of faith, the hard paradox of the resurrection, with the valence "Take it or leave it." Over the centuries millions have chosen to take it. We can understand why others, both Jews and Gentiles, have preferred to leave it.

5

THE
MEANING
OF EASTER

W̲H̲A̲T̲ ̲W̲E̲ ̲H̲A̲V̲E̲ ̲J̲U̲S̲T̲ ̲S̲A̲I̲D̲ is to a certain degree unfair. Popular
devotions and bad theology notwithstanding, Christians do not
believe in the resurrection of Jesus *because of* the empty tomb. No
matter how vigorously the church may proclaim the Easter stories
found in the Gospels, she does not believe in what those stories say.
She believes, rather, in what the stories *mean*. Saint Thomas Aquinas
is clear on this point: The object of faith is not the words of a text
but the divine reality they point to. Thus, the church herself acknowl-
edges that her scriptural texts and doctrinal pronouncements are only
interpretations that require further interpretation.

If we allow, despite appearances to the contrary, that the "official"
Christian interpretation of Easter is not the literalist one of a physical
resuscitation on Sunday morning, April 9, 30 c.e., we are faced with
the double task of discerning what that official interpretation is and
whether or not we agree with it. However, the problem here is that
the church has never clearly stated what she means by the "resurrection." Or rather (and this comes down to the same thing), her theologians have very clearly stated what it means, but in very different and
often conflicting ways.

Let us begin by surveying the spectrum of interpretations of Easter offered by Christian theologians in our own day. Our treatment is necessarily schematic. It covers three major positions, which I shall call the "traditionalist," the "moderate," and the "liberal."

The traditionalist, or conservative, understanding of the resurrection is roughly the one outlined above, characterized by a literalization of the Bible's apocalyptic imagery. It accepts the gospel texts at face value and insists that the resurrection was a historical event that happened on the first Easter Sunday. In its more extreme form the traditional position maintains that the resurrection included the resuscitation of Jesus' body and its exit from the tomb, an event that could have been seen by eyewitnesses, or at least by believers. In this popular form, the traditionalist position goes beyond the New Testament and follows the lead of the Gospel of Peter. But whether in such extreme form or more moderate forms, the traditional approach takes the resurrection as an event that happened *ante nos*—before us in time.

The middle ground of the spectrum is occupied by the moderates, who maintain that something happened objectively to Jesus after his death, but that this "something" was not a historical event but an eschatological or supernatural happening that lay beyond time and human perception. That is, Jesus is somehow alive with God because of his resurrection; and this resurrection is generally taken to mean that Jesus, by his own divine power, overcame death and "physically" (the meaning of this is left somewhat open) entered into eternal glory.

In other words, moderate theologians tend to interpret the resurrection ontologically rather than apocalyptically: They purport to say what in fact really happened to Jesus after his death, but without emphasizing the Bible's mythical imagery. The moderates hold that the resurrection is not historically *ante nos* but ontologically *extra nos* (outside of us), that is, a supernatural reality that objectively "happened" to Jesus, quite apart from whether or not anyone believes in it.[75] By saving what they think is the religious sense of resurrection (Jesus' triumph over death) and relativizing the apocalyptic language in which it was originally cast, these moderate theologians remove some of the obstacles that the biblical accounts, especially when taken literally, put in the path of modern people who wish to believe in Jesus.

The third, or liberal, position tends to bypass the resurrection not only as a historical event *ante nos* but also as an ontological happening *extra nos*. Liberal theologians are concerned not with the "resurrection" so much as with *the genesis of the early church's faith in Jesus*. They emphasize less the objective and historical (what really is or was the case with Jesus himself) and more the subjective and functional, that is, how Jesus continued to have significance for his disciples after he died, what he *meant* to the early believers and could mean to Christians today. The focus is on the significance of Jesus *pro nobis* (for us), almost without regard to what may have happened to him after the crucifixion.

In other words, the liberal position not only deemphasizes the resurrection but also tends to relativize Jesus himself by making his meaning for believers more important than his personal history either before or after he died. Some liberal theologians, like the late Rudolf Bultmann, say that Jesus rose only "into the kerygma," and that the "resurrection" is only a proclamational symbol for the salvific meaning his death had for early Christians. Others, like the German theologian Willi Marxsen, argue that "resurrection" is merely an apocalyptic way of saying that the "cause" of Jesus—his message of the kingdom of God —continues to have meaning today.[76] What may have happened to Jesus "after" he died is not particularly emphasized by these liberal theologians. The more cautious will assert that Jesus is *somehow* alive with God; the more radical will assert that Jesus is presumably dead; and almost all of them will insist that the question is irrelevant to the point being made: that the *meaning* of Jesus is still alive regardless of what happened to him. Nonetheless, even the radicals who presume that Jesus is dead still consider themselves Christians insofar as they believe in the "cause" of Jesus, if not in his continuing personal existence. They believe that Jesus was fundamentally right in what he said and did and that he is a timeless example for others, even if he ended up permanently in the grave.

The interpretation of the resurrection that I propose draws on the best elements in all three of these positions but then goes beyond them. Like the traditionalists, I take the gospel *text* seriously—but *as* a text, a work of religious literature and not a document of history. Like the moderates, I recognize that Christian faith, at least on its own claims, is based on something that is independent of an individual's subjective psychological states. I maintain, however, that this "something" is not that Jesus is alive with God. Like the liberals I believe that the resurrection texts are about present meaning rather than past history. I hold, however, that the resurrection texts are not about the meaning of Jesus for Christians but about the end—the fulfillment and therefore the undoing—of both Jesus and Christianity. With reference to these three positions as a whole, I hope to show: that the Easter legends are not about the "resurrection"; that they proclaim the fundamental datum of faith to be the absolute absence of Jesus; and that they show the futility of searching for Jesus at all.

What, then, is the meaning of "Easter"? In what follows I use the word "Easter" as a heuristic device, a stand-in for the as-yet-unknown "X" that is the object of Christian faith and that has been interpreted apocalyptically in such legends as the resurrection story. Was Easter a historical event that took place three days after the crucifixion? or a transhistorical "happening" in which Jesus somehow triumphed over death? or the birth of faith in Jesus? Or is it something else? To answer these questions, let us return once more to the Easter legend and the historical events that underlie it.

SEEKING

Of the five lines the angel recites in Mark's Easter legend, the most important one is not "He has been raised" but the preceding sentence: "You seek Jesus, the one who was crucified" (16:6). The word "seek" (zēteite, zēteis) appears in all the gospel accounts of the empty tomb, whether it is spoken by an angel, as in the Synoptic Gospels (Matthew 28:5, Luke 24:5), or by Jesus himself when he appears to Mary Magdalene ("Whom do you seek?": John 20:15; cf. 1:38).

It is significant that in all these accounts the word "seek" always comes *before* any mention of either the resurrection or the appearances of Jesus. We have seen that both those formulae—"He has been raised" and "He has appeared"—are secondary and tertiary apocalyptic interpretations of a prior experience. Even the *primary* interpretation

("Jesus will usher in the kingdom") is an apocalyptic one. But behind all these apocalyptic interpretations, we find the meaning of Easter expressed nonapocalyptically within a hermeneutical circle of a "seeking" and a "sought-for." To put the matter in general and formal terms, Easter is the "object" of a certain kind of seeking, it is *something correlative to and inseparable from that seeking.* With this we come to the "origin" of Easter, that is, to a primordial, preapocalyptic interpretation of what it means. And at these origins we find not history but hermeneutics, a circle of interpretation consisting of a certain kind of experience and its inseparable content. There is no way of knowing what that content is apart from the experience of seeking.

This much may not seem like a significant step toward understanding Easter, but in fact it is. By discovering that "Easter" is inseparable from the seeking which all the Gospels mention, we have accomplished two things. On the negative side, we have called into question the notion that Easter is an objective event, whether historical or eschatological, that happened to Jesus; that is, *Easter is not about the "resurrection."* We have also challenged the idea that Easter was an "appearance" in the sense of an objective revelation that befell the disciples like a bolt from heaven. Easter (whatever it may be) "happens" only to those who seek it (whatever that seeking may be). At the origin of Easter we find not a past historical event but an ongoing hermeneutical task.

On the positive side, we have at last found what seems to be the primordial "place" where the first Easter happened, and it is not a tomb but a hermeneutical circle. It is here at this nonapocalyptic site that we must construct our own interpretation of Easter. And from now on, everything we can say about Easter comes down to what is meant by "seeking."

In general and formal terms, all seeking is bound up with some kind of absence. No one seeks for what is already present and is known as such. But on the other hand, no one can search for what is totally absent, entirely unknown or unknowable. Plato makes the point in a negative way when he has Meno say to Socrates: "A man cannot search for what he knows, for since he knows it, there is no need to search for it. And he cannot search for what he does not know—because he does not know what to look for" (*Meno* 80e). To put this negative thesis in positive terms: What makes the seeking possible is something sought-for which is absent but not totally absent. All seeking is initiated and guided by the absent as seekable, something desired but not possessed, something guessed at but not fully known, something partially present in its absence. Even if it is only an idea or an illusion, this absent "sought-for" is what prompts the search, gives it meaning along the way, and perhaps finally fulfills the search by being found at the end. The sought-for is the meaning of the search, inseparable from it and yet, in a logical sense, "prior" to (the *a priori* of) the search. And yet it can be known—to whatever degree that is possible—only by understanding the seeking, by following out its teleology.

THE END OF THE SEARCH

Let us flesh out these formal remarks on "seeking" with what the gospel text says about it and with what we ourselves can supply. The Easter legend is about two kinds of seeking and, therefore, two kinds of absence. The interpretation I shall give of Easter is based on yet a third kind of absence.

At the beginning of the Easter story the women are engaged in one kind of search that is guided by one kind of absence: the absence of the Jesus who was once alive. Like all who mourn for the dead, the women come to the tomb not primarily to look for the corpse but above all to look for what can no longer be found: the person they loved, who is gone forever. Their mourning is their search—their way of living into an absence that is excruciatingly present precisely because the absent loved one is not. These mourning women cling to two forms of the already fading presence of the now absent Jesus: a corpse—the tangible presence of a no longer tangible life—and a memory.

But in the legend (and apparently on the first Easter morning as well) that search was caught up short: no body, no vestige of his life to be seen and touched. Let us leave aside for a moment what may actually have happened to the body. What counts at this point is that the women's search for Jesus was doubly frustrated because Jesus was doubly absent: Not only was he dead, but his corpse was gone. There were no remains at all. This search had come to absolutely nothing.

At this point there are two choices: either to invent an angel who will declare a resurrection, or to accept that Jesus is quite dead (wherever his corpse may be) and to draw out the consequences of that.

The church chose the first possibility. Enter the angel, and the meaning of the Christian search for Jesus is elevated to a higher, heavenly level. The Apocalyptic Messenger, speaking for the Jerusalem community, informs the women that the absence which brought them to the tomb was the wrong kind of absence, and that their search is the wrong kind of seeking. Jesus is absent from life, and his body is gone from the tomb, because the whole of him is present with God: "He has been raised, he is not here." To this new level of absence there corresponds a new kind of search, and so Mark has the angel say: "He goes before you; you will see him." In these Christian interpretations, Easter is Jesus, raised to a higher presence, the object of a higher search. For those left behind, Jesus' presence in heaven means that his current absence from earth is only temporary, and it calls forth a temporary and provisional seeking, which will one day be rewarded with a final find.

Before we decide whether or not to follow the church's path, let us for a moment step outside the Christian legend of Easter. Let us stand at the tomb with the women who actually came there on the first Easter Sunday. What do we find? No angel, no proclamation of the resurrection—and no corpse. This empty grave has, of and by itself, no resurrectional meaning. But to whoever discovers it, whether the women who were originally there in person or we ourselves who read a text, the historical fact of the emptiness of the tomb does have some meaning, even if it is only negative. What was the significance of the empty tomb before that emptiness came to be interpreted in terms of a resurrection?

Some women came to the tomb on April 9, 30 c.e., seeking the corpse of Jesus. They found nothing. They did not discover that Jesus was alive elsewhere, in heaven. They found, quite simply, that Jesus was unfindable. After his burial he was never seen again in any form, dead or alive. The primordial, preapocalyptic meaning of that scene at the grave on that Sunday morning is *the utter absence of Jesus* and *the futility of the women's search for him.*

It is worth standing for a moment in front of that empty hole before we decide to invent an angel to interpret it for us. Jesus is gone, and there is no forwarding address. He is lost, and, short of a miracle, he will never be found again. Some people did dream of such a miracle, and we can easily understand why. It is hard to lose a person who has so dramatically freed you, who has shown you the ultimate scheme of things and your place at the center of it. It is hard to lose a hero, an extraordinary man who woke you up from the pettiness of the everyday and led you beyond yourself, a liberator who proclaimed that you were living at the denouement of a cosmic drama that was being realized in his very words and deeds: God himself, your loving Father, was arriving and would live with you forever. It is hard to see all that die, to hear the prophet's words fade into silence, to feel his presence dissolve into an utter and total absence. If, as the disciples hoped, these were the "last days," the moment of the eschatological arrival of God, and if Jesus identified himself so entirely with that hope that he seemed to become it, could his Father really desert him in death? Would not God have assumed Jesus into the eschatological future which the prophet had so perfectly embodied when he was alive?

If God did not save Jesus, who was so close to God that he could call him "Abba," what hope could there be for the rest of us? The confusion provoked by the empty tomb almost had to be turned into the certainty of Jesus' resurrection; the women's silence had to give way to the angel's words, "He has been raised." The seeking of Jesus that motivated the first pilgrimage to the tomb demanded an angelic messenger who would direct the search to a higher level: Jesus' abiding presence with his Father, his merely temporary and provisional absence from those who sought him.

ABSOLUTE ABSENCE

The Easter legend is focused on two kinds of seeking that are correlative with two kinds of absence: the women's fruitless search for the dead body of the crucified Jesus, and Christianity's faithful search for the risen body of the glorious Jesus, who is absent from earth because he is present in heaven. In the Christian understanding of the tomb, the hopefulness of the second search is the answer to the despair that motivated the first one. The correlation of the *provisionally absent Jesus* and *the faithful search for him* is what believers mean by "Easter," that fundamental "X" which lies at the base of Christianity. Easter is neither an event that happened to Jesus in the historical past (as traditional theologians believe) nor some transhistorical triumph that he experienced after he died (as the moderates maintain).

Then, does Easter "happen" (as some liberal theologians hold) whenever a person interprets the meaning of his or her own life in terms of the experience of "seeking Jesus"? This third position poses as many problems as the other two. In the first place, what does "seeking Jesus" mean? It is open to any number of interpretations, ranging from "looking for him in heaven" to believing that "his cause goes on" even though Jesus is dead.

Is there, underlying these three strands of interpretation, some basic and normative interpretation of Easter, some solid criterion of faith by means of which we could decide what is and what is not a life dedicated to "seeking the risen Jesus"? If there is, who would supply that interpretation? Roman Catholics, for example, hold that Jesus, in his revelation, established an official teaching authority (the pope and the bishops) and gave them the divinely delegated power to make infallible pronouncements on what "seeking Jesus" properly means. But since the New Testament is, at best, ambiguous on the question of episcopal authority, those allegedly infallible interpreters of revelation must first interpret revelation as constituting them infallible before they can start making universally binding pronouncements about the correct way to "seek Jesus."

In short, from its Easter foundations upward, Christianity is caught in a hermeneutical circle—in fact, Christianity *is* that circle—and you are either inside or outside. What is more, it is impossible to know whether you are inside or outside. At the very best you can declare —that is, interpret—yourself as being in one place or the other.

The problem (if it is that) of the hermeneutical circle of Easter lies in Christianity's insistence that the ultimate meaning of human seeking is bound up with Jesus. And the only way out of that problem is to *surrender Jesus:* to leave him dead and to see that the meaning of Jesus is that Jesus himself no longer matters.

One last look, then, at the empty tomb—the real tomb of history, not the one of the Christian legend. As we peer into that emptiness, the absence of the living Jesus and even of his dead body allows us to identify a unique form of seeking: the desire for that which can never be had. This unique kind of seeking is the experience that makes human beings different from any other kind of entity, and we see it exemplified in the women who actually found the tomb empty on the first Easter Sunday. Such seeking is not something we occasionally get caught up in; rather, it is what makes us human, constitutes us as the futile passion, the unfulfilled and presumably unfulfillable desire that we are. If we were not this endless *eros*, either we would be God, who cannot seek because he has already found everything, or we would be animals, those living entities that lack an "ontological imagination" and therefore never have a desire that exceeds the possibility of being fulfilled.

This fundamental desire, this seeking that constitutes human nature, is correlative to what I shall call "absolute absence." Others might call this absence "the absurd," that which is absolutely deaf *(surdus)* to our desire to render it present in any way. Absolute absence would seem to annul any search for itself—because it annuls itself: It does not and cannot exist. But the amazing thing is that the desire for it refuses to be quenched. This absolute absence, even though it does not exist in itself, continues to live a parasitic life within our futile desire for it. It dwells like a ghost in the rooms of our everyday lives, haunting all our doings with the dream of the impossible. Thus, beyond all our seeking for things that can be found (whether or not we actually find them), we find ourselves still directed to a "more" that does not exist. We remain, fundamentally, an act of questioning to which there is no answer. We find this endless and unfulfillable seeking, for example, in all kinds of faith, and in more ordinary forms of fruitless nostalgia, such as mourning for the dead. Perhaps its most dramatic manifestation is mysticism (from the Greek *myein*, "to keep silent"), that form of devotion to the absolutely unreachable in which the devotee is confined not just to silence about the "object" of his or her search, but even to silence about that silence.[77]

If we prescind from the usual Christian interpretations, the historical fact of the empty tomb is about such mysticism and such silence. The alternative to inventing a resurrection is accepting the fact that Jesus, regardless of where his corpse ended up, is dead and remains dead.

This historical fact of the complete absence of Jesus does have religious significance: It means the *end of religion*. In a symbolic sense, the empty tomb was the last word that Jesus the prophet uttered. His mission had been to undo religion and its God and to put radical mercy, the living of the present-future, in its place. And at the end of his mission he, so to speak, dissolved even himself, wiped out every trace, left not even a corpse, only an absolute absence.

There is no Jesus to be found anywhere anymore, neither here nor elsewhere. The women who went to the tomb and found absolutely nothing—and we too who observe their pilgrimage—may leave the grave with the awareness that, as regards Jesus and his God, there is nothing to be found and therefore nothing to be searched for. The meaning of the dead prophet is an unsurpassable absence that cannot be changed into any form of presence. The absolute absence of the prophet and his God makes room at last for silent, unadvertised, and groundless mercy.

No one knows what happened to the body of Jesus. Stolen? Buried elsewhere? Miraculously resurrected? The point is that it does not matter and that we should not care. For believers, indeed for anyone who would seek the real meaning of Jesus, the proper response to the empty tomb is silence, even silence about that silence. The women who came to the tomb had the correct reaction. They took the path that led away from the tomb and away from Jesus himself. They went back to their own lives and to the meaning that Jesus' message had taught them to find therein. *Oudeni ouden eipon* (Mark 16:8): They did not say anything to anyone.

THREE

HOW JESUS BECAME GOD

THE FIRST MENTION of Jesus anywhere in literature was made twenty years after he died, and is found in a text that records the already developed status of his reputation. Writing around 50 C.E., Saint Paul began a letter to a group of his converts in Greece with the following greeting:

> To the Church of the Thessalonians
> in God the Father and
> the Lord Jesus Christ:
> Grace to you and peace. (I Thessalonians 1:1)

This greeting—the very first sentence of Christian Scripture ever to be written—shows that within two decades of Jesus' death the Christian community had already elevated the prophet beyond his own understanding of his status and had endowed him with two titles, "Lord" and "Christ," neither of which he had dared to give to himself.

Paul also asserts that Jesus is soon to return from the heavens in order to bring God's kingdom to earth. To be sure, it is likely that Jesus, before he died, had come to believe he was the long-awaited eschato-logical prophet; and it is possible that Jesus expected God the Father to vindicate his message in the very near future by sending a separate apocalyptic figure—the Son of Man of the Book of Daniel—to usher in the fullness of the kingdom of God that Jesus was preaching. But in this letter to the Thessalonians the apocalyptic scenario of the Book of Daniel is reworked so as to make Jesus himself be the Son of Man, soon to appear in glory. The Son of Man, that formerly mysterious apocalyptic figure whom pious Jews earnestly awaited, now had a recognizable human face: He was Jesus of Nazareth.

> You turned to God from idols, to serve a living and true God and to wait for his Son from heaven, whom he raised from the dead, Jesus, who delivers us from the wrath to come. (I Thessalonians 1:9–10)
>
> For the Lord himself will descend from heaven with a cry of command, with the archangel's call, and with the sound of God's trumpet. And the dead in Christ will rise first; then we who are alive, who are left, shall be caught up together with them in the clouds to meet the Lord in the air; and so we shall always be with the Lord. (4:16–17)

Paul, of course, was not alone in his belief. By the middle of the century there were several thousand converts scattered around the Mediterranean who, thinking that they were living at the brink of history, had readied themselves for the Last Day. And that day was imminent.

> As for the times and seasons, brethren, you have no need to have anything written to you. For you yourselves know well that the day of the Lord will come like a thief in the night. When people say, "There is peace and security," then sudden destruction will come upon them as labor pains come upon a pregnant woman, and there will be no escape. (5:1–3)

Clearly, by mid-century when Paul wrote his first epistle, Christian-ity was well on its way to establishing Jesus' reputation as we have known it for almost two millennia. If by 50 C.E. the prophet was already acknowledged as Lord and Christ, before the end of the century he would be thought of as the equal of God himself.

The odyssey of Jesus of Nazareth from crucified prophet to divine ruler of the cosmos is an extraordinary event in Western intellectual history and, given the current state of biblical scholarship, one of the best documented. The process consisted in a gradually increasing identification of Jesus himself with the kingdom of God that he had preached; and one of the major results of this process was a dramatic change in the sense of time and history that Jesus' proclamation had introduced into Judaism.

The heart of Jesus' message had been the presence of the future: the arrival of God among men and women. Jesus heralded the end of religion and religion's God insofar as he proclaimed the present-future as the fulfillment of what religion had always claimed to be about. In that sense Jesus did announce the "end of history": the end of alienation from God and oneself, from one's fellow men and women and the entire created world. Paradoxically, however, Jesus' message of the present-future became the basis of its own undoing. After the prophet's death his disciples identified God's presence with Jesus himself and relegated that presence to an apocalyptic future when Jesus would return to usher in the kingdom once and for all.

This third part of the book is about that twofold process: the growth of Jesus' reputation and the corresponding undoing of his message.[1] Our objective is to examine the evolution of the Christian faith over its first fifty years, from its earliest formulations to its full-blown interpretation of Jesus as the Son of God. I will trace this evolution via the church's transformation of Jesus' notion of history. We will examine how Jesus' ideal of the present-future disintegrated as his own reputation grew in the decades after his death. Although this evolutionary process was quite complicated, we can distinguish three general phases within a broad spectrum of christological variations:

STAGE ONE: THE APOCALYPTIC FUTURE. Whereas Jesus had dissolved the future of Jewish apocalyptic expectations into the presence of that future (the dawning kingdom), Christianity reconstituted the apocalyptic future by recasting Jesus as the future Son of Man.

STAGE TWO: THE HEAVENLY PRESENT. Christianity then drew that apocalyptic future back into the present moment by reinterpreting Jesus as the Lord and Christ who was already reigning in heaven.

STAGE THREE: THE CHRISTOLOGICAL PAST. Finally the church projected the Lord Jesus into the past history of the cosmos by declaring that he had preexisted from before creation as the savior of the entire world.

These three stages in the evolution of early Christianity are associated with three more or less distinct groups of early converts to belief in Jesus, two of them made up of Jews and the third of Gentiles.

The first members of the Jesus-movement were Aramaic-speaking Jews who lived in Palestine. Some, like Simon Peter and the first disciples, had heard Jesus preach the kingdom of God when he was alive; others came to faith through the preaching of the original disciples in the first years after Jesus had died. It was this community that first projected Jesus' reputation into the *future* by declaring that he would be the coming Son of Man.

Alongside these Aramaic-speaking believers there grew up in Palestine a second and distinct group of converts to the Jesus-movement: the Hellenistic Jews of the Mediterranean Diaspora, who had absorbed Greek language and culture. At the time of Jesus some of these Hellenistic Jews, or their ancestors, had returned to Palestine from the Diaspora, and they continued to speak Greek rather than Aramaic, to read the Scriptures in the Septuagint (Greek) translation, and probably to worship in their own Greek-speaking synagogues throughout Palestine. Within a few years of joining the Jesus-movement, they (apparently unlike the Aramaic-speaking believers) were persecuted by the local religious authorities, probably for vigorously proselytizing on behalf of their new and unorthodox beliefs. As a result of this persecution, many Hellenistic Jews left Palestine for Samaria and the Diaspora, most notably Antioch in Syria, where they first acquired the name "Christian." It was these Hellenistic Jewish believers in Palestine and the Diaspora who, within a few years of the crucifixion, effected a momentous shift in the interpretation of Jesus. If the Aramaic-speaking believers had projected Jesus into an apocalyptic future—the end of time, when Jesus would begin to reign—the Hellenistic Jewish Christians pulled the moment of Jesus' glorification back into a heavenly *present* by declaring him to be already reigning as the Lord and Christ, who was now enthroned at God's right hand until his second coming in glory.

The third group of early believers was composed of Gentile converts. The Jesus-movement was originally a Jewish affair, and until the middle of the century, Gentile converts to the movement were expected to join Judaism, that is, to undergo circumcision and observe the Jewish law. It was most likely the Hellenistic Jewish believers who began evangelizing pagans, and these Gentile converts were originally associated with the liberal synagogues of Greek-speaking Jews in the Diaspora.

Around mid-century, however, the more conservative Jerusalem community apparently agreed that Gentile converts to the Jesus-movement did not have to be circumcised so long as they obeyed certain basic Jewish laws, mostly dietary in nature. This decision, which is usually attributed to the "Council of Jerusalem" (ca. 48 or 49 C.E.), made possible a new and freer mission to the Gentiles and the formation of distinct communities of Gentile converts to Christianity.[2] It was these new communities, rooted as they were in both Judaism and the Graeco-Roman world, that projected Jesus' reputation into the mythical *past* by declaring that he had preexisted as a divine being before becoming a man.

All three groups maintained a basic unity and continuity in their faith, although they articulated their beliefs in different ways. These differences in expression help to reveal the evolution of Jesus' status after his death. Even though there is a great deal of overlapping, we may characterize three more or less distinct interpretations of Jesus, each of which points to one of the three groups of believers:

(1) THE APOCALYPTIC JUDGE: The Aramaic Jews held that Jesus had been appointed by his Father to assume the role of Son of Man in the near future.

(2) THE REIGNING LORD AND CHRIST: The Hellenistic Jews declared that Jesus, was already reigning as the messiah in the interim before his glorious return.

(3) THE DIVINE SON OF GOD: The Gentile converts came to believe that Jesus was God's divine Son who had preexisted even before creation, had become a human being to save mankind, and had returned to heaven after his death.

1

THE
APOCALYPTIC
JUDGE

FAITH IN JESUS BEGAN as, and for a long time remained, a movement within Judaism. The first disciples saw themselves not as be-
longing to a new religion, not even as an exclusive sect within Judaism,
but rather as orthodox Jews who were proclaiming what Israel had
always awaited but only now had attained: the fullness of Yahweh's
presence.

The disciples began preaching the victory of Jesus in the spring of
30 C.E. in the synagogues of northern Galilee, probably starting in
Simon's home village of Capernaum. We may imagine Simon, like
Jesus before him, entering the synagogue on the sabbath with a small
group of believers.[3] Simon's reputation as a follower of the prophet
has already become well known in the area, and he is invited to read
from the Scriptures. He chooses a text from the prophet Isaiah:

> The Spirit of the Lord is upon me,
>   because the Lord has anointed me
>   to bring good tidings to the poor. . . .
> He has sent me to proclaim release to the captives
>   and recovering of sight to the blind,

To free those who are oppressed
and to proclaim the year of the Lord's favor. (cf. 61:1–2)

Then, referring the text to Jesus, Simon proclaims:

This scripture was fulfilled before your very eyes
in Jesus of Nazareth,
a man attested to you by mighty works
that God did through him in your midst.
For Moses said:
"The Lord shall raise up for you
a prophet from among your brethren, as he raised me up.
You shall listen to him in whatever he tells you.
And whoever does not listen to him shall be destroyed."

This Jesus was crucified and killed
at the hands of lawless men.
But the God of Abraham, Isaac, and Jacob,
the God of our Fathers,
Has glorified his servant Jesus.
And of that we are witnesses.
He has loosed the pangs of death,
for it was not possible for Jesus to be held by death.
And heaven must receive him
until the time of restoration of all things.

But you are the heirs of the covenant
that God made with our forefathers.
Repent, therefore, and turn again,
that your sins may be blotted out.
And the Lord will send the time of comfort.
(See Luke 4:21; Acts 3:13–25 and 2:22–24)

Simon proclaimed that time was running short. The eschatological
spirit was already being poured out—they had already received him.
It was as Yahweh had promised through his prophet Joel:

In those days
I will pour out my Spirit

And I will display portents in heaven above
and signs on earth below.
The sun will be turned into darkness
and the moon into blood
Before the great Day of the Lord dawns.
(Acts 2:18–20, citing Joel 2:29–32)

And so Simon and the others went down to Jerusalem from Galilee to await that Day of the Lord.[4] There they invoked the God of the end-times: "Abba, may thy kingdom come!" And they called out to Jesus: *"Maranatha.* Come, master!" (I Corinthians 16:22; Revelation 22:20). They prayed and preached, but above all they waited for the *apokatastasis pantōn,* the final establishment of all God had promised to Israel (Acts 3:21). They lived as an eschatological community totally given over to their coming Lord and to each other. In what is most likely an idealized portrait of those first days in Jerusalem, Luke writes that

the faithful all lived together and owned everything in common. They sold their goods and possessions and shared out the proceeds among themselves according to what each one needed.

They went as a body to the Temple every day but met in their houses for the breaking of the bread. They shared their food gladly and generously. They praised God and were looked up to by everyone. Day by day the Lord added to their community those destined to be saved. (Acts 2:44–47)

The preaching of the earliest believers took place during the period of the "literary blackout"—the years before the New Testament was written—that covered the first twenty years of the Jesus-movement. We possess no Christian Scriptures earlier than Paul's First Epistle to the Thessalonians in about 50 C.E., but numerous fragments of oral tradition from that period have survived (often much changed by later circumstances) in the writings of the New Testament, and from those fragments exegetes have been able to reconstruct a plausible version of the original Aramaic-Jewish interpretation of Jesus in the period immediately after he died.

That first interpretation was composed of two moments, one of which dealt with Jesus' earthly life, the other with his eschatological future. That is, the earliest disciples thought Jesus *had been God's eschatological prophet* during his life on earth and *would soon become the Son of Man* at the end of time. Let us consider each moment in turn.[5]

Jesus certainly had thought of himself as a prophet; and even though he did not explicitly designate himself as the eschatological prophet, there was no doubt that he presented his mission in eschatological terms and that his disciples hoped he would soon prove to be that long-promised herald of the end. Many Jews believed that when this final prophet came, he would be "anointed" with God's Spirit. That is, he would be a "messiah," although not in a nationalistic or political sense.

In the broadest terms, a messiah ("anointed one"; in Greek translation, *christos*) was a deputy of God, one who had received the Spirit and was appointed to act in Yahweh's name. One such anointed figure was the future Davidic king whom many Jews awaited as a national and political savior; but Judaism likewise expected an anointed prophet, whom Moses himself had promised:

> Moses said, "The Lord God will raise up for you a prophet from your brethren as he raised me up. You shall listen to him in whatever he tells you." (Acts 3:22, citing Deuteronomy 18:15, 18)

This "prophet like Moses" would preach conversion, interpret the Law properly, serve as a "light to the Gentiles," and announce God's definitive arrival among his people. It was this kind of prophetic (not political) messiah that the Aramaic Jewish believers understood Jesus to have been. In so doing they were simply turning their earlier hope about Jesus into an explicit declaration of faith in him. This first moment of the early Aramaic interpretation of Jesus was in strict continuity with what his disciples had believed him to be before he died.

However, the second moment of the interpretation—Jesus as the future Son of Man—represented a qualitative leap in the disciples' faith. In one sense, this "leap" was only an adjustment, although a momentous one, in the then-current Jewish expectation. The disciples gave a recognizable human face—that of Jesus—to the heretofore anonymous apocalyptic judge whom Daniel had called the Son of Man. However, the consequences for Jesus' message were tremendous. Jesus himself had never spoken of returning at the end of time; in fact, at one point in his ministry he may well have expected to be still alive at the end. At most Jesus may have believed—this is much debated—that the definitive arrival of the kingdom would be signaled by the appearance of God's apocalyptic deputy, the Son of Man. Whenever Jesus mentioned this Son of Man (if indeed he did mention him), he always referred to him as a future figure separate from Jesus himself.

Soon after the crucifixion, however, believers invented and put into Jesus' mouth statements which implied that at the eschaton Jesus himself would return as the Son of Man. For example, when Mark wrote his account of Jesus' trial, he constructed it so as to have the high priest ask Jesus whether he was the messiah. And Mark had Jesus respond:

I am; and you will see the Son of Man sitting at the right hand of the Power and coming with the clouds of heaven. (14:62)

But even in inventing such claims, the early believers maintained a distinction between the Jesus of the past, who had preached the kingdom of God, and the Jesus of the future, who would reappear as God's apocalyptic deputy. They did not think that Jesus, during his life on earth, had been an incarnation of the future Son of Man; nor did they claim that he was now fulfilling that role in heaven, that is, that he had already become the apocalyptic judge. Rather, they believed Jesus *would become* the Son of Man *in the near future,* that he had been "ordained by God [to become] the judge of the living and the dead" (Acts 10:42). They believed that when he was raised to heaven, Jesus had been designated or appointed for that role but that he would not begin exercising it until the end arrived.

The first disciples thought that between Jesus' past mission as eschatological prophet and his future mission as Son of Man there lay a brief interval during which God was gathering his people together in readiness for the end. The brevity of that in-between time was the source of the eschatological urgency both of their message and of their style of life. The brevity of the interval also had a negative consequence for christology: It left the disciples with little or nothing to say about who Jesus was or what he was doing during this supposedly short period. They could say only that "heaven must receive him until the universal restoration comes" (Acts 3:21). Jesus was, so to speak, "on hold" for a short while until God would put him into action again at the end of time.

The disciples understood the interval of time between Jesus' death and his second coming less as a chronological moment in time with a before-and-after than as the frozen and breath-catching instant between seeing the flash of an explosion and feeling its full impact. The assumed brevity of the interval provided the earliest believers with little incentive for working out christological theories about Jesus. The title "Son of Man" was soon enough replaced by "messiah" (in Greek, *christos*) as a way of speaking of the role for which Jesus was designated. And since God had appointed Jesus the future judge at the moment when he rescued him from death, the church began to apply the names "Messiah" and "Christ" to Jesus in his suffering and crucifixion. Similarly the title "Son of God" (which was the equivalent of "Messiah" and had no reference to divinity) became another way of identifying Jesus' future role, just as the title "Son of David," which indicated Jesus' qualification for messiahhood, came to apply to Jesus during his earthly life. But all such titles were meant only to spell out the two moments that made up the eschatological faith of the first believers: Jesus had been the final prophet, and he was now momentarily in heaven until his return as apocalyptic judge.

During the interval between his resurrection and the parousia, Jesus was operatively present in the disciples' proclamation of the kingdom. But he was not the object of their preaching so much as its motivation. His words and deeds had been functionally associated with the arrival of the kingdom, and indeed Jesus would function that way again in the future. But the Church did not yet make an ontological identification of Jesus with God's presence among men. During his life he was perceived as the locus of the kingdom of God, just as after his death he became the focus of the disciples' preaching. But he was not yet understood to be the *content* of the kerygma. The early Jewish believers did not think that Jesus was already enthroned and reigning at God's right hand or that he was currently acting with God's power. All that was to come only when Jesus returned at the end of time. During the brief interval he was only the messiah-designate. The fulfillment of God's plan was soon to come, and thus everything about the interval was charged with an overwhelming sense of urgency.

But as this supposedly brief instant dragged on, the status of Jesus during the interval became problematic. Even if his absence from earth could be accounted for by "appearances" from heaven, what was Jesus actually doing in heaven during the lengthening time before his return? It will not do to say that Simon and the early disciples believed that Jesus was alive only in their preaching ("Jesus rose into the kerygma," as Rudolf Bultmann phrased it) or in the continuation of his ideals in the church ("Jesus' cause goes on," as Willi Marxsen puts it). On the contrary, in the eyes of the early church, the kerygma and the continuing cause of the eschatological prophet derived all their meaning from the future return of Jesus. If he was not about to come back, then the entire eschatological business—"resurrection," "appearances," kerygma, and even Jesus himself—would be called into question. And in fact it soon was. The months and years passed without the parousia happening; the brief interval began to turn into a long period of waiting. How long would God keep Jesus in heaven before sending him again?

The next stage in the enhancement of Jesus' status came in large measure as a response to that delay; and that step was taken by the second group of early believers, the Hellenistic Jews. But before moving on to that, let us take stock of the first evaluation of Jesus.

As we have seen, after the crucifixion the disciples came to believe that, by God's initiative, the kingdom Jesus had preached—the presence of God among men and women—was still dawning and in fact was soon to arrive in its fullness. The proper response of the believer to that eschatological event was to live God's present-future in hope and love. The disciples were convinced that the Father had ratified the "word" of his prophet—not just what Jesus had said about the kingdom, but first and above all *how Jesus had lived*. That was what had effected the Father's presence among his people.

Among the earliest interpretations that accrued to this belief were the formulae "Jesus has appeared [from the eschatological future]" and "Jesus has been raised." In these early proclamations we can discern a momentous twofold shift away from Jesus' original message of the kingdom. To begin with, these proclamations presume the identification of the word of Jesus (the efficacious way he lived the present-future) exclusively with Jesus himself; and then further, they announce the identification of Jesus himself with the coming kingdom of God.

This twofold shift lies at the origins of Christianity, and its importance can scarcely be exaggerated. To believe that the way Jesus had lived effected the dawning of the kingdom was to identify an exemplary praxis, imitable by all, for realizing God's presence among men. That was the "word" of Jesus: not his "words" as pieces of information, but his *deed*, what he had lived out and embodied. Jesus' deed had been his all-consuming hope for the Father's presence, a hope that he lived out among his fellow men. The future had become present, and Jesus lived that present-future by turning hope into charity, eschatology into liberation. He lived that hope-as-charity so intensely that he became it. In that sense, yes, Jesus "was" his word, and his word "was" (that is, effected) the kingdom. But the proper way for his followers to affirm that belief was to live the present-future as Jesus had lived it. Strictly speaking, this is what they believed God had ratified: Jesus' *lived hope*, which could remain effective only in the further living of it.

However, the disciples' original mistake lay in exchanging that lived hope for the man who had lived it. And in turn the disciples projected that man into the apocalyptic future as a pledge that their own hope would soon be fulfilled. They surrendered a lived hope for a dead hero whom their faith brought back to life. The memory of the hero grew —first of all into an apocalyptic future, when he would supposedly bring what in fact he had already brought: God's presence. Soon enough the weight of that expected future (what Jesus would do at the parousia) would shift back toward the present (what Jesus was now doing in heaven). And finally that weight would be spread over the whole of history, the past as well as the present and future: The church would interpret Jesus as God himself, the preexistent creator as well as the now reigning Lord and the future judge of the world.

This whole process began when the first disciples gave God back his future and identified it with Jesus of Nazareth. As far as Jesus had been concerned, there was no longer a future any more than there was a past. He stood, so he thought, at the moment when God's future had begun to become present and to abolish the reign of sin. But his disciples exchanged that presence of God's future for the future of God's presence. Jesus had freed himself from religion and apocalypse by transforming hope into charity and by recasting future eschatology as present liberation. But his disciples redirected their attention into a fantastic future and thus reinserted Jesus into the religion he had left behind. They remade God's presence-among-men into God's presence-yet-to-come and eventually into Jesus himself. Henceforth one's relation to God (who Jesus had said was already present) was determined by one's relation to Jesus (who the disciples now said was temporarily absent).

The future-oriented christology of the first disciples did not yet identify the kingdom with the person of Jesus. The earliest disciples did see their master as the unique embodiment of what the kingdom meant, but in so doing they were identifying Jesus with what they took to be his *functions* of prophet (in the recent past) and judge (in the very near future). The process of a full *ontological* identification of Jesus with the kingdom, and eventually as the equal of God, would require more time and would climax in the development of a normative christology that interpreted Jesus—not just in his functions but in his very being—as divine.

But at this earliest stage of christology, the disciples were in fact beginning the process of undoing Jesus' message by reconstituting an apocalyptic future. They started reifying what had begun as a challenge: the challenge of living with one's neighbor in a way that befit the Father's irrevocable commitment to be God-with-men. There at the beginning the disciples missed the point, even if ever so slightly. But the consequences were to be enormous. As Aristotle once said, "The smallest initial deviation from the truth is multiplied later a thousand-fold; what was small at the start turns out a giant at the end."[6]

2

THE
REIGNING
LORD AND
CHRIST

THE JESUS-MOVEMENT was soon to be in trouble. The problem was not that the disciples frequently met resistance from the religious establishment: That, in fact, was grist for their mill. The threat of excommunication from the synagogue, the martyrdom of some believers and the forced emigration of others, even the start of the Zealot uprising in 66 C.E. that would end in the destruction of the Temple in Jerusalem four years later—all such problems fit the apocalyptic program. They were the eschatological woes that signaled the imminent end of the world that the disciples so earnestly awaited. Jesus had predicted:

> When they persecute you in one town, flee to the next; for truly,
> I say to you, you will not have gone through all the towns of Israel,
> before the Son of Man comes. (Matthew 10:23)

The serious problem, rather, was the lengthening of the supposedly brief interval between Jesus' hidden vindication at his death and his public reappearance in glory. Not only was the parousia being progressively delayed, but within thirty years of Jesus' death the founders of this eschatological movement within Judaism would begin dying off, with no return of Jesus yet in sight. This state of affairs occasioned major adjustments in the way the movement looked at history and how it evaluated Jesus himself. The clue to understanding the progressive enhancement of Jesus' status from failed prophet to divine savior lies in the early believers' response to this "problem of the interval."

The period that we now consider stretches from the first years of the Jesus-movement, through the composition of Saint Paul's epistles (about 50–55 C.E.) up to the writing of the Synoptic Gospels (about 70–85 C.E.). Our focus is on the Hellenistic Jewish Christians who began spreading the message beyond the geographical confines of Palestine and the religious limits of Judaism. The development of christology during this period is rich and very complex, but some general lines can be discerned: (1) a gradual deemphasizing of eschatology;[7] (2) a heightening of Jesus' status during the so-called interval;[8] and (3) the "backward migration" of Jesus' messianic status, first from the parousia to the resurrection, then back to his baptism, and then even further back to his conception.[9] Whereas the Aramaic-speaking Jews hoped Jesus would become the messiah at the end of the world, the Hellenistic Jewish converts came to believe that he had already been constituted the messiah from his mother's womb. The Jesus-movement, which originally looked forward, now started glancing over its shoulder to what was believed to have occurred in the past and was now a cosmic fact: that Jesus was already the Lord and Christ, the messianic Son of God.

Properly speaking, Christianity begins with these Hellenistic Jewish believers. They were the first to introduce Jesus into the Western world with the Greek title *christos,* thus earning themselves the name "Christians" (Acts 11:26). More important, the changes they wrought in the movement's theology elevated Jesus to an intermediate christological plateau, from which he would later be launched to the heights of divinity.

The Aramaic-speaking believers, for all their "liberalism" vis-à-vis the religious establishment, were rather conservative in comparison with Hellenistic Jewish Christians. The Palestinian Jewish members of the Jesus-movement regularly visited the Temple, obeyed the Mosaic

THE GROWTH OF CHRISTOLOGY AND SALVATION HISTORY

The savior's powers are increased as his role in history is extended from the future toward the past.

(THE CHART READS FROM RIGHT TO LEFT.)

STAGE THREE Gentile Christians "THE PAST"			STAGE TWO Hellenistic Jewish Christians "THE PRESENT"			STAGE ONE Palestinian Jews "THE FUTURE"
DIVINE SON OF GOD			**CHRIST, LORD, SAVIOR**			**SON OF MAN**
Preexistent Eternally God *before* *Creation*	*Incarnate* Becomes God-man *at* *Incarnation*	*Hidden* Begotten as Savior *at* *Conception*	Adopted as Christ *at* *Baptism*	*Enthroned* Exalted as Lord *at* *Resurrection*	*Revealed* Becomes Son of Man *at* *Parousia*
ca. 50 to 100 C.E. (Collossians hymn, John)		by 85 C.E. (Matthew/Luke)	by 70 C.E. (Mark)	by 50 C.E. (Paul)	ca. 30 C.E. (Simon)

DIVINE PREEXISTENCE

INCARNATION

EARTHLY LIFE

RESURRECTION

EXALTED REIGN

PAROUSIA

(HISTORY OF JUDAISM)

(HISTORY OF CHRISTIANITY)

N.B.: *This chart does not show the overlapping between stages.*

Law (even if in a different spirit from that of some of the Pharisees), and looked forward to the coming apocalyptic end. On the other hand, the Greek-speaking converts, who breathed the cosmopolitan air of Hellenism, were more liberal when it came to the minutiae of the Law and the Temple cults (even though they were quite strict about the Ten Commandments), and were less interested in eschatology and futuristic messianism than their Aramaic-speaking colleagues. The Hellenistic Jewish Christians also took it upon themselves to widen the circle of evangelization to include Gentiles as well as Jews, and in so doing they liberalized some of the strictures, particularly regarding observance of the Law, that more conservative Jewish believers imposed on converts to the movement. As a consequence, the Hellenistic Jewish Christians soon found themselves in conflict not only with their conservative Aramaic-speaking colleagues but also with the religious establishment in Jerusalem, which began persecuting them in the early thirties (Acts 8:1). Within a very few years after Jesus' death many of them left Palestine for the Diaspora, taking with them a new ferment of ideas about who Jesus was and what he was currently doing in heaven.

At first, the Hellenistic Jewish Christians merely translated from Aramaic into Greek the christological titles that expressed the early Church's understanding of Jesus. For example, they rendered the Aramaic *masiah* ("anointed one") and *mare* ("lord") with, respectively, the Greek words *christos* and *kyrios*. But pressured by the continuing delay of the parousia, they then took a momentous step and revised their notions of Jesus' status during the ever-lengthening interval. They began a process within christology which would continue for the rest of the century until Jesus would be recognized as the equal of God himself.

That process consisted in *enhancing Jesus' status prior to the parousia.* (See the accompanying chart.) This enhancement, which was begun by the Hellenistic Jewish Christians and continued by their Gentile converts, moved in the opposite direction from the christology of the first believers. The original impulse of the church had been to augment Jesus' status in a forward direction, toward the future parousia, when he would be revealed as God's chosen messianic son. However, the Hellenistic Jewish believers began enhancing Jesus' status in a *backward* direction. They disconnected the "christological moment" (the point where, according to faith, Jesus became the chosen one of God) from the parousia and began edging it backward toward earlier moments: first to Jesus' resurrection, then to his baptism in the Jordan, and finally to the very moment of his conception. The third group of early believers, the Gentile Christians, would later take the climactic step and declare that their savior had preexisted in heaven as God's divine Son before he became incarnate as Jesus.

This "backward migration" of christology brought about a major change in the church's vision of history. The Hellenistic Jews took the first step by toning down the eschatological thrust of the original believers and pushing Jesus' "christological moment" back through his resurrection to the beginning of his earthly life. But by the end of the century the Gentile Christians went further and formulated a cosmic view of history controlled by their vision of Jesus. Their savior had existed in heaven as God's divine Word—his instrument of creation and revelation—even before the beginning of the world; he had become incarnate as a human being and had suffered and died for the sins of mankind; and at his resurrection he had been exalted to heaven, where he now reigns in glory until the end of the world.

The present section focuses on what the chart designates as Stage Two of christology and salvation history, that is, the period of the backward enhancement of Jesus' christological status, first from the future parousia to the *resurrection;* then further back to his *baptism in the Jordan;* and finally back to the very moment of his *conception.* Later we shall consider Stage Three of the christological progression: how the Gentile Christians came to interpret Jesus as divine.

THE RESURRECTION: JESUS EXALTED AS LORD

Whereas the Aramaic-speaking believers thought Jesus had only been designated to be the future messiah, the Hellenistic Jewish Christians believed that he had already been enthroned as Christ and Lord from the time he was raised from the dead. Instead of a brief and temporary "assumption" into a heavenly limbo of inactivity with the promise of an imminent return, Jesus was now thought to be already "exalted" (enthroned) and ruling at his Father's right hand even before the parousia. The church took two psalms which celebrated the royal coronation of a past Davidic king and interpreted them as applying to Jesus, who they now thought was reigning alongside his Father. Note the following excerpts from two sermons, one attributed to Simon Peter, the other to Paul, which use those psalms:

Acts 2:32–35:

This Jesus God raised up, and of that we are all witnesses. Being therefore exalted at the right hand of God, and having received from the Father the promise of the Holy Spirit, he has poured it out, as you see and hear. . . . For David himself says:

The Lord [Yahweh] said to my Lord [Jesus]:
"Sit at my right hand,
till I make thy enemies
a footstool for thy feet." [Psalm 110:1]

Acts 13:32–33:

We bring you the good news that what God promised to our fathers he has fulfilled to us their children, as it is written in the second psalm,

"Thou art my son,
this day I have begotten thee." [Psalm 2:7]

Now thought to be ruling as the Christ and "Son of God" (God's chosen one, not his ontological son), Jesus becomes the *functional equivalent of God himself*.[10] That is, without yet sharing the nature of God, Jesus is now seen as carrying out functions previously attributed to his Father. Jesus pours out the eschatological Spirit upon those who are to be saved; in fact, he becomes a "life-giving spirit" (I Corinthians 15:45). He receives power from his Father and is made the Lord of the living and the dead (Romans 1:4, 14:9). Above all, he becomes the *Savior* through whom God reconciles the world to himself: "Jesus . . . delivers us from the wrath to come" insofar as he "gave himself for our sins to deliver us from the present evil age" (I Thessalonians 1:10; Galatians 1:54).

The idea of Jesus as the Savior who atoned for the sins of the world (which is a commonplace among Christians today) was far from obvious to the early church. In fact, it took some years before Christians settled on the now normative interpretation of Jesus' death as an expiatory sacrifice for sin. To begin with, Jesus in fact was not condemned to death by the Sanhedrin for claiming to be the messiah. (That claim was from Mark, not Jesus.) Not only did he refuse to advance that claim, but many men before and after him did claim to be the messiah without having any trouble with the Sanhedrin. The most plausible reason that history can currently give for the condemnation of Jesus was that he was perceived as defying the authority of the religious establishment.

However, in a first effort to give a theological meaning to Jesus' death, his disciples interpreted the crucified Jesus as a martyred prophet who had been rejected by men but glorified by God.[11] Although this early interpretation is quite simple when compared with later understandings of Jesus' death, it did bring together into one christological evaluation the heretofore separate themes of (1) the Jewish saint or holy person as God's suffering servant and (2) the coming Son of Man. In support of this schema of rejection and glorification, the church applied to Jesus the words of the psalmist:

> The stone which the builders rejected
> has become the cornerstone.
> This is the Lord's doing;
> it is marvelous in our eyes. (Psalm 118:22f.)

At a second stage of reflection the church enhanced this interpretation by providing the crucifixion with an apocalyptic meaning that changed it from a historical accident into an eschatological inevitability. According to this view, in the days of eschatological woe before the final end, Jesus, like all just and God-fearing Jews, was bound to undergo suffering at the hands of sinners, but with the assurance that God would not forever abandon him to death.

Only at a third stage—perhaps before mid-century—did Hellenistic Jewish Christians begin to think of Jesus' death as a vicarious atonement for the sins of mankind. For those believers, and especially for Saint Paul, Jesus' death and resurrection took on a transcendent and cosmic significance. It was God's universal saving act, his transformation of the very being of the world, the apocalyptic beginning of a "new creation" (II Corinthians 5:17; Galatians 6:16). With Jesus' death and resurrection God's will to save all mankind, which was understood to have been his purpose from the beginning of the world, was seen as becoming a cosmic force now operating through the mediation of the exalted and enthroned messiah.

Jesus himself was that force personified, the human (yet somehow suprahuman) Lord and Christ who was no longer merely the prophetic locus of the coming of the kingdom nor the apocalyptic focus of the disciples' preaching. Jesus as Lord, Christ, and Savior was now the content of the Hellenistic Jewish Gospel. In one sense this Gospel continued the central theme of Jesus' own message—the fact that God had given himself over to be henceforth present among mankind—but on the other hand it changed Jesus' preaching in a fundamental way. Henceforth the God-for-man whom Jesus had proclaimed would be understood as God-*in*-Jesus saving the entire world. In the words of Saint Paul, "God was in Christ reconciling the cosmos to himself" (II Corinthians 5:19).

This Hellenistic Jewish "enthronement christology," which took the resurrection as the moment when Jesus became Lord and Savior, marked Christianity's first important step beyond its original Jewish roots. The earlier "parousia christology" had merely refocused Judaism's expectations by giving the coming Son of Man a known and recognizable face, that of Jesus of Nazareth. This first Jewish christology did not claim that Jesus was now operating with God's power; during the interval it awarded him only the proleptic role of messiah-designate. But the Hellenistic Jewish Christians pulled that future role, and the titles that went with it, back into the present. Jesus, now enthroned in heaven, was *already functioning* with the power he would later exercise in the sight of all at the future parousia. That is, the Hellenistic Jewish Christians made up for the delay in Jesus' future coming by enhancing his present powers. If the first disciples exchanged an earthly present-future for an apocalyptic future, this second wave of believers began dissolving the apocalyptic future into a heavenly present. The parousia slipped into the penumbra of the Church's concern, and Christianity slowly changed from a movement focused on the future to a religion centered on a present redeemer.

THE BAPTISM:
JESUS ADOPTED AS CHRIST

Within twenty years of his death, "Jesus the future Messiah" had become "Jesus the already reigning Christ." But within two more decades—that is, by the time of Saint Mark's Gospel—Jesus' "christological moment," the point when, according to believers, he entered into his complete glory, would migrate one step further back: to his baptism in the Jordan. A text that expresses this new evaluation of Jesus is found at the beginning of Saint Mark's Gospel:

> In those days Jesus came from Nazareth in Galilee and was baptized by John in the Jordan.
>
> And when Jesus came up out of the water, immediately he saw the heavens opened and the Spirit descending upon him like a dove. And a voice came from heaven,
>
>> "Thou art my beloved Son.
>> With thee I am well pleased." (1:9–11)

This text documents the growing interest of Hellenistic Jewish Christians in Jesus' earthly life and ministry and not just in the cosmic saving event of his death and resurrection. Their concern was not "historical" in our modern sense but religious: They wanted to know the prophet of Galilee and Judea as their Savior. Therefore, this first mention of the "historical" Jesus dates his adoption by God as the chosen one not to the resurrection but to the beginning of his public life.[12] This viewpoint is echoed in a later text in which Simon Peter reminds his listeners of

> the word which was proclaimed throughout all Judea, beginning from Galilee after the baptism which John preached: how God anointed Jesus of Nazareth with the Holy Spirit and with power; how he went about doing good and healing all that were oppressed by the devil, for God was with him. (Acts 10:38)

Neither of these two Scripture texts clarifies what Jesus' status was before that moment at the Jordan when God chose him to be the messiah. The presumption is that Jesus was simply a pious Jew and that he was "adopted" by God for the office of proclaiming the eschatological kingdom. Once he was adopted and constituted as God's messianic deputy, his words and works were thenceforth charismatically directed by the Spirit of God. Therefore, even before his resurrection he was the Christ, the messianic "Son of God."

In Mark's Gospel, however, God's adoption of Jesus as the Christ was a hidden affair, known only to Jesus and to the demons whom he exorcized (3:11, 5:7). According to Mark, Jesus never tells his disciples that he is the Christ, and when God miraculously announces the fact to Peter, James, and John during a heavenly vision, Jesus enjoins them to tell no one about the matter (9:9). But during his passion and death the "messianic secret" comes out at two crucial moments. According to Mark, Jesus tells the Sanhedrin that he is the Christ, and for that he is condemned to death (14:61–64). Then, having been rejected by his own religious leaders, Jesus is recognized as messiah by a Gentile, the Roman centurion who was supervising the crucifixion: "Truly this man was the Son of God" (15:39).

The "secret" of Jesus' election to the office of messiah is a literary device employed by Mark for theological purposes. It allowed him to take the christological moment—which believers had already shifted from the parousia to the resurrection—and move it one step further back to the beginning of Jesus' prophetic ministry. However, it was not Mark who invented the messianic interpretation of Jesus' ministry, for the early title of eschatological prophet already embodied the conviction that Jesus' life had been directed by the power of God. What Mark did, rather, was to stabilize this conviction under the stronger rubric of "messiah" or "Christ." In this way, Jesus the Mosaic prophet was seen as permanently endowed, from his baptism onward, with the gift of the Spirit that God had reserved for the end of time.

Intentionally or not, Mark leaves the impression that Jesus, before being adopted at his baptism to be God's messianic son, was an ordinary human being and not the Christ. Other believers apparently found this "adoptionist christology" inadequate to express their conviction that Jesus was already constituted as the Christ from the very beginning of his life. Therefore, the next stage in enhancing Jesus' status would consist in pushing the christological moment one step further back: to his physical conception.

THE CONCEPTION:
JESUS BEGOTTEN AS SAVIOR

Mark's Gospel opens with the preaching of John at the Jordan and has nothing to say about Jesus' life before he was baptized. But some fifteen years later (ca. 85 C.E.), Matthew and Luke begin their Gospels with narratives about the infancy of Jesus—stories which purported to show that Jesus was the Christ from the first moment of conception in his mother's womb. These narratives, which make up the first two chapters of both these Gospels and from which Christians have forged the story of Christmas, are not at all historical accounts of Jesus' earthly beginnings but testimonies of faith that grew out of the burgeoning christology of the Hellenistic Jewish Christians.

Popular ideas notwithstanding, the infancy narratives in the first two chapters of the Gospels of Matthew and Luke say nothing about an "incarnation" of God as man. Quite the contrary, the fetal Jesus whose conception is narrated in these two stories is *entirely human,* despite his miraculous beginnings. Neither Gospel claims that God the Father sent his preexistent and ontologically divine Son to take on human flesh in the Virgin Mary's womb. Such an "incarnation christology" would be the product of the next stage in the enhancement of Jesus' status (for example, in John's Gospel).[13] At this point, rather, we find a more modest "conception christology," which maintains simply that the human fetus that would eventually be born as Jesus of Nazareth was conceived with the blessings of God and was the Messiah from the beginning of his human life. These Gospels do not claim that God was Jesus' physical or ontological Father, or that Jesus was born of a *hieros gamos,* a sacred marriage between the Virgin Mary and the Holy Spirit. Despite popular interpretations, these Gospels are not concerned with the anatomical aspects of Jesus' conception. Their point, rather, is that however the conception may have come about (Luke allows for the possibility that Jesus was conceived in the natural way), that conception was the work of God and the child who was born was God's messiah.

Despite the religious biologism to which they later gave rise, and quite apart from whatever curiosity about Jesus' biography these accounts may have satisfied *en passant,* the "conception christologies" of the Gospels of Matthew and Luke were aimed primarily at correcting earlier adoptionist theories by showing that Jesus was the Christ from the first moment he was human.

In a few short years the Hellenistic Jewish churches of the Diaspora managed to create much of what we know as Christianity. The climactic step, the proclamation of Jesus as the divine Son of God, was still to come; but within fifty years of the crucifixion, the groundwork for that was solidly laid. The consequences were momentous.

FROM ESCHATOLOGY TO HISTORY. Hellenic Jewish Christianity revamped the early believers' eschatological sense of history. For Simon and his brethren—the first generation of believers—the present and the recent past were seen as being entirely ruled by the future parousia. The present existence of these believers was nothing but an expectation of the future, and that future would publicly vindicate all that the prophet Jesus had once been. But with the new emphasis on Jesus' messiahhood—reaching from the past moment of his conception to the present moment of his heavenly reign—Christianity began surrendering its focus on eschatology. However, Christianity did not thereby regain Jesus' sense of the present-future but rather began fashioning its notion of history as a progression toward the eschaton.

One response to the delay of the parousia was the writing of the Gospels. To counter the climate of doubt aroused by Jesus' failure to return, some gospel accounts embellished the Easter experience with elaborate apocalyptic stories that concretized the "resurrection" of Jesus by providing him with a preternatural body that was physically seen, touched, and elevated into heaven. Other New Testament texts portrayed Jesus comforting his disciples by warning them that the parousia might be delayed: "It is not for you to know the times and seasons which the Father has fixed by his own authority" (Acts 1:7); "I am with you always, to the close of the age" (Matthew 28:20). Some believers even declared that the eschaton had already arrived with the first appearance of Jesus and that the kingdom was continuing to grow through the ministry of the Church. (Classical Roman Catholic ecclesiology was built in large measure on this notion of "realized eschatology.")

As the future continued to recede into the distance, the period of the present gained in importance. We have noted how the Aramaic-speaking believers reclaimed the apocalyptic future that Jesus had already left behind. But when that misplaced eschaton failed to come about, the Hellenists created a present that weighed more heavily on Christianity than the apocalyptic future ever could. By opting for a once hidden and now currently ruling Lord and Christ, the Hellenistic Jewish Christians created a heavenly present and the beginnings of a sacred past that would soon become the vertebrate structure of Christian salvation history. In the process, they began substantializing Jesus' salvific functions and identifying the kingdom of God with those functions, thus opening the way to a substantialized divinization of the person of Jesus himself. The message of Jesus became less a challenge to live the reign of God-with-mankind and more an invitation to revere this *one particular man* who had now assumed God's functions.

From that point on, history was dated and centered. The dawning eschatology preached by Jesus, which had become the anticipated apocalypse proclaimed by Simon, now gave way to the present rule of Christ with, at very best, a parousia postponed until a far-distant future. The Christian church stepped firmly into history, which now seemed to move forward on two parallel lines, one celestial, the other terrestrial. Celestial history was the trajectory of Christ's reign in heaven, with his saving work basically accomplished and his second coming indefinitely delayed. Terrestrial history was the parallel trajectory of the church's patient movement toward the ever receding future of the parousia. And even though Christianity's feet were firmly planted in earthly history, its head was in the clouds.

> We know that while we are at home in the body we are away from the Lord. We would rather be away from the body and at home with the Lord. (II Corinthians 5:6, 8)

> My desire is to depart and be with Christ. (Philippians 1:23)

FROM FUNCTIONAL TO ONTOLOGICAL CHRISTOLOGY. The change in the church's sense of history followed from its reevaluation of Jesus. From an early emphasis on his prophetic functions (what he had done in the recent past and would do again in the near future), the church began to stress his nature (who he had been in the past and who he now was in heaven). Strictly speaking, Hellenistic Jewish christology did not take this leap, but it did prepare the way. As the retrospective evaluation of Jesus increased and as the powers he was to exercise at the parousia were extended backward through the "interval" to the beginning of his life, the question of who Jesus was (ontological christology) began to gain importance alongside the question of what he had done (functional christology). Could he have been just a man? Once the "conception christology" of Matthew and Luke had raised the stakes over the "adoptionist christology" of Mark, momentum built up for an even higher wager: that Jesus' origins stretched back beyond his merely human beginnings, to divine preexistence in heaven.

3

THE DIVINE
SON OF GOD

D URING THE FIRST CENTURY of Christianity, pagan religion in
the Mediterranean was characterized by a syncretism of Greek
philosophy, Jewish theology, and a variety of mystery cults. This rich
mixture defies synthesis, but we can identify within it a widely diffused
interest in personal and cosmic salvation. This was an interest to which
Christianity responded as it took the third step in enhancing the status
of Jesus.

The Graeco-Roman world was in social and religious ferment when
Christianity was born. Three centuries earlier, with the conquests of
Alexander the Great, the tidy world of the Greek city-state had begun
to crumble, and with it went the security of living one's life within
a cohesive whole in which politics, religion, and social intercourse
were integrated. In the less stable cosmopolitanism which ensued,
Greek culture found itself bound under Roman political authority and
confronted with the strange practices of Oriental religions. The old
gods seemed to have fled. They had lost their footing in the everyday
life of the polis and disappeared into the transcendent Beyond, which
philosophers attempted to divine. Their traces could still be found in
the ancient poems of Homer and Hesiod, but the gods' crude morals

and fickle ways, as depicted in those works, hardly seemed models for ethical and political action. The ancient divinities had lost their power to do the one thing they had once been good for: holding the world and the social order together.[14]

At the time when Christianity was entering the Diaspora, there was a general sense among the Mediterranean peoples that the whole cosmos was in the grip of forces and spirits that imposed a hard fate on the course of natural and human events. For ancient peoples, Greeks and Romans included, the world of the stars and planets had never been a neutral or strictly "natural" realm. The sky was the abode of the immortal gods, the realm of eternity, stability, and bliss, in contrast with earthly change and human suffering. In both popular religion and learned philosophy, the sky was thought to be filled with gods and demigods who influenced everything from the course of history to the humors of the body. Even in postexilic Judaism, when Yahweh seemed to retreat into the further reaches of transcendence, angelic intermediaries were multiplied to fill the gap left by Yahweh's absence and to guarantee both his contact with, and his detachment from, the world. In popular Jewish cosmology, each planet, star, and material substance, as well as every nation on earth, was governed by an angel who guaranteed God's presence and dominion in the world.

Perhaps never before had the oppressive sense of cosmic fate weighed so heavily on Mediterranean peoples. There was a widespread sense, derived in good measure from Near Eastern cults, that the "lower heavens" (the area of sky beneath the moon) was controlled by obscure cosmic forces that held one's life and destiny within their power. The Greeks had long had a sense of the tension between order and chaos and knew the difference between nature's purposeful activity and its raw, unshaped power. But these were distinctions made by reason in an effort to know and control the irrational, or at least to hold it at bay. The new religious forces, on the other hand, lay beyond the power of reason and the orderliness of nature. These forces constituted a system of ironclad fate—*heimarmenē*—that defied human comprehension and control. All one could do was to achieve harmony with the cosmic system. Even in Stoic philosophy, where the power of fate was seen as hypostasized Reason *(Logos)*, men and women were powerless to do anything but surrender themselves to its inevitability. As Seneca put it, "The fates lead the willing and drag the unwilling."[15]

In most of these systems, whether pagan or Jewish, the cosmos was seen as divided between the heavenly and the earthly realms, each of which in turn was divided into two.

HEAVENLY $\begin{cases} \text{Upper Heavens} \\ \text{Lower Heavens} \end{cases}$

EARTHLY $\begin{cases} \text{The Earth} \\ \text{Below the Earth} \end{cases}$

The upper ethereal heavens, sometimes called *epourania,* were where the highest God or gods dwelt; in Jewish and Christian models of the cosmos, this was the dwelling place of Yahweh. The lower heavens were the abode of demons and spirits, both good and bad. In some systems it included the region of the stars and planets, in others it was confined to the "air" (Greek *aēr*), that is, the atmosphere under the moon. In the epistles of Paul and his colleagues, these cosmic powers were given various names: "principalities," "authorities," "powers," "the world-rulers of the darkness of this age," "the spirits of evil in the upper heavens," and in general "the god of this world." Sometimes they were angels, sometimes the personified "elements of the cosmos," which had become mythologized into living beings who determined the course of earthly events. These elements were seen as intermediaries of the higher gods, and one had to worship them to gain access to the fullness *(plērōma)* of divine power and, ultimately, to immortality.

The third level was the dwelling place of men and women during their earthly subjection to the power and influence of demons and angels. And finally, below the earth, according to some systems of Jewish apocalypse, were subterranean caves where the fallen angels were enchained. Such demonology and mythical cosmology was common in both paganism and apocalyptic Judaism, and was part even of certain Stoic theories of the universe. All these mythologies shared a common notion: The destiny of men and women was out of their control.

The need for salvation from the cosmic forces of the lower heavens was strongly felt and took various forms. One way to achieve liberation was to placate these powers by observing astrological holy days and abstaining from certain foods. Another means was participation in mystery cults that promised initiates the wisdom and knowledge that would save them. The older Greek mystery religions of Demeter, Dionysos, and Orpheus were augmented by still others coming from the East: the cults of Isis and Osiris from Egypt, of Cybele and Attis from Phrygia, of Atargatis and Adonis from Syria, and later, from Persia, the religion of the Aryan deity Mithra. These rites answered a felt need for spiritual rebirth by associating the participants with a god who died or disappeared and then either returned to life or in some way shared divine power with the initiates. At a more sophisticated level, the Stoics taught that one must achieve harmony with, or resign oneself to, the universal principle of Reason, which ruled the cosmos in the form of fate, or providence *(pronoia)*. In all such systems, whether astrologism, mystery religions, or Stoic philosophy, the desired salvation was both individual (spiritual redemption, ethical conversion) and cosmic (reconciliation with, or resignation to, the forces ruling the world).

Hellenistic Jewish Christians lived in the midst of this religious ferment, influencing it and being influenced in turn. As they gained converts among Gentiles and as these new believers took up the work of evangelization, the Christian proclamation of the person and works of Jesus was gradually adapted to the new religious situation. In the process, Christian evangelists rewrote their vision of Jesus and made him into the cosmic redeemer who had conquered the malevolent powers of the world.[16]

In the previous section we saw how Greek-speaking Jewish Christians promoted Jesus beyond the original roles of eschatological prophet and future Son of Man by moving his future parousial powers back into a present reign. This second-stage Hellenistic christology was continuous with first-stage Aramaic christology on two points. First, it maintained a *functional* emphasis on Jesus' saving actions and did not yet hazard an ontological evaluation of his nature. And second, even though Hellenistic christology shifted the historical focus from the future to the present, it still kept the parousia at least in the peripheral vision of Christianity.

However, all of that began to change in the last half of the century. As the church became more populated by Gentiles and as the parousia continued to be delayed, Christians reshaped their faith in two important ways. First, they began to affirm the *ontological divinity of Jesus*.

And second, they scored this belief in the key of an *elaborate cosmic drama* which comprised three acts: (1) the savior's preexistence as God in heaven, (2) his incarnation as the God-man Jesus, and (3) after his redemptive death and resurrection, his re-exaltation as Lord and Christ and his recognition as God (see chart, p. 194).

In constructing this cosmic drama Christianity drew upon a late-Jewish tradition that spoke of the odyssey of God's "Wisdom" through the cosmos. In the years after the exile, when Yahweh seemed to withdraw from the earth and become more transcendent, Judaism began to hypostatize and personify various features of his divinity—for example, his "Spirit" and his "Word"—which were represented as distinct from him, yet closely related to God. These hypostatizations mediated between Yahweh and mankind, thus preserving both God's transcendence and his presence to the world.[17]

One of the most important of these hypostatizations was God's "Wisdom" (Hebrew *hokhma;* Greek *sophia*), which was personified as a woman. She was the first of God's creations, brought into being "at the beginning of his work, the first of his acts of old" (Proverbs 8:22), and she was a perfect image of God himself.

> [Wisdom] is a breath of the power of God and a pure emanation
> from the glory of the Almighty; therefore can nothing defiled
> enter her.
> She is a reflection of eternal light, a spotless mirror of the working
> of God, and an image of his goodness. (Wisdom 7:25–26)

As a hypostatization of God, Wisdom assumed two of God's functions toward the world: She was the agent of the rest of his creation, "the fashioner of all things" (Wisdom 7:22); and she was the mediatrix of revelation who reveals "all things that are either secret or manifest" (7:21). As God's own revelatory word seeking to find a place among mankind, Wisdom periodically entered the world, either directly or through intermediaries, to offer Israel the liberating knowledge of the Law. The Book of Proverbs asks:

> Does not wisdom call?
> Does not understanding raise her voice?
> On the heights beside the way,

in the paths she takes her stand.
Beside the gates in front of the town,
    at the entrance of the portals she cries out:
"To you, O men, I call,
    and my cry is to the sons of men. . . .
Hear, for I will speak noble things,
    from my lips will come what is right. . . .
Take my instruction instead of silver,
    and knowledge rather than choice gold. (8:1–5, 6, 10)

On the basis of these beliefs, Hellenistic Jewish circles created a cosmic myth of Wisdom's voyage through the world. At first she dwelled in heaven as God's companion. Then, as the medium of his revelation, she entered the world in search of those who would receive her. Finally, rejected by mankind, she returned to heaven to take her place with God. We can see that threefold pattern in the following passage from the apocalyptic book of I Enoch, chapter 42:1–2:

[*Preexistence*]
Wisdom found no place
    in which she could dwell,
but a dwelling place was found for her
    in the heavens.

[*Descent and rejection*]
Then Wisdom went forth to dwell
    with the children of the people,
but she found no dwelling place.

[*Reascent and exaltation*]
So Wisdom returned to her own place,
    and she settled permanently among the angels.

This is the pattern of descent and ascent (Greek: *katabasis* and *anabasis*) that Christianity took over and modified in order to express its belief that Jesus was the human incarnation of the divine savior who had preexisted from all eternity. In certain Jewish Diaspora traditions, notably in Philo of Alexandria, this heavenly Wisdom had become associated with the hypostatization of God's "Word" or *Logos*, and even with an ideal heavenly Adam (not the Adam who fell into sin), a "first man" who was sometimes described as neither male nor female, who was created in God's image and dwelled with him in heaven. This Jewish tradition of Wisdom/Logos/heavenly Adam was adapted to fit Christianity's new conviction that their savior had preexisted as God, had become incarnate as Jesus of Nazareth to save mankind from sin, and had reascended to his former divine station.

Although this cosmic redemptive drama had its roots in Jewish intertestamental literature, there is little doubt that the mission to the Gentiles was sensitive to the mood of the pagan world and adapted its message to the perceived religious needs of its new converts. Paul's Epistle to the Philippians, written perhaps in the late fifties, contains an earlier Christian hymn (2:6–11) that expresses one version of the cosmic redemptive drama that Hellenistic Jewish Christians preached in the pagan world. Using Paul's text in his Epistle to the Philippians, scholars have reconstructed the original, underlying Christian hymn about the savior as follows:

[*Preexistence*]
Though he was in the form of God,
    he did not count equality with God
    a thing to be clung to,

[*Incarnation*]
but emptied himself,
    taking the form of a slave,
    being born in the likeness of men.

And being found in human form,
    he humbled himself,
    and became obedient unto death.

[*Exaltation and Universal Homage*]
Therefore, God has highly exalted him,
    and bestowed on him the name
    which is above every name,

that at the name of Jesus
    every knee should bow,
    in heaven and on earth and under the earth,

and every tongue confess
"Jesus Christ is Lord"
—to the glory of God the Father.

This hymn clearly shows how the Hellenistic Jewish Christians adapted and enhanced the Jewish Wisdom myth to fit the needs of their mission to the Gentiles. The modifications are visible in all three states of the redemptive cosmic drama.[18]

THE PREEXISTENCE OF THE SAVIOR: The hymn dramatically shifts the valence of christology by placing the work of redemption within the framework of a cosmic history that begins with the savior's preexistence. To be sure, there are New Testament texts earlier than the hymn in Philippians which do speak of God "sending" the savior to earth (for example, Romans 8:3; Galatians 4:4), but those texts do not elaborate the preexistence of the savior, and in fact they are focused on the eschatological nature of his mission. In the Philippians hymn, however, the church's original focus on the eschaton is entirely absent, and instead we are swept back in the other direction, to the beginning of God's plan of salvation. Gone, too, is the simple "contrast model" of the early church, according to which God raised up the prophet whom men had rejected, and exalted him to his present reign in heaven. Here, rather, the drama of salvation begins outside of time, in heaven with an already enthroned divinity. The hymn transcends even the Jewish Wisdom tradition insofar as it declares the preexistence savior to be actually divine and equal to Yahweh ("in the form of God") rather than merely a vague hypostatization of his being. However, while it is clear in the hymn that the savior existed in heaven before becoming a man, it is not stated that he existed prior to creation.

THE INCARNATION: Here the hymn takes a daring stride beyond the Wisdom myth. First, the divine savior is not "sent" by God, but freely and of his own accord chooses to leave his heavenly station. Second, and more important, this savior, unlike the Wisdom of late Judaism, empties himself *(heauton ekenōsen)* and becomes a specific, individual human being, Jesus of Nazareth. Such a self-emptying *(kenōsis)* and appearance in human form was unheard-of in the Jewish Wisdom tradition. The text in Philippians goes beyond the "conception christology" of the Gospels of Matthew and Luke, in which God makes a human child be the Christ from the first moment of his life. In this epistle we find a qualitatively different "incarnation christology," in which a preexistent divine being becomes the Christ by becoming a human being. What is more, in becoming human the savior makes himself a "slave"—but not just God's obedient prophetic servant of earlier christologies who "makes himself an offering for sin" (Isaiah 53:10). Rather, in the lexicon of pagan religions "slavery" meant the state of being subject to the supernatural demonic powers that ruled the "lower world." Thus, according to the Philippians hymn, the savior descended from God's heaven and not only took his place lower than the spiritual beings who rule the sky and the planets but also submitted, like any other human being, to their domination. Which means he submitted to the ultimate power of these forces of evil: He became obedient unto death.

EXALTATION AND UNIVERSAL HOMAGE: Here the hymn transcends the earlier enthronement christology of Hellenistic Jewish Christianity. In that second stage of christology, as we have seen, Jesus' enthronement at God's right hand had an element of provisionality about it: Jesus was already reigning, to be sure, but his full triumph still lay in the future, when God would completely submit the powers of the world to him. ("Sit at my right hand until I make your enemies your footstool," Psalm 100:1). In the earlier "enthronement christology" we can still see a remnant of the Church's original focus on a future parousia.

According to the Philippians hymn, however, Jesus received *all* power from the very moment of his reassumption into heaven after his crucifixion. After the savior's death God "highly exalted" *(hyper-ypsōsen)* him, lifted him above the demonic powers to which he was formerly subjected. God took Jesus into the highest heaven, where he bestowed upon him the name which is above any other, the divine title "Lord." The savior's divine powers, which previously were hidden from the cosmic forces, are now fully revealed, so that enthroned on high, he commands worship from all three of the lower levels of the universe: "Every knee should bow, in heaven [the "air" ruled by demons] and on earth and under the earth." God the Father now exercises his divine power toward the world through this exalted

God-man Jesus, who reigns as Cosmocrator, the Lord of the entire universe.

With the vision that is expressed in the Philippians hymn, belief in Jesus took a major step beyond earlier functional christologies and entered ontological christology. Jesus not only *acted* with divine power; he also *was and is* divine. This cosmic vision of the divine savior —preexistent, incarnate, and exalted over all the powers of the world —set christology on the high road along which it would continue to develop for the next two millennia.

We find further elaborations of this understanding of Jesus in later texts of the New Testament. The Epistle to the Colossians, for example, continues the adaptation of the Jewish Wisdom tradition when it speaks of the preexistent savior as "the image of the invisible God, the first-born of all creation" (1:15). He is the origin and sustainer of the cosmos; he is its head and it is his body. The present text from Colossians, like the Philippians hymn, does not assert that the savior existed with God before creation (rather, he is the "first-born" of creation). But in saying that Jesus was exalted as "the beginning [of the new creation], the first-born from the dead," the text is asserting that Jesus is now the heir of God's own powers:

[*The first creation*]
He is the image of the invisible God,
    the first-born of all creation.
For in him all things were created
    in heaven and earth,
    visible and invisible—
    whether thrones or dominions
    or principalities or authorities—
All things were created through him and for him.
He is before all things,
    and in him all things hold together.

[*The new creation*]
He is the head of the body, the church.
He is the beginning, the first-born from the dead,
    that in everything he might be preeminent.
In him all the fullness of God was pleased to dwell,

and through him to reconcile all things to himself,
    whether on earth or in heaven,
    making peace by the blood of his cross. (Colossians 1:15–20a)

This New Testament christology of the divine savior achieves its highest expression in the hymn to the preexistent and incarnate savior that serves as the prologue to the Gospel of John.[19] That hymn is older than the Gospel itself (which was composed during the last decade of the first Christian century) and draws upon the Jewish Wisdom tradition at that point in Hellenistic Judaism where Wisdom had already come to be combined with another hypostatization of Yahweh: his Word (Greek *Logos*). In fact, it is possible that the prologue-hymn is a combination of a Jewish hymn to Wisdom-Logos (roughly, verses 1–12) and a specifically Christian hymn (verses 14 and 16) about the incarnation of the savior. (The final editor of the Gospel inserted into the combined hymns a number of verses that are not relevant to this discussion and that are omitted below.)

Unlike Colossians, which speaks of the savior as the first-born of all creation, the prologue to John's Gospel pushes the existence of the Word back to a point even prior to creation.

In the beginning was the Word,
And the Word was with God,
And the Word was God.
He was in the beginning with God. (1:1–2)

Unlike the Wisdom of late Jewish tradition, this Word, or *Logos*, is not merely a hypostasis of one of God's attributes, but rather exists in his own right *as* God and *with* God. Although there is no mention here of the Trinity—Father, Son, and Holy Spirit—the text is certainly on the way to that later doctrine.

Like the Wisdom of the Jewish tradition, this Word is the agent of all of God's creation:

All things were made through him
    and nothing that has been made
        was made without him. (1:3)

And also like Wisdom, the Word is the mediator of God's revelation to the world. Even before he becomes incarnate as a man, the Word shines into the world as God's light. We notice here the same pattern as Wisdom's odyssey through the world, with rejection by some and acceptance by others:

> In him was life,
> and the life was the light of men.
> And the light shines in the darkness
> and the darkness has not overcome it.
>
> He was in the world
> yet the world knew him not.
> He came to his own
> and his own received him not.
> But to all who received him
> he gave power to become children of God. (1:4–5, 10–12)

Up to this point, if we were to make the slight change of "he" to "she," the prologue could well be a hymn to Wisdom in the pre-Christian Jewish tradition, and in fact it originally may have been just that. What follows, however, is a specifically Christian assertion of the incarnation of the preexistent Word as the man Jesus of Nazareth:

> And the Word became flesh
> and dwelt among us. . . .
> And we beheld his glory,
> glory of the only one from the Father,
> full of grace and truth.
>
> And of his fullness we have all received:
> grace upon grace. (1:14, 16)

With this text the christological moment takes the final and climactic step in its backward migration: It moves back earlier than the miraculous but still human conception of Jesus in his mother's womb to the incarnation of the divine Word as a human being. That is, to the earlier "conception christologies" of Matthew and Luke there is now superadded an "incarnation christology," which asserts that God himself has appeared in human form to lead men and women back to the same heavenly abode from which he descended. The arrival of the Word on earth is no longer, as it was in the Epistle to the Philippians, the savior's "emptying" himself of his divinity in order to take on humble human status. The incarnation is now seen as a resplendent divine epiphany, the very appearance of God himself: "we beheld his glory." The words that Jesus spoke and the works he performed will, from now on, be understood as the miraculous acts of a God-man who sojourned awhile on earth in order to show mankind the way to heaven.

In the view of such an incarnation christology, the proper question to put to this divine human being is not the one the first disciples put to Jesus—"Rabbi, where do you dwell?" (John 2:38)—so much as it is the question that Pilate reportedly put to the God-man on the day of his crucifixion: "Where do you *come from*?" (John 19:9). At this stage of christology, the answer to that question is clear; and equally clear is the path that this God-man now opens up to believers by means of his death and glorification: "Christ died for sins, once for all . . . so that he might bring us to God" (I Peter 3:18). The challenge to search for the kingdom of God-with-man on earth has now become an exhortation to "seek the things that are above, where Christ is, seated at the right hand of God" (Colossians 3:1).

The odyssey of christology continued to develop from the height it reached in Saint John's Gospel. Later generations of Christians would define the status of this God-man as the only-begotten Son of God. And after the "Spirit" of God had been fully hypostatized, he would be proclaimed as the Second Person of the divine Trinity. But that story belongs to the later development of Christianity. We stop our investigation here at the end of the first Christian century, at the point where Jesus' status had evolved from eschatological prophet to preexistent Son of God. Within a few short decades of his death, the man who had heralded the end of all religion had been transformed into the divine guarantor of the one, true, and universal religion.

RECOVERING THE KINGDOM

W E HAVE STUDIED how the kingdom of God became Christianity, how Jesus' message of the Father's presence devolved into one more form of religion.

We saw how Jesus proclaimed the incarnation of God, the mystery of the heavenly Father coming to dwell among his people. And we saw how the disciples, by announcing the resurrection of Jesus and by generating various christologies, changed the prophet's radical message about God into a doctrine about Jesus himself.

The genesis of Christianity—the interpretation of Jesus as the savior —distorted the message of Jesus in three major ways.

First of all, Christianity hypostatized the kingdom. Whereas Jesus preached that God was arriving in the present-future, that is, in the enactment of justice and mercy, the church reified that living presence and narrowed it down to God's incarnation as and in one person, Jesus of Nazareth. Christianity's first sin was idolatry: It turned what Jesus was about into Jesus himself. It took the mystery he proclaimed—the utterly unfathomable mystery of God's disappearance into humankind —and reduced it to the Procrustean dimensions of the one who proclaimed it. By elaborating functional christologies initially and onto-logical christologies eventually, Christianity turned Jesus, in the phrase of the third-century theologian Origen, into *hē autobasileia*, the king-dom-of-God-in-person.[1]

Second, Christianity abandoned the prophet's radical sense of time. By interpreting Jesus as savior, the church surrendered the present-future—the only place where the Father henceforth would dwell—and in its place constructed the mythical past-present-future of a cosmic "salvation history," according to which God had become man in the past, was reigning in heaven at present, and would return to earth in the future. In so doing, Christianity lost the core of the prophet's message of forgiveness: that the future was already present—grace was everywhere—and therefore that the arrival of the heavenly Father was transformed into the praxis of earthly liberation.

Third, Christianity reconstituted religion. Jesus did not undertake his prophetic mission in order to bring people more religion (surely there was enough available already) or a different religion (Judaism was quite adequate, as religions go) or the true and perfect religion (which would be a contradiction in terms). Nor was his goal to reform the religion into which he was born. Rather, Jesus preached the *end* of religion and the beginning of what religion is supposed to be about: God's presence among men and women. And the paradox of the prophet's message was that God's presence meant God's disappearance —into his people. In a sense then, yes, it meant the death of God, his *kenōsis*, or outpouring of himself. But Christianity, in place of God's reign with man (or rather, in the hope of realizing it), reintroduced religion in a variety of forms: apocalyptic eschatology (Jesus as the future judge), messianic salvation (Jesus as the reigning Redeemer), and cosmic mythology (Jesus as the preexistent, incarnate, and exalted Son of God).

Paradoxically, to say that Christianity distorts the message of Jesus is not to say that it is wrong. Christianity is not a false interpretation but one possible interpretation of the meaning of the kingdom of God. And insofar as the Christian interpretation enables some people to live loving and meaningful lives, it is even "true," at least in the sense of making possible what the Greeks called *eu zēn*, "living well." But Christianity is certainly not the only interpretation of Jesus' message, and arguably not the best one. I have suggested that in seizing upon Jesus, the church has missed what Jesus was about, that in elaborating her christological doctrines, she has covered over the mystery of the present-future. It is not that the church is at a loss for answers about Jesus; but maybe she has forgotten the question.

Can one recover the kingdom? Surely not in the sense of developing more precise christological answers to the question of who Jesus is in his divine self, or what Jesus does to save mankind. We will not recover the kingdom by fashioning a new Christ. Nor will we recover the kingdom by clinging to Jesus the way Simon did, and by making him—his particular words and deeds—into the absolute and sufficient law for everyday life. All such ways of clinging to Jesus are the very way to lose what he was about, for they take Jesus as an answer, whereas the point is to discover oneself as a question.

Perhaps one could begin to recover the kingdom by learning to ask the question that started things off in the beginning, the question about where one dwells. The focus now is on ourselves, not on Jesus. And in learning to do without Christ (that is, the Christian inter-pretation of Jesus) and even without Jesus (taken as the answer to anything), we may catch a glimpse of how to recover the *question* that Jesus was.

Where do we dwell? To be human means to be condemned to having the things of one's world not simply and directly (as supposedly God does) but only indirectly, that is, through interpretation. We dwell in our interpretations. In interpreting a phenomenon, we always take it *as* this or that, *in terms of* such and such a viewpoint. (For example, Jesus *as* God; or Jesus *as* merely a human being.) This means that we always understand things partially, inadequately, and with prejudice—in a word, through language rather than through a God-like omniscient intuition. If "perfect truth" means perfect identifica-tion of our language with what we are talking about, then all our truths are fraught with falsehood, and all our taking of phenomena *as* this or that is also a mis-taking of them.

The interpretation of the kingdom of God that I have advanced in this book is certainly not traditional or orthodox. But what was just said about interpretation and the inevitability of mis-take raises the possibility that even the traditionally orthodox interpretation of the kingdom, which we call Christianity, is as much a heresy as is any "heretical" interpretation, including the one in this book.

In the broadest sense, heresy (from the Greek *hairēsis:* taking, choosing, taking sides) is an essential constituent of all hermeneutics (in Greek *hermēneia:* interpretation, taking something *as* something). The history of Christianity through the centuries is, in fact, a history of its hermeneutical heresies, not just the heresies that the church has condemned and excluded, but also, and above all, the orthodox heresies, the acceptable takes/mis-takes that have come to constitute mainstream Christianity. Thus, over against the heresy that is Christianity I propose another, one that consists in understanding the message of the kingdom of God without Christ and without Jesus: (1) "without Christ," that is, without interpretations that equate the kingdom of God with Christ's salvific acts (functional christology) and ultimately with his divine person (ontological christology); (2) "without Jesus," that is, not dismissing the prophet, but also not turning him into an idol. "Without Jesus" means without attributing to him any power beyond the natural, human power everyone has: that of being a culturally determined, historically relative interpreter of one's world and one's own life. This means that for all the natural gifts and talents he once displayed, and regardless of whether one chooses to take him as a model for enacting the kingdom, Jesus is ultimately dispensable. He is not irreplaceable—in fact, he demands to be displaced so that one can get to what he is about. Jesus is not the object of the message he preached. The proclaimer of the kingdom gives way to the reality he proclaimed.

"The kingdom of God" is a language, an interpretation of human existence that was preached and lived by Jesus in the past and that can be reinterpreted and lived out by people today. The reinterpretation that I propose—recovering the kingdom without Christ or Jesus—entails taking the prophet *at* his word and *as* his word.

(1) To hear Jesus' message of the kingdom of God "without Christ" and the Christian interpretation means to take Jesus *at* his word. This requires understanding what he said about eschatological forgiveness and its enactment in one's own life: "Live the present-future, for God has disappeared into justice and mercy" (cf. Mark 1:15). This most certainly entails not turning Jesus into the Christ or the Son of God or the kingdom incarnate or any other form of religion. Taking Jesus

at his word means living God's eschatological future in and as the worldly task of human liberation, and doing this in a context where it is no longer possible or necessary to distinguish, as religion does, between nature and grace, between the worldly and the divine. The incarnation of God, his act of eschatological forgiveness, is what makes these distinctions impossible. In the postreligious dispensation that Jesus inaugurated, faith—that is, living the present-future—means maintaining the *undecidability* of what is human and what is divine. This is what the Jewish scholar Philo of Alexandria, a contemporary of Jesus, seems to be expressing when he writes:

> When the righteous man searches for the nature of all things, he makes his own admirable discovery: that *all is God's grace.* . . . Everything in the world, and the very world itself, manifests the blessings and generosity of God.[2]

(2) To hear the message of the kingdom of God "without Jesus," that is, without attributing to the prophet any unique or extraordinary powers, means to take Jesus *as* his word. That means cutting through the words and deeds in which Jesus preached the kingdom of God, in order to discover what gave rise to those acts and made them possible. Taking Jesus *as* his word means understanding that he is what everyone else is: a finite, fallible, mortal act of interpretation. Every human being is just that and no more: a hermeneusis, a lived interpretation (in action, in play, in language and thought) of what one's existence is and is about. Simply by living, one enacts such an interpretation and expresses it in the words of one's dialect, one's culture, one's moment in history.

Jesus summarized everything he understood about the world and mankind in the idiosyncratic and culturally determined words "The kingdom of God is at hand." That phrase expressed, within the eschatological language of intertestamental Judaism, Jesus' vision of what human existence is: a present prolepsis of the once-future God, in a word, the incarnation.

Jesus' words, of course, are an interpretation that requires yet further interpretation, and so on ad infinitum. But in all these efforts at understanding the message of his kingdom of God, the point is to see the *inevitability of interpretation,* that is, to see that what makes us be human is our inexorable finitude, which condemns us to being acts of indirection and mediation, where all is "hints and guesses / Hints followed by guesses."[3] If, as we suggested above, living the kingdom means maintaining undecidability (the impossibility of distinguishing the worldly from the divine), then human existence itself, as an act of interpretation, is the *enactment* of undecidability. We are the inevitability of taking and mis-taking ourselves and the world as this or that; we are the inevitability of heresy. That is to say: All of us, including Jesus, are inevitably and forever a question to which there is no answer. Taking Jesus as his word means understanding and accepting that. Therefore, yes: The message of the kingdom of God is about Jesus of Nazareth—but only insofar as it is about every man and woman.

Recovering the kingdom "without Christ"—that would mean getting to what Jesus *said:* the present-future, the incarnation. Recovering the kingdom "without Jesus"—that would mean getting to what Jesus *was:* a hermeneut, a heretic, that is, a human being. The point in recovering the kingdom is to recover oneself as the place of the mystery of the present-future, and thus as one called to enact liberation.

We are brought back full circle to where we started. The crisis Christianity faces today is not sociological or administrative; it has little to do with the otherwise important facts that family life and sexual morality are in revolution, that church attendance and clerical vocations are decreasing, that women are demanding their rightful place in a heretofore masculine church. Christianity will survive all such crises by reshaping its outer form, as it has repeatedly done over the last twenty centuries. The major decision Christianity faces today is not how it might continue as before, or even how it might reform itself so as to return to its origins, to the surety of Simon's vision, to the pristine power of his Easter experience. No, the decision is whether or not Christianity can dissolve itself in order to become what it is about.

The crisis in Christianity is about its origins, its founding story, but not in the sense that its doctrines have been found to be myths (all religious doctrines are mythical) or to be totally lacking in truth (they are presumably as true, and as false, as any other decent religion's) or that they have no more meaning in the sophisticated modern world. Rather, the crisis is that at last Christianity is discovering what it always was about: not God or Christ or Jesus of Nazareth, but the endless, unresolvable mystery inscribed at the heart of being human.

This is a chastening insight, but a salutary one, fraught with new possibilities for recovering the radically original impulse behind Jesus' preaching. The prophet announced that the time had come (Mark 1:15), that the beginning of the end of religion was at hand. Since then, the church has wrestled with the challenge of putting herself out of business the way Jesus himself did: in the name of God's incarnation. That means learning to live at the uncertain point that is the present-future, without appeal to any "beyond." It is there, in the present-future, that all the reified and self-perpetuating structures of religion dissolve into what they were supposed to be about—this is the kingdom's "protestant" moment of calling faith back to its origins. But there too the "catholic" moment, when one discovers the simple, universal meaning of those origins. It is the same message that Jesus preached when he came back to Galilee after his baptism in the Jordan: Grace is and always has been everywhere. The task is to make it so.

Appendix
Notes on
Rabbinical Literature

A. THE MISHNAH

In the centuries after the closing of the Pentateuch (ca. 400 B.C.E.), and particularly from 270 B.C.E. onward, there grew up alongside the Written Law of the Pentateuch a rich *oral* tradition of ethical casuistry, generated by the scribes and Pharisees but not accepted by the Sadducees. The purpose of this Oral Law, according to its proponents, was to "build a fence around the [Written] Law."

At first this tradition was elaborated via running commentaries (*midrash:* "explanation" or "exposition") on the Torah and more broadly on the whole Tanackh. These scriptural commentaries eventually took the form either of Midrash Halakhah ("the way"), which generated legal principles in a quasi-systematic manner, or the more imaginative Midrash Haggadah ("tale"), which expanded on biblical history and developed ethical and/or devotional ideas. These two forms of commentary continued, usually mixed together, with one or the other dominating according to the document, in later rabbinical literature.

After the Maccabean revolt the scribes developed a systematic, but still oral, tradition of deriving legal opinions. This elaborate and meticulous oral jurisprudence, over which Jesus and the Pharisees frequently clashed, was at first taught by scribes and, after 70 C.E., by teachers (Tannaim) through the process of repetition (Hebrew *mishnah;* Greek *deuterōsis*). Therefore, when the famous Galilean Rabbi Judah the Prince collected, codified, and wrote out the corpus of received legal opinions in postbiblical Hebrew around 200 C.E., it took the name Mishnah.

The Mishnah, as Jacob Neusner has noted, "stands at the beginning of a new and stunningly original epoch in the formation of Judaism" (*Midrash in Context*, 4) insofar as it leads to the Talmud, Judaism's *Summa Theologiae*. But more important, as "the oldest extant code of traditional Jewish law" (Schürer, *The History of the Jewish People* I, 71), the Mishnah is a valuable source of information about Jewish traditions reaching as far back as the first century C.E. It is composed of six Orders (*Seder*, plural *Sederim*), each of which is composed of tractates, which are divided into chapters and these in turn into paragraphs. In its final form the Mishnah comprises sixty-three (originally sixty) canonical tractates (along with seven extracanonical ones, which are sometimes printed at the conclusion of the Fourth Seder). The Sederim are listed here with an indication of their general content as well as the number of tractates contained in each one. (A complete list, with the names of the individual tractates, is found in Strack-Billerbeck, V: *Rabbinischer Index*, edited by Joachim Jeremias and elaborated by Kurt Adolph, vii-viii; and Schürer, I, 71–74 and 80.)

The Orders (Sederim) of the Mishnah:
  (1) Zeraim (Agriculture; 11 tractates)
  (2) Mo'ed (Feasts, Appointed Times; 12 tractates)
  (3) Nashim (Women; 7 tractates)
  (4) Nezikin (Damages; 10 tractates, plus 7 extracanonical ones)
  (5) Kadashim (Holy Things; 11 tractates)
  (6) Torohoth (Purities; 12 tractates)

Texts in the Mishnah are usually cited according to the name of the tractate, the chapter, and the paragraph, *without* the name of the Seder. For example, the citation "Berakoth, 2, 3" refers to the tractate Berakoth (on benedictions), chapter two, paragraph three. (The tractate Berakoth happens to be the first one in the First Seder, Zeraim.) However, I cite both Seder and tractate.

B. THE TOSEPHTA

Legal opinions that continue and comment on the Mishnah were collected around 300 C.E. into the Tosephta ("supplement"), which, although it cites sources older than the Mishnah and is four times longer, has not achieved the same status as the Mishnah. The Tosephta follows the same plan as the Mishnah but is composed of fifty-nine rather than sixty-three tractates. Omitted are the tractates Aboth (Sayings of the Fathers) from the Fourth Seder, and Tamid (Perpetual Sacrifice), Middoth (Measures), and Kinnim (Nests) from the Fifth Seder. In some editions of the Talmud the Tosephta commentaries are inserted at the end of each tractate.

C. THE TALMUD (THE GEMARA)

After its compilation around 200 C.E. the Mishnah itself became an object of commentary and exegesis, especially in the form of the Gemara ("completion"), written in Aramaic and Hebrew and composed of casuistic interpretations of the Mishnah along with the views of the third- and fourth-century Mishnah scholars called Amoraim ("speakers"). The combined texts of the Mishnah and the Gemara make up the Talmud ("teaching," "doctrine"), although the word "Talmud" often refers only to the Gemara.

The Talmud exists in two forms: the earlier and shorter *Jerusalem* (or *Palestinian*) *Talmud* (ca. 425 C.E.), composed basically of only the first four Sederim of the Mishnah along with the corresponding Gemara texts—thirty-nine tractates in all; and the later and four-times-longer *Babylonian Talmud* (ca. 500 C.E.), which comments on about thirty-six tractates and which is the one usually referred to.

The Talmud is usually cited (1) with an abbreviation indicating the Talmud in which the Gemara is found: for example, "J." or "Y." or "P." for the Jerusalem/ Yerushalmi/Palestinian Talmud; and "B." or *no indication at all* for the Babylonian Talmud (Strack-Billerbeck cite the two Talmuds respectively as "p" and "b"); (2) then comes the name of the Mishnah tractate that is being commented on—for example, Berakhoth; in Strack-Billerbeck, for example, bBerakoth; (3) then follows an indication of either the *chapter and paragraph* of the Mishnah text under considera- tion (e.g., Y. Berakhoth 2, 4) or the *page number and column letter* in the particular Talmud (e.g., Y. Berakhoth 4 d). (Strack-Billerbeck cites the Jerusalem/Palestinian Talmud [according to the German edition published in Cracow in 1609] by chapter, page, column, and line; thus "pBerakhoth 1, 2a, 37" refers to: Palestinian Talmud, the Gemara-commentary on the Mishnah tractate Berakhoth, chapter 1, page 2, sheet on reader's left [cf. infra], line 37 in the Cracow edition.)

Regarding reference by page and column: In the Talmud, which of course reads from right to left, a single page is made up of the sheet on one's left and its verso. In the Jerusalem Talmud, each sheet has two columns. Columns a and b are found on the sheet on one's left, columns c and d on the verso. Thus "Y. Berakoth 4 d" refers to: page 4, verso, second column. In the Babylonian Talmud each sheet has only a single column. After the page reference the letter *a* indicates the sheet on one's left; the letter *b* indicates its verso.

D. THE MIDRASHIM

The Midrashim, or commentaries on the Tanackh, grew out of the edifying lectures and sermons delivered in synagogues and schools rather than out of the legal academic discussions that gave birth to the Mishnah and the Talmud. Whereas the Talmud is, to be sure, filled with scriptural commentary, it is not organized as a book of exegesis the way the Midrashim are.

The four oldest Midrashic commentaries (250–350 C.E.?), sometimes called the Tannaitic Midrashim, are Mekhilta (devoted to Exodus 12–23), Sifra on Leviticus, Sifra on Numbers 3–35, and Sifra on Deuteronomy. Among the later commentaries, dating from the fifth to the eighteenth centuries C.E., are: the extensive Midrash Rabba, a collection of midrashim on the Pentateuch and on the Megilloth (Song of Songs, Ruth, Lamentations, Ecclesiastes, and Esther); the three Pesikta (on the Bible texts read at feasts); Pirke (on Pentateuchal history from Adam to Moses); Tanhuma (on the whole Pentateuch); Yalkut (on the whole Tanackh); and Lekah Tob (on the Pentateuch and Megilloth).

E. THE TARGUMIM

The Targumim ("interpretations") are explanatory Aramaic translations of the Hebrew Bible, giving evidence of the popular and traditional expositions of the Tanackh provided in the synagogues. The Targumim date mostly from the second century C.E. and later but provide information on traditions reaching back to pre-Christian times.

Notes

INTRODUCTION

[1] The question of how Jesus understood himself and whether he asserted messianic or divine claims is treated in Part One as well as later in this introduction. The question of the difference/discontinuity—or the identity and continuity—between the "Jesus of history" and the "Christ of faith" is the subject of the entire book.

Concerning whether or not Jesus intended to found a new religion, see Lohfink, "Hat Jesus eine Kirche gestiftet?" Compare Küng, *On Being a Christian*: "Jesus did *not found a Church* during his lifetime. Today this is no longer a matter of dispute between the denominations" (285 and 648, n. 42, with bibliography). A brief introduction to the question of the "primacy" of Peter and the problem of papal succession in New Testament times is given in Pesch, *Simon-Petrus*, 163–170.

[2] For general introductions to contemporary Catholic theology see McCool, *Catholic Theology*; Schoof, *A Survey of Catholic Theology*; on Catholic exegesis, Brown, *Biblical Reflections*, 3–19, and *The Critical Meaning of the Bible*, 45–95; Crehan, "The Bible in the Roman Catholic Church from Trent to the Present Day."

[3] See Brown, *Biblical Reflections*, 110–118. Concerning recent Vatican statements on exegesis see Thomas Aquinas Collins and Raymond E. Brown, "Church Pronouncements," in *The Jerome Biblical Commentary* II, 624–632.

[4] Moreover, some Catholic theologians consider it discussable whether Jesus' mother, Mary, remained a virgin in the act of conceiving him, or whether Jesus was begotten by a natural father like everyone else. The question of the virginal conception of Jesus is treated in Brown, *The Birth of the Messiah*, 517–533, and more fully

in his *The Virginal Conception*, 21–68. (Brown, let it be noted, emphatically maintains that the Catholic Church teaches infallibly that Mary conceived as a virgin.) The Lutheran-Catholic study *Mary in the New Testament*, edited by Brown and others, concludes that in the questions of both the virginal conception and the perpetual virginity of Mary, "church tradition will be the determining factor in the view that one takes, with the important difference that while the tradition of the virginal conception is based on N[ew] T[estament] evidence, the doctrine of Mary's perpetual virginity goes beyond anything said of her in the Scriptures" (292).

5 See Ott, *Fundamentals*, 143–161 and 69. On Jesus' knowledge, see Brown, *Jesus, God and Man*, esp. 79–102, and *Biblical Reflections*, 35, n. 27.

6 Steiner, *In Bluebeard's Castle*, 9. (Compare 7: "the long liberal summer.")

7 Marx and Engels, "The Manifesto of the Communist Party," translation here slightly modified, in Marx and Engels, *Collected Works* VI (1976), 487.

8 See Neill, *The Interpretation of the New Testament*, 1–103; Kümmel, *The New Testament*, 62–205; Krentz, *The Historical-Critical Method*.

9 The threefold distinction of early Christian communities was long in developing and continues to undergo refinements. Heitmüller's article "Zum Problem Paulus und Jesus" (1912) marked a major breakthrough in identifying Hellenistic Christians as the first group "to grasp the kernel of universalism that lay in Jesus' preaching" (329) and "to break through the particularist and nationalistic limitations connected with it" (332). Hahn, *The Titles of Jesus in Christology*, has made a major contribution to the study of early Palestinian Christianity and Hellenistic Jewish Christianity, in part by showing the overlapping between the two groups. See also Hengel, *Between Jesus and Paul*, 32–44, as well as the further specifications in Pesch, Gerhart, and Schilling, " 'Hellenisten' und Hebräer: Zu Apg 9,29 und 6,1." (See Riches's suggestion that the "enthusiastic church" of the Hellenistic Jewish Christians "[preserved] the more radical teaching of Jesus and arguably [was] more receptive to it than the Jerusalem community itself," *Jesus and the Transformation of Judaism*, 60.) On the overlapping of Hellenistic and Palestinian culture before Jesus, see Bickerman, *From Ezra to the Last of the Maccabees.*

In Brown and Meier, *Antioch and Rome*, 1–9, Brown distinguishes four groups of Jewish Christians and their Gentile converts: (1) strongly conservative: those (of the Pharisee sect) who insisted on full compliance with Mosaic Law, including circumcision; (2) moderately conservative: those, like James and the early Peter, who insisted that their Gentile converts observe some Jewish laws but need not be circumcised; (3) liberals: those, like Paul, who required of their converts neither circumcision nor observance of Jewish food laws; and (4) radicals: those who not only did not require circumcision or observance of food laws but also "saw no abiding significance in Jewish cult and feasts" (6).

10 See, for example, Reimarus, *The Goal of Jesus and His Disciples*, 35–143 = *Reimarus: Fragments*, 61–269. See also the editor's notes in Lessing, *Gesammelte Werke* VII, 871–872, VIII, 640–641, and X, 327–336; also Talbert's essay in *Reimarus: Fragments*, 18–57, and Buchanan's in *The Goal of Jesus*, 10–11. Also Schleiermacher, *Das Leben Jesu: Vorlesungen an der Universität zu Berlin* [May 14–August 29] *im Jahr 1832*, edited posthumously by K. A. Rütenik, Berlin: Georg Reimer, 1862 (English translation, *The Life of Jesus*, 1975); Strauss, *Das Leben Jesu, kritisch bearbeitet*, 2 vols., Tübingen: C. F. Osiander, 1835–1836 (English translation, *The Life of Jesus, Critically*

Examined, 1846); Renan, *Vie de Jésu,* Paris: Michel Levy, 1863 (English translation, *The Life of Jesus,* 1864). The classical text on the nineteenth-century "quest for the historical Jesus," with the relevant literature cited at the beginning of each chapter, is Schweitzer's *Von Reimarus zu Wrede: Eine Geschichte der Leben-Jesu-Forschung,* Tübingen: J.C.B. Mohr (Paul Siebeck), 1906 (English translation, *The Quest for the Historical Jesus,* 1910). On Strauss, see Barth, *From Rousseau to Ritschl,* 362–389.

[11] Adolf von Harnack, *Das Wesen des Christentums,* Leipzig: C. J. Hinrichs, 1900 (*What Is Christianity?,* 1901). The citations in this paragraph are from the second, revised, English edition (1902), 56, 60, and 61. See Alfred Loisy's controversial response to Harnack: *L'Évangile et L'Église,* Paris: A. Picard, 1902 (English translation, *The Gospel and the Church,* London: Isbister, 1903).

[12] On source criticism see Neill, *The Interpretation of the New Testament,* 104–136; Fuller, *A Critical Introduction to the New Testament,* 69–81; Frederick Gast, "Synoptic Problem," *Jerome Biblical Commentary* II, 1–6; and John S. Kselman, S.S., "Modern New Testament Criticism," *Jerome Biblical Commentary* II, 11; and n. 13, below. A helpful popular introduction to New Testament criticism can be found in Harrington, *Interpreting the New Testament.*

[13] The chronological priority of Mark, which had been suggested since the late eighteenth century, was systematically argued by Karl Lachmann in his "De ordine narrationum in evangeliis synopticis" in *Theologische Studien und Kritiken,* 8 (1835), 570–590. The hypothesis of the "Q-document" (although without that name) apparently was first postulated either by Johann David Michaelis (1717–1791) in *Introduction to the New Testament,* 1793–1801, or by Johann Gottfried Eichhorn, *Über die drey ersten Evangelien,* in *Allgemeine Bibliothek der biblischen Literatur,* Leipzig, (1794), 5:759–996. (See M. Devisch, "La source dite des Logia et ses problèmes.") The Q-hypothesis was strongly advanced in terms of verbal concordances, doublets, and common sequences of pericopes by Christian Hermann Weiss, *Die evangelische Geschichte kritisch und philosophisch bearbeitet,* two volumes, Leipzig: Breitkopf and Hartel, 1838. Twenty-five years later Heinrich Julius Holtzmann carefully verified the two-source theory in *Die synoptischen Evangelien: Ihr Ursprung und geschichtlicher Charakter,* Leipzig: Engemann, 1863. (See Schweitzer, *The Quest for the Historical Jesus,* 88, 121–136, 203ff.) The four-source theory was advanced in its first and imperfect form by B. H. Streeter, *The Four Gospels,* in 1924.

T. W. Manson notably advanced the research on the Q-material (without, however, sufficient attention to form criticism) in Major, Manson, and Wright, *The Mission and Message of Jesus,* 1937, Part II of which Manson republished as *The Sayings of Jesus,* 1949; see also Manson, *The Teaching of Jesus.* In 1959 Heinz-Eduard Tödt *(The Son of Man in the Synoptic Tradition)* showed that the Q-document was not a mere "manual of instruction in the Christian life" (thus T. W. Manson) but a collection of texts with strong theological and christological preoccupations. On Q, see also James M. Robinson, "LOGOI SOPHON: On the Gattung of Q," in Robinson and Koester, *Trajectories Through Early Christianity,* 71–113, and Schillebeeckx, *Jesus,* 100–102. Farmer has challenged both the Q-hypothesis and the priority of Mark and has reproposed the priority of Matthew (*The Synoptic Problem,* 1963). Some of the documents of the (continuing) debate for and against the Q-hypothesis and the priority of Mark are found in Bellinzoni, *The Two-Source Hypothesis.* Bellinzoni, while not necessarily endorsing the two-source hypothesis, calls it "the *status quo* in synoptic studies" (7) and notes that "most contemporary New Testament scholarship continues to assume the theory" (11); Joseph B. Tyson concludes (*ibid.*, 438, 452) that serious questions raised against the hypothesis have not succeeded in completely dislodging it.

14 See Ritschl, *Die christliche Lehre von der Rechtfertigung und Versöhnung*, 3 vols., Berlin: Marcus, 1870–1874 (English translation of Volume III: *The Christian Doctrine of Justification and Reconciliation*, 1900). On Ritschl, see Philip Hefner, "Albrecht Ritschl: An Introduction," in Ritschl, *Three Essays*, 1–50.

15 Ritschl, *Unterricht in der christlichen Religion* (first edition), 15 = *Three Essays*, 265, n. 5; and n. 8. (The translation of *Unterricht* that appears in *Three Essays* is made from the third edition [1886] of the German, but the variant readings of the first edition [1875] are reflected in the footnotes.)

16 Ritschl, *The Christian Doctrine of Justification*, 285. This attitude is reflected to some degree in Ritschl's student Nietzsche: "The Kingdom of Heaven is a condition of the heart (—it is said of children 'for theirs is the Kingdom of Heaven'): Not something 'above the earth.' The Kingdom of God does not 'come' chronologically-historically, on a certain day in the calendar, something that might be here one day but not the day before: it is an 'inward change in the individual,' something that comes at every moment and at every moment has not yet arrived—": *The Will to Power*, No. 161, 98–99.

17 Ritschl, *The Christian Doctrine of Justification*, 12.

18 Weiss, *Die Predigt Jesu vom Reiche Gottes*, Göttingen: Vandenhoeck & Ruprecht, 1892 (English translation, *Jesus' Proclamation of the Kingdom of God*, 1971). The citation here is from the English edition, 108. On Weiss see: the editor-translators' introduction to the English edition, 1–54; David Larrimore Holland, "History, Theology and the Kingdom of God," 54–66 and bibliography at 54, n. 3; Kümmel, *The New Testament*, 236–240; Schweitzer, *The Quest for the Historical Jesus*, 238–241.

19 Barth, *Der Römerbrief*, Bern: Bäschlin, 1919 (reworked, second edition, 1922); the citation here is from the English translation *Epistle to the Romans*, "The Preface to the First Edition," 1.

20 In this regard Bultmann was influenced by the distinction that Martin Kähler had drawn between *Historie* and *Geschichte* in *Der sogennante historische Jesus und der geschichtliche, biblische Christus*, second, expanded and clarified, edition, Leipzig: Deichert, 1896 (English translation: *The So-Called Historical Jesus and the Historic, Biblical Christ*, 1964). The first edition of Kähler's book, published by the same press in 1892, ran to only forty-seven pages and bore the subtitle *Vortrag auf der Wupperthaler Pastoralkonferenz*.

21 Schmidt, *Der Rahmen der Geschichte Jesu: Literarkritische Untersuchungen zur ältesten Jesusüberlieferung;* Dibelius, *Die Formgeschichte des Evangeliums*, Tübingen: J.C.B. Mohr (Paul Siebeck), 1919 (English translation, *From Tradition to Gospel*, 1935); Bultmann, *Die Geschichte der synoptischen Tradition*, Göttingen: Vandenhoeck & Ruprecht, 1921 (English translation, *History of the Synoptic Tradition*, 1963). For a virtually complete bibliography of works by and about Bultmann, see Kwiran, *Index*, Section III. A bibliography on demythologizing is found in Küng, *On Being a Christian*, 637, n. 32; for works *against* Bultmann, see *ibid.*, 627, n. 17. Bultmann's interpretation of Jesus is presented in *Jesus and the Word*, 27–219, and *Theology of the New Testament* I, 3–32.

[22] For a list of gospel texts under the categories of pronouncement stories (and apothegms), miracle stories, and "stories about Jesus" (Bornkamm's *Christusgeschichten*), see Fuller, *A Critical Introduction to the New Testament*, 85–89.

[23] The literature on form criticism is vast; see, for example, Kwiran, Section III, s.v. "Form Criticism"; Fuller, *A Critical Introduction to the New Testament*, 81–94; McKnight, *What Is Form Criticism?*; and the literature listed in *Jerome Biblical Commentary* II, 7.

[24] At the turn of the century William Wrede, in his *Das Messiasgeheimnis in den Evangelien: Zugleich ein Beitrag zum Verständnis des Markusevangeliums*, Göttingen: Vandenhoeck & Ruprecht, 1901 (English translation, *The Messianic Secret*, 1971), had already challenged one of the presuppositions of the source criticism (and liberal theology) of the time, according to which Mark's Gospel was in effect a factual history of Jesus without dogmatic christological embellishments. Wrede showed that from the very opening of his Gospel Mark was reflecting the Christian community's belief in the messiahship and divinity of Jesus. On Wrede, see Schweitzer, *The Quest for the Historical Jesus*, 330–348.

[25] On redaction criticism, see Rohde, *Rediscovering the Teaching of the Evangelists*, 9–30; Perrin, *What Is Redaction Criticism?*; and the bibliography listed in Tatum, *In Quest of Jesus*, 177, n. 13.

[26] From among the immense literature on the "new quest," see: Robinson, *A New Quest of the Historical Jesus*; Fuller, *The New Testament in Current Study*, 25–53; Braaten and Harrisville, editors, *The Historical Jesus and the Kerygmatic Christ*; and the works listed in Perrin, *Rediscovering the Teaching of Jesus*, 262–265, and in Küng, *On Being a Christian*, 626, n. 16.

[27] On the criteria for authentic sayings, see Fuller, *A Critical Introduction to the New Testament*, 94–98; Hahn, *Historical Investigation and New Testament Faith*, 52–54; and Schillebeeckx, *Jesus*, 81–100.

[28] Boethius, *The Theological Tractates* (Loeb No. 74), 36, 37, translated by H. F. Stewart and E. K. Rand, revised by S. J. Tester, 1978. The text is in the last sentence of the letter introducing the Second Theological Tractate, "Utrum pater et filius et spiritus sanctus de divinitate substantialiter praedicentur," addressed to the future Pope John I. The text is cited correctly (*poteris*, not *poterit*) in *Patrologia Latina* LXIII (1847), 1302.

ONE: HOW JESUS LIVED AND DIED

[1] The Christian bishop Ignatius of Antioch (74–117 C.E.) reports the Docetist claims that Jesus only seemed to be human (*Ad Trallianos*, 10) and only apparently suffered (*Ad Smyrnaeos*, 2, 1): J.-P. Migne, ed., *Patrologia Graeca* V (1894), 792 and 709 respectively. See the variant readings of these texts in *The Apostolic Fathers* I (Loeb No. 24), 220–221 and 252–255, translated by Kirsopp Lake, 1919.

Docetism, which goes back to early Gnosticism and which continued into the Middle Ages in the form of Manichaeism, was condemned indirectly in 1274 at the Second General Council of Lyons and explicitly in 1441 at the General Council of Florence: Denzinger and Rahner, editors, *Enchiridion Symbolorum*, n. 462 and n. 710; English translations in Denzinger, *Sources*, 183 and 227.

[2] Useful studies of the period from the Maccabees to the revolt of Simon ben

Kosibah (Bar Cochba) include: Bickerman, *From Ezra to the Last of the Maccabees;* Safrai and Stern, eds., *Compendia;* Freyne, *Galilee;* Stone, ed., *Jewish Writings of the Second Temple Period;* Hengel, *Judaism and Hellenism* and *Jews, Greeks and Barbarians;* Pfeiffer, *History of New Testament Times;* Schürer, *The History of the Jewish People;* Wright, Murphy, and Fitzmyer, "A History of Israel," in *Jerome Biblical Commentary* II, 671–702.

Maps and chronological and genealogical tables can be found in: Safrai and Stern, *Compendia* I, 82–83, 100–101, 120–121; Bickerman, 183–186; Schürer, I, 607–614 (including a helpful chart of the parallel calendars of the Olympic, Seleucid, and Christian eras; see as well Finegan, *Handbook*, 134–135); Grant, *Herod the Great,* 250–264; Barrois, "Chronology, Metrology, Etc.," in Buttrick, ed., *The Interpreter's Bible* I, 142–164, and Terrien and Knox, "Literary Chronology," *ibid.*, XII, 668–672; Duncan, "Chronology," in Buttrick, ed., *The Interpreter's One-Volume Commentary on the Bible,* 1271–1275.

3 On Israel's notions of time and history: Bultmann, *The Presence of Eternity,* 23–31, and *Primitive Christianity,* 80–86; Eliade, *Cosmos and History,* 102–112; Pidoux, "À propos de la notion biblique du temps"; von Rad, *Old Testament Theology* II, 99–125. For chronological data: Finegan, *Handbook of Biblical Chronology.*

4 Strack, *Introduction to the Talmud and Midrash,* 201, notes that Ezra is described in this text as a "student of the law (*sopher,* not 'scribe')."

5 The canonical Hebrew Scriptures (called the "Old Testament" by Christians) are properly called Tanackh, a word composed of the first consonants in: Torah (Law), Nebiim (Prophets), and Katubim (Writings). On the redaction history of the Pentateuch, see such standard introductions as Kaiser, *Introduction to the Old Testament,* 78–133; E. A. Speiser, *Genesis,* xxii–xlii. A useful historical chart is given by Terrien in Buttrick, ed., *The Interpreter's Bible* XII (1957), 669.

6 See Appendix, "Notes on Rabbinical Literature."

7 On the Jewish Law and related matters, see: Berger, *Die Gesetzesauslegung Jesu,* passim, but esp. 56–136 and 258–361; Brown, "Jewish Law," in *Jerome Biblical Commentary* II, 558–560 and the bibliography on 560; Bultmann, *Primitive Christianity,* 59–71; Schillebeeckx, *Jesus,* 230–233 and bibliography on 229–230; Schürer, I, 68–114 (on rabbinical literature), II, 314–380 (on Torah scholarship), and 464–487 (on the Law and Jewish life); Strack, *Introduction to the Talmud and Midrash;* Wright, *The Literary Genre of Midrash;* von Rad, *Old Testament Theology* II, 338–409.

8 The phrase "build a fence around the Torah" is from the Mishnah: "Moses received the Torah at Sinai and transmitted it to Joshua, Joshua to the Elders, and the Elders to the Prophets, and the Prophets to the Men of the Great Synagogue [= the legendary body of 120 men established after the Captivity]. The latter used to say three things: Be patient in [the administration of] justice, rear many disciples and make a fence round the Torah": Epstein, ed., *The Babylonian Talmud,* Seder Nezikin, Volume VIII, Tractate Aboth, chapter I, paragraph 1, translated by J. Israelstam (1935), p. 1. Referring to the last phrase, n. 6 on p. 1 reads: "The Torah is conceived as a garden and its precepts as precious plants. Such a garden is fenced round for the purpose of obviating wilful or even unintended damage. Likewise, the precepts of the Torah were to be 'fenced' round with additional inhibitions that should have the effect of preserving the original commandments from trespass."

9 The question of wearing a false tooth on the Sabbath is treated in Epstein, ed.,

The Babylonian Talmud, Seder Mo'ed, Tractate Shabbath (Volume I), chapter VI, 64b and 65a, translated by H. Freedman (1938), pp. 306, 309. (A silver tooth apparently could be worn on the Sabbath, but not a gold one.) The matter of wearing artificial limbs is discussed *ibid.:* "A stump-legged person may go forth with his wooden stump: This is R[abbi] Meir's view; while R[abbi] Jose forbids it" (65b–66a, p. 312); "An artificial arm [lukitmin] is clean, but one may not go out therewith" (66a, p. 313).

[10] Seder Nezikin, Volume VIII, Tractate Makkoth, chapter III, 23b, translated by H. M. Lazarus (1935; the translation is slightly changed here), p. 169. Some rabbis confirmed the number 613 from the letter-value of the word "torah" (taw [400] + waw [6] + resh [200] + he [5] = 611) with two more units added for "I am" and "Thou shalt have no other gods" *(ibid.).*

[11] The dualism that is at least implicit and more often explicit in Jewish apocalyptic eschatology can be seen in IV Ezra 7:50 (late first century C.E.): "For this reason the Most High has made not one world but two": Charlesworth, I, 538 = Charles, II, 585 (see n. 12, below; also Schillebeeck's cautionary remark on dualism in *Jesus,* 149f).

[12] On eschatology and apocalypse as treated in the following paragraphs see, besides works listed in n. 2, above: Collins, *The Apocalyptic Imagination,* and (ed.) *Apocalypse: Morphology of a Genre* (he defines apocalyse as "a genre of revelatory literature with a narrative framework, in which a revelation is mediated by an otherworldly being to a human recipient, disclosing a transcendent reality which is both temporal, insofar as it envisages eschatological salvation, and spatial, insofar as it involves another, supernatural world": *Apocalyptic Imagination,* 4; italicized in the original); Hengel, *Judaism and Hellenism* I, 175–196; McKenzie, "Aspects of Old Testament Thought," *Jerome Biblical Commentary* II, 764f.; Russell, *The Method and Message of Jewish Apocalyptic;* Stone, "Apocalyptic Literature," in Stone, ed., *Jewish Writings of the Second Temple Period,* 383–437 and bibliography on 437–441; Stuhmueller, "Post-Exilic Period: Spirit, Apocalyptic," *Jerome Biblical Commentary* I, 343; Wifall, "David—Prototype of Israel's Future" (apocalypse as a blending of prophetic and wisdom traditions; the rise of eschatology in reaction against non-Davidic Hasmoneans). The classical texts not found in the Bible are in Charles, ed., *Apocrypha and Pseudepigrapha,* and in Charlesworth, ed., *Old Testament Pseudepigrapha.* The real burgeoning of apocalyptic literature comes after the fall of Jerusalem in 70 C.E. Schillebeeckx notes: "As compared with these two climaxes [ca. 55 B.C.E. and 70 C.E.] . . . , Jesus' own time was rather a quiet one where the literature of apocalyptic is concerned. We should not push the feverish outburst of apocalypticism after the fall of Jerusalem (with its obvious influence on a great part of the New Testament) back into Jesus' own lifetime": *Jesus,* 715, n. 82; cf. also 122.

On Zoroaster and Zoroastrianism: Corbin, "Cyclical Time in Mazdaism and Ismailism," 115–126; Duchesne-Guillemin, *La Religion de l'Iran ancien* (dualism: 189–193; ages of the world: 212–214) and "Zoroastrianism and Parsiism"; Eliade, *Cosmos and History,* 124–126; Zaehner, *Dawn and Twilight of Zoroastrianism,* 248–264.

Concerning "original sin," note that Jesus never mentions the fall of Adam (Genesis 3), although Paul did (cf. Romans 5:12ff.), as did Jewish apocalyptic literature contemporary with the early church. Cf. IV Ezra 4:30 (late first century C.E.): "For a grain of evil seed was sown in Adam's heart from the beginning, and how much ungodliness it has produced until now, and will produce until the time of threshing comes!": Charlesworth, I, 530f. = Charles, II, 566. Also II (Syriac) Baruch 23:4 (early second century C.E.): "For when Adam sinned and death was decreed against those who were to be born [etc.]": Charlesworth, I, 629 = Charlesworth, II, 495. On Jewish demonology, see n. 47, below. Descriptions of cosmic eschatological woes can be found in Joel 2:30–32 (quoted at Acts 2:19–20); IV Ezra 5:1–13, in Charlesworth, I, 531f. = Charles, II, 569f. *The Testament* [or *Assumption*] *of Moses* 10:1–10 (first century C.E.) describes cosmic events ("the sun will not give light," etc.) that accompany God's arrival: Charlesworth, I, 931f. = Charles, II, 421f. See Russell, 271–276.

13 Later, Christians would read these texts in terms of the "Antichrist," a term that first appears in I John 2:18, 22, and II John 7. For the history of the Antichrist theme in Christianity see Alexander, *The Byzantine Apocalyptic Tradition*, 193–225; Bousset, *The Antichrist Legend*, esp. Part II, 121–252; Russell, 276–280.

14 Hahn, *The Titles of Jesus*, 15–21, esp. 17–19, and Tödt, *The Son of Man in the Synoptic Tradition*, 22–31, hold that the "Son of Man" in pre-Christian Judaism was an individual heavenly figure, but Dunn, 65–82, shows to the contrary that "we lack any sort of firm evidence that the 'one like a son of man' in Dan[iel] 7 was understood within pre-Christian Judaism as the Messiah, pre-existent or otherwise" (72; cf. also 81, 95); Kümmel, *Theology of the New Testament*, 89–90, agrees with that position. Lindars, *Jesus Son of Man*, 1–16, and passim, similarly maintains that there was not "a single, identifiable concept [of the "Son of Man"] in Judaism of the time of [Jesus]," in fact, that "the assumption that the Son of Man could be recognized as a title of an eschatological figure in Jewish thought . . . has now been demolished" (8). Nonetheless, he admits: "At the same time the figure of one like a Son of Man in Dan[iel] 7:1–14 was clearly an important factor in New Testament times" as I Enoch shows (11f.). See n. 51 below.

See also T. W. Manson, *The Teaching of Jesus*, 175–188 (with 211ff.) for an interpretation of "Son of Man" as designating collectively the faithful Remnant; Perkins, *Resurrection*, 80–84; Russell, 324–352 (cf. his list of psychological terms in apocalyptic literature, 396–405); Schillebeeckx, *Jesus*, 460–467 (who dates I Enoch to 50 B.C.E.) and bibliography, 459–460; Vermès, *Jesus and the World of Judaism*, 89–99. See the bibliography in Küng, *On Being a Christian*, 649, n. 59.

Collins, "The Son of Man and the Saints of the Most High in the Book of Daniel," maintains that the "one like a man" in Daniel represents the angelic host collectively, as well as its leader Michael, "who receives the kingdom on behalf of his host of holy ones [angels], but also on behalf of the people of Israel" (64). But he also represents faithful Jews insofar as they are associated with the heavenly host in the eschatological era (hence, as angelic beings). Wifall, in "David—Prototype of Israel's Future?" and "Son of Man—A Pre-Davidic Social Class?," presents a theory that the notion of the Son of Man originated in the royal traditions of pre-Israelite Jerusalem (second millennium B.C.E.), where the title applied to the nobility and ruling class; the term was eventually applied to David (in the light of whose rise and fall the Yahwist story of creation and Adam was constructed), was later "demo-cratized," and during the Maccabean period was reintegrated into its original royal setting but in an apocalyptic context; see further bibliography on this theory in Dunn, 292–293, n. 17.

Kraeling, *Anthropos and Son of Man* (151–165), following Bousset (*Hauptprobleme der Gnosis*, Göttingen: Vandenhoeck & Ruprecht, 1907) and Richard Reitzenstein (esp. *Das iranische Erlösungsmysterium*, Bonn: Marcus & Weber, 1921), held that the origin of the Son of Man in Daniel (as well as of the Heavenly Adam) was the *gayamaretan* (or Gayomart: "mortal life") of ancient Iranian mythology. This figure, after identification with Mesopotamian Marduk (Baal Merodach), "was received into Judaism in the second pre-Christian century, and furnished the inspiration for the properly nameless 'man-like one' of Daniel . . . [insofar as] his humanity abetted the transformation of the Hebrew conception of the protoplasm, the common origin of the Bar Nasha and celestial Adam": Kraeling, 187–188. However, Thomas H. Tobin has convincingly shown that the notion of the Heavenly Adam arises in intertestamental Judaism from an interpretation of Genesis 1:27 and 2:7 rather than from Indian cosmology or Iranian speculation: *The Creation of Man*, 102–134.

[15] See Nickelsburg, *Resurrection;* Hengel, *Judaism and Hellenism* I, 196–202; Russell, 353–390; Schillebeeckx, *Jesus*, 518–523; Schubert, "Die Entwicklung der Auferstehungslehre." Hope in an eschatological resurrection was not universal in Judaism even at this point, the Sadducees being the obvious example. Sirach 38:21 ("Remember him not, for he hath no hope" [or: "for there is no returning"], Charles, I, 452) was taken by some as denying resurrection.

[16] Cf. also *Testaments of the Twelve Patriarchs* (second century B.C.E.), Judah 25:4: "And those who died in sorrow shall be raised in joy; / and those who died in poverty for the Lord's sake shall be made rich; / those who died on account of the Lord shall be wakened to life," and Zebulon 10:2: "And now my children, [said Zebulon,] do not grieve because I am dying, nor be depressed because I am leaving you. I shall rise again in your midst": Charlesworth, I, 802 and 807; Charles, II, 324 and 332. Also II Maccabees 7:9,14 ("the King of the world shall raise us up"; "they shall be raised up by God again"); 12:43 ("[Judas Maccabeus,] bearing in mind the resurrection"); 14:46 ("[Razis] tore out his bowels with both hands and flung them at the crowds. So he died, calling on Him who is lord of life and spirit to restore them to him again"): Charles, I, 141, 150, 152.

[17] On the Zadokite line and more generally on the priestly aristocracy, see Jeremias, *Jerusalem in the Time of Jesus*, 181–198.

[18] On the Pharisees and on messianism: Davies, *Introduction to Pharisaism;* Hengel, *Judaism and Hellenism* I, 253–254; Jeremias, *Jerusalem in the Time of Jesus*, 246–267; Neusner, *Judaism in the Beginning of Christianity*, 45–61; Russell, 304–323; Schürer, II, 388–404, 488–554; Schillebeeckx, *Jesus*, 450–459.

[19] See *The Dead Sea Scrolls in English*, translated by Vermès; Dimant, "Qumran Sectarian Literature," 483–547, in Stone, *Jewish Writings*. On the Essenes: Schürer, II, 555–590; Hengel, *Judaism and Hellenism* I, 218–247; Vermès, *Jesus and the World of Judaism*, 126–139; 100–125.

[20] On the eschatological prophet and what Schillebeeckx describes as "an original Palestinian prophet Christology" at the time of Jesus (*Interim Report*, 69) see, for example: Hahn, *The Titles of Jesus*, 352–406; Schillebeeckx, *Jesus*, 442–449 and *Interim Report*, 64–74; Teeple, *The Mosaic Eschatological Prophet;* Vermès, *Jesus the Jew*, 94–99. See also n. 52, below.

[21] On the date of Jesus' baptism, Finegan, *Handbook*, 259–280, 300–301, thinks that "some preference may be given" to November, 26 C.E. (with Jesus' birth ca. 5/4

B.C.E.), but allows as well for 28 C.E., a date that I favor (Finegan specifies: the autumn). Ruckstuhl, *Chronology,* maintains that "Jesus must have received John's baptism several weeks before the paschal feast of 28 A.D. His public life lasted thus about two years" (136). Hoehner, *Herod Antipas,* 307–312, concludes that *if* Jesus died in 30 C.E. (a date that I maintain is correct, although Hoehner prefers 33 C.E.), John probably began his ministry between September/October 27 C.E. and September/October 28 C.E., a period that corresponds to the following dates:

A. *The Greek calendar:* Olympiad 201, years 3–4. The Olympic year began in midsummer.

B. *The Roman calendar:* September/October 780–September/October 781. Since AUC 601 (= ca. 153 B.C.E.), the Roman year was calculated as beginning on January 1 (when consuls entered their office) rather than on the traditional April 21 of the Varronian year.

C. *The Seleucid calendar:* 1 Hyperberetaios (September/October) 339–Hyperberetaios 340. The Seleucid year began ca. October 1).

D. *The Jewish calendar:* 1 Tishri 3787–1 Tishri 3788. The Jewish calendar (dating from ca. 360 C.E.) counts from the presumed date of creation and calculates the beginning of the official year as the autumn equinox (Hoehner, 309).

22 In a passage about John the Baptist that is contested on certain points but generally accepted as authentic, Flavius Josephus (cf. n. 23, below) wrote ca. 93/94 C.E.: "But to some of the Jews the destruction of Herod's army [by the Nabataean king Aretas IV of Petra, ca. 36 C.E., at Gabala, Idumaea] seemed to be divine vengeance, and certainly a just vengeance, for his treatment of John, surnamed the Baptist. For Herod had put him to death, though he was a good man and had exhorted the Jews to lead righteous lives, to practise justice towards their fellows and piety towards God, and so doing to join in baptism. In his view this was a necessary preliminary if baptism was to be acceptable to God. They must not employ it to gain pardon for whatever sins they committed, but as a consecration of the body implying that the soul was thoroughly cleansed by right behaviour. When others too joined the crowds about him, because they were aroused to the highest degree by his sermons, Herod became alarmed. Eloquence that had so great an effect on mankind might lead to some form of sedition, for it looked as if they would be guided by John in everything that they did. Herod decided therefore that it would be much better to strike first. . . . John, because of Herod's suspicions, was brought in chains to Machaerus . . . , and there put to death": *Jewish Antiquities* XVIII (v, 1 = Niese 116–119), in *Josephus* IX (Loeb No. 433), 80–85, translated by Louis H. Feldman, 1965.

23 The earliest mention of Jesus in *any* extant literature comes some twenty years after he died and is found in Saint Paul, in the salutation of I Thessalonians: "To the Church of the Thessalonians in God the Father and the Lord Jesus Christ [en . . . kuriōi Iēsou Christōi]" (1:1). The letter was probably written in Corinth (but possibly in Athens) between the autumn of 49 and the summer of 51 C.E. (See Fuller, *A Critical Introduction to the New Testament,* 14; Hengel, *Acts and the History of Earliest Christianity,* 137.)

The earliest mentions of Jesus in secular literature are as follows:

(1) *93/94 C.E.:* The Jewish historican Flavius Josephus (37/38–100 C.E.) mentions Jesus in passing when reporting the murder of the apostle James, which took place ca. 62

C.E.: "[The high priest Ananus] convened the judges of the Sanhedrin and brought before them a man named James, the brother of Jesus who was called the Christ, and certain others": *Jewish Antiquities* XX (ix, 1 = Niese 200), *Josephus* IX, 494–497, translated by Louis H. Feldman, 1965. Jesus is mentioned in another passage in Josephus, which is sometimes called the *Testimonium Flavianum*, but the text is generally considered inauthentic: *Jewish Antiquities* XVIII (iii, 3 = Niese 63–64), *Josephus* IX, 48–51. The text is cited by Eusebius, *Historia ecclesiastica* I, 11, in Migne, *Patrologia Graeca* XX (1857), 117, and, with some textual changes, in *Demonstratio evangelica* III, 5 (no. 124), *Patrologia Graeca* XX (1857), 221. See also Brandon, *Jesus and the Zealots*, New York: Scribner, 1957, 359–368.

(2) *Between 110 and 112 C.E.:* Gaius Pliny the Younger (ca. 61–112 C.E.), who served as imperial legate in the province of Bithynia-Pontus in northwest Asia Minor between 110 and 112 C.E., reported to Trajan during those years the hearsay evidence that Christians in the province "were in the habit of meeting on a certain fixed day before it was light and singing in alternate verses a hymn to Christ, as to a god": *Letters* X, 96, in *Letters and Panegyricus* (Loeb No. 55) II, 400, 401, translated by William Melmoth, revised by W.M.L. Hutchinson, 1927.

(3) *Before ca. 115 C.E.:* The Roman historian Cornelius Tacitus (ca. 56–ca. 115 C.E.), in discussing Nero's persecution of Christians for allegedly burning the city of Rome in 64 C.E., opines that the origin of the name "Christian" was the man Christ, who was put to death by the procurator (actually the prefect) Pontius Pilate during the reign of emperor Tiberius: *Annals* XV, 44, in *Tacitus* (Loeb No. 322) V, 282, 283, translated by John Jackson, 1956.

(4) *Before 120 C.E. (?) or 150 C.E. (?):* The Roman historian Gaius Suetonius Tranquillus (ca. 69–ca. 150) wrote that around 42 C.E. the emperor Claudius "expelled the Jews from Rome because, incited by Chrestus [*sic;* perhaps 'Christus'?], they were constantly creating disturbances": *The Lives of the Caesars: The Deified Claudius* XXV, 4, in *Suetonius* II (Loeb No. 38), 52, 53, translated by J. C. Rolfe, 1924.

[24] On Jesus' name, see Brown, *Birth of the Messiah*, 130–131; Dalman *Jesus—Jeshua*, 6. Concerning "Nazorean" (Matthew 2:23), Brown, *Birth of the Messiah*, 209–213 and 223–225. The Patristic debate about whether or not Jesus was physically ugly was based on a mistaken, literalistic application to Jesus of passages like Isaiah 52:14 and 53:2–3; see Clement of Alexandria, *Paedagogus* III, 1, in Migne, *Patrologia Graeca* VIII (1891), 557, 558, and the further references there in n. 85.

It is probable that Jesus was born before the spring of 4 B.C.E., when Herod the Great died, but not long before, if Luke is right in saying (3:1, 3:23) that Jesus was "about thirty years of age" when he began his ministry in the fifteenth regnal year of the emperor Tiberius (which according to one calculation may be dated from October 1, 27 C.E., to September 30, 28 C.E.). Thus Jesus was born probably during the 193rd Olympiad (which stretched from the summer of 7 B.C.E. to the summer of 4 B.C.E.), between 748 and 750 years from the founding of the city of Rome. The Jewish year 3755 corresponds to about 6 B.C.E. See Finegan, *Handbook*, 215–259 (nos. 337–408); 260 (no. 414), and 262 (table 116); 298–299 (nos. 463–464) and 301 (table 143)—but no. 464 and table 143 omit the option given in no. 414! See also Brown, *The Birth of the Messiah*, 166–167, 547–555; and Wright et al., "A History of Israel," in *Jerome Biblical Commentary* II, 696.

On the question of whether Jesus was born at Bethlehem see Brown, *Birth of the*

Messiah, 513–516; cf.: "If Herod and all Jerusalem knew of the birth of the Messiah in Bethlehem (Matt[hew] 2:3), and indeed Herod slaughtered the children of a whole town in the course of looking for Jesus (2:16), why is it that later in the ministry no one seems to know of Jesus' marvelous origins (13:54–55), and Herod's son recalls nothing about him (14:1–2)?": *ibid.,* 31–32.

As to whether Jesus' home (and/or native town) was Nazareth or Capernaum (see Mark 2:1: "And when he returned to Capernaum after some days, it was reported that he was at home," and 3:19), Bornkamm holds unproblematically: "His native town is Nazareth": *Jesus,* 53. See the bibliography in Brown, *Birth of the Messiah,* 516.

Mark 6:3 and Matthew 13:55 name the four brothers *(adelphos/-oi)* of Jesus and refer to his unnamed sisters *(adelphai).* For a brief history of the discussion about the brethren of Jesus, see Taylor, *The Gospel According to St. Mark,* 247–249: "The three main hypotheses are the *Helvidian* (maintained by Helvidius, *c.* A.D. 380), which claims that the *adelphoi* were brothers by blood; the *Epiphanian* (Epiphanius, *c.* A.D. 382), which maintains that they were the sons of Joseph by a former wife; and the *Hieronymian* (Jerome, *c.* A.D. 383), that they were cousins of Jesus, the sons of Mary the wife of Clopas and the sister of the Virgin" (247). Taylor concludes: "There can be little doubt that the Helvidian view stands as the simplest and most natural explanation of the references to the brothers of Jesus in the Gospels" (249). Likewise the Protestant-Catholic collaborative study *Mary in the New Testament,* edited by Brown and others, notes the various problems (65–72; cf. 72, n. 138, and 292, n. 667) and concludes that "there is no convincing argument from the N[ew] T[estament] against the literal meaning of the words 'brother' and 'sister' when they are used of Jesus' relatives" (292). Also Bornkamm, *Jesus,* 199, n. 4; and "Jesus Christ," 149: "There is no basis in the text for making them [Jesus' *adelphoi* and *adelphai*] into half brothers and half sisters or cousins, and to do so betrays a dogmatic motive." See also A. Meyer and W. Bauer, "The Relatives of Jesus," in Hennecke/ Schneemelcher, especially 418–425.

Compare Brown (who most emphatically holds to the orthodox Catholic doctrine of Mary's virginal conception of Jesus), *The Birth of the Messiah,* 131, 513–542, and *The Virginal Conception,* 21–68. The traditional Catholic position that these are all cousins of Jesus is argued by Blinzler, *Die Brüder und Schwestern Jesu.*

25 For the following paragraphs, see: Bornkamm, *Jesus,* 44–53; Meagher, *Five Gospels,* 21–67; Schillebeeckx, *Jesus,* 116–139; Scobie, *John the Baptist;* Steinmann, *St. John the Baptist;* Wink, *John the Baptist in the Gospel Tradition.*

26 Pesch, for example, holds that with the phrase "the one who is coming" *(ho erchomenos:* Matthew 3:11; cf. Mark 1:7, Luke 3:16, John 1:30, Acts 13:25), John the Baptist was referring to the Son of Man: "Zur Entstehung des Glaubens . . . : Ein neuer Versuch" (1983), 94. Cf. Brown, *The Gospel According to John* I, 44, 52–54.

27 See Hoehner, *Herod Antipas,* 184–250 (Antipas and Jesus), and especially 224–250 (Jesus' trial).

28 Among the general works I have drawn on for what follows are: Bornkamm, *Jesus of Nazareth* (see also his helpful article "Jesus Christ"); Bultmann, *Jesus and the Word,* 27–219, *Theology of the New Testament* I, 3–32, and *Primitive Christianity,* 86–93; Schillebeeckx, *Jesus,* 140–271, and *Interim Report;* Kasper, *Jesus the Christ,* 65–123; Mackey, 52–85, 121–172; Meagher, 69–141; Schelkle, II, 59–220; Vermès,

Jesus and the World of Judaism, 30–43. Useful bibliographies on Jesus are provided in Küng, *On Being a Christian,* 626, n. 17, and 636, n. 2, and in Schelkle, II, 317, n. 35.

²⁹ On "Abba" (cf. Mark 14:36, Romans 8:15, Galatians 4:6), see Dalman, *The Words of Jesus,* 191f.; Jeremias, *The Central Message,* 9–30: "The stress [in 'abba'] is on the final syllable" (10, n. 1); Schillebeeckx, *Jesus,* 256–269; also, 625: Jesus' "exceptional *Abba* experience" as the ground of his certainty of God's reign, and as "soul, source and ground of his going out and his coming in, his living and dying" (658). Abba is "a concept borrowed from the Jewish family life of the period" (652) and "does not occur in Jesus' time in the language of prayer addressed to God" (260). See Dunn, *Christology,* 26–33 (and his challenge to the last assertion: 27); also Vermès, *Jesus the Jew,* 210–213.

³⁰ On the Aramaic word(s) for "the kingdom of God" see Dalman, *The Words of Jesus,* 91–96 (and further to 147), and *Jesus—Jeshua,* 129f., 181f., 197f. On the meaning of "messianic kingdom" in apocalyptic literature, see Russell, 285–297.

³¹ In Jesus' preaching about the Father's presence, Küng says, "God is not seen apart from man, nor man apart from God": *On Being a Christian,* 251. On God's identification of himself with the well-being of mankind, *ibid.,* 253; on God as "intent upon humanity," see Schillebeeckx, *Jesus,* 162, 213, 241, 267, 269, 317, 625, and 652.

Regarding marriage as a symbol of God's identification with mankind, Lindars interprets Mark 2:18 ("Can the wedding guests fast while the bridegroom is with them? As long as they have the bridegroom with them, they cannot fast") as follows: "Though it is inevitable that [in early Christianity] the bridegroom should have been supposed to be a reference to Jesus himself (hence the addition of verse 20 ["when the bridegroom is taken away from them . . . then they will fast"], justifying the church's practise of fasting), it is much more likely that Jesus is alluding to the well-known Old Testament idea of God as the husband of Israel. The response of the common people is that God is gaining his bride" (*Jesus Son of Man,* 174).

³² On Jesus' Beatitudes, see Schillebeeckx, *Jesus,* 172–178, and the bibliography in Küng, *On Being A Christian,* 641, n. 22.

See Pixner, "Tabgha on Lake Gennesareth," for a discussion of the history and archaeology of what may well have been Jesus' preferred retreat—present-day el-Tabgha (from the Greek "Heptapegon," Seven Springs) just west of Capernaum —and the setting for such gospel stories as the Beatitudes (the hill to the north), the first multiplication of the loaves (Mark 6:32–44, Matthew 14:13–21), and possibly the post-Easter appearance to Peter and six other disciples (John 21:1–23).

³³ *The Works of Pindar,* edited by Lewis Richard Farnell. 3 vols. London: Macmillan, 1931. III *(The Text),* 56.

³⁴ Whereas the word "repentance" has its root in the Latin *poena* (indemnification, satisfaction; cf. the Greek *poinē,* blood money paid by the killer to the kinsmen of the slain), the Greek *metanoia,* used in the Gospels, stresses change of heart or mind (*noos/nous,* mind, perception, heart; *meta,* prepositional prefix, here with the sense of "change"). Edersheim, I, 510, notes that the equivalent in the Tanackh is *teshubhah,* "return." See also Bornkamm, *Jesus,* 82–84.

³⁵ See Schillebeeckx, *Jesus,* 233–243. Bultmann holds to the contrary: "The upshot [of Jesus' preaching] is that the Old Testament in so far as it consists of

ceremonial and ritual ordinances, is abrogated": *Primitive Christianity,* 74. This appears to be a change from Bultmann's earlier position in *Theology of the New Testament* I, 16, where he says that Jesus supported the validity of the Old Testament Law as much as the scribes did and that he contested only the legalistic application of it. See also Sloyan, *Is Christ the End of the Law?*, 38–69.

36 Philo Judaeus of Alexandria (*floruit* ca. 20 B.C.E.–40 C.E.) notes: "[The Sabbath] extends also to every kind of tree and plant; for it is not permitted to cut any shoot or branch, or even a leaf, or to pluck any fruit whatsoever": *On the Life of Moses* II, iv (= II, 22), in *Philo* VI (Loeb No. 289), 460, 461, translated by F. H. Colson, 1935. Edersheim, II, 56, cites a similar prohibition from the Jerusalem Talmud, Seder Mo'ed, Tractate Shabbath, 10a.

37 Within the Written Law found in the Torah, or Pentateuch, the Jews of the Hellenistic Diaspora and, later, Hellenistic Jewish Christians made an important distinction (which the more Levitical-oriented Aramaic-speaking Jews of Palestine generally did not maintain) between: (A) the *primary* law: the Decalogue, or Ten Commandments (Greek, *entole*, plural *entolai,* Exodus 20:2–17; Deuteronomy 5:6–21; cf. Mark 10:19), which all Jews believed God gave to Moses on Mount Sinai and which the Hellenistic Jews took to be God's life-giving (Deuteronomy 30:15–20) authentic law, grounded in the order of creation; and (B) the *secondary,* post-Sinaitic, man-made "Mosaic Laws" (including laws relating to the Temple, to the Sabbath, and to other feast days—the laws, in fact, that Antiochus IV forbad), which are also recorded in the Pentateuch and which Hellenistic Jews believed God gave Israel as an intolerable burden because of the hardness of their hearts (cf. Ezechiel 20:25–26). In Mark 7:3–8, which in this case reflects the views of Hellenistic Jewry, these laws are called "the tradition of the elders" or "the injunctions of men" (*paradosis ton presbyteron, entalmata ton anthropon*), as contrasted with "the [authentic] commandment of God" (*he entole tou theou*), to which the Hellenist Jews sought to return.

See Berger, *Gesetzesauslegung,* 16–23. For the relation between "reform Judaism" and the decrees of Antiochus IV see Hengel, *Judaism and Hellenism* I, 292–303.

38 Küng comments on the God of Jesus' ethical preaching: "This would certainly be a new God: a God who has set himself free from his own law, . . . not a God of God-fearers, but a God of the Godless": *On Being a Christian,* 313.

39 On the "timing" of the eschaton according to Jesus' preaching, see Perrin, *The Kingdom of God,* 13–89; Schillebeeckx, *Jesus,* 148–154; Küng, *On Being a Christian,* 220–226; etc. Fuller, *Foundations,* chapter five, and Fitzmyer, *A Christological Catechism,* 27–29, delineate current positions on Jesus' understanding of the eschaton (with the representative spokesmen for the positions) roughly as follows:
(A) *Eschaton as Present.* The eschaton is already realized ("realized eschatology") in the words and deeds, indeed in the very person, of Jesus: Dodd.
(B) *Eschaton as Future.* The eschaton is either (1) future but imminent ("consequent eschatology"): Weiss, Schweitzer, Buri, Werner; or (2) future but already beginning to dawn in the words and deeds of Jesus: Bultmann, early Fuller.
(C) *Eschaton as Present-Future.* The eschaton has already been inaugurated and either is now in the process of being realized: Jeremias; or is present in a hidden way and will soon be consummated in a revealed way: Kümmel, later Fuller; see also Schillebeeckx, *Jesus,* 149–150 on this hidden/revealed, nondualistic model.

Was Jesus an apocalyptist? According to Schillebeeckx, *Jesus:* "There are no texts known to us which suggest that Jesus ever mentioned the 'aeon to come' " (149; cf. 684, n. 76) and "Christian expectations of the end [of the world] cannot be traced back directly to Jesus' teaching" (152). But Fitzmyer, *A Christological Catechism*, 28, notes: "In reality, one cannot be certain about what Jesus of Nazareth might have said about the imminence of the kingdom." On the timing of the end in apocalyptic literature in general, see Russell, 263–284.

⁴⁰ Compare Philo: "All things are God's grace . . . , everything in the world and the very world itself [charin onta tou theou ta sympanta . . . ta panta hosa en kosmōi kai autos ho kosmos]": *Allegorical Interpretation of Genesis II, III [Legum Allegoria]*, III, xxiv (= 78) in *Philo* I (Loeb No. 226), 352, 353, translation (not used here) by F. H. Colson and G. H. Whitaker, 1956.

⁴¹ Schillebeeckx maintains that Mark 2:1–12 (esp. v. 10) and Luke 7:36–50 (esp. v. 47f.), in which Jesus speaks explicitly of forgiving sins, "are not authentic sayings of the historical Jesus" but are "early Christian affirmations on the part of the Church about Jesus, already acknowledged as the Christ"; nonetheless, Schillebeeckx holds that "the ground of this power to forgive sins, of this tender of salvation or fellowship-with-God, which the Christian community ascribes to Jesus after his death, really does lie in the concrete activity of Jesus during his days on earth": *Jesus*, 179; cf. also 209. On the other hand, Lindars (*Jesus Son of Man*, 176–178) does accept Mark 2:10 as authentic, and he maintains: "The point at issue is the authority of Jesus to announce forgiveness *in the name of God*" (177; my emphasis). Fitzmyer (*A Christological Catechism*, 25) holds that Jesus "acted as an agent of Yahweh, as one who could forgive sins," and that he taught "that God's forgiveness was available for [sins]—precisely through himself."

⁴² On Jesus' parables see the bibliography in Küng, *On Being a Christian*, 637, n. 26. Adolf Jülicher (the teacher of both Barth and Bultmann) initiated modern research on the parables by delimiting the nature of the genre as over against allegory: *Die Gleichnisreden Jesu* (Freiburg: J. C. Mohr, 1888). C. H. Dodd, *Parables*, took the next major step by establishing that the *Sitz im Leben* of the parables is Jesus' *eschatological* message (for Dodd a "realized" eschatology). The standard work today remains Jeremias, *The Parables of Jesus* (see 18–22 for a sketch of scholarly approaches to the parables from 1900 to 1970). Crossan distinguishes three genres of parable according to modes of temporality: those of advent of God's kingdom as a gift from the future; those of reversal of the recipient's world; and those about the empowering of life and action in the present *(In Parables, 27–36 and passim);* see also Mackey, *Jesus*, 128–142; Perrin, *Jesus and the Language of the Kingdom*, chapters 3 and 4, and *Rediscovering the Teaching of Jesus*, 77–206, bibliography at 257–259.

⁴³ On Jesus' miracles: Bultmann, *History of the Synoptic Tradition*, 209–244, and *Jesus and the Word*, 172–179; Fuller, *Interpreting the Miracles* (with a helpful list of miracles and sayings referring to miracles, with textual references, 126–127); Küng, *On Being a Christian*, 226–238 and bibliography at 638, n. 1; Kasper, *Jesus*, 89–99; Schelkle, II, 68–86 and bibliography at 319, n. 44, and 320, n. 48; Sanders, *Jesus and Judaism*, 157–173; Schillebeeckx, *Jesus*, 180–200 (". . . there is among the majority of critical exegetes a growing conviction that Jesus carried out historical cures and exorcisms," 189). On the importance of miracles in the mission of the early church, see Fiorenza, ed., *Aspects of Religious Propaganda:* Elisabeth Schüssler Fiorenza, "Miracles, Mission, and Apologetics: An Introduction," 10–16; and Paul J. Ach-

temeier, "Jesus and the Disciples as Miracle Workers in the Apocryphal New Testament," 149–186; and on role of magic in Judaism, Judah Goldin, "The Magic of Magic and Superstition," 115–147. Vermès recounts many examples of charismatic Jewish figures during the time of Jesus, many of them with miraculous powers: *Jesus the Jew*, 69–82, and 241, n. 53.

44 Quadratus' text, which is known only through Eusebius' *Ecclesiastical History* (Part IV, chapter 3), goes so far in its enthusiasm to prove Jesus' divinity via miracles that it claims that some of those cured and raised by Jesus were still alive even a century later *(eis tous hēmeterous chronous): Patrologia Graeca* XX (1857), 308.

45 See Schillebeeckx, *Jesus*, 186f.

46 Examples of Jesus' "nature miracles" include: Matthew 14:13–33, 15:32–39, 17:24–27, 21:19. For a tradition-history analysis of a miracle text that combines both a cure and a nature miracle, see Pesch, "The Markan Version of the Healing of the Gerasene Demoniac," where Pesch suggests that the story (Mark 5:1–20) of Jesus allowing demons to possess and kill two thousand swine is a pre-Marcan addition to a story of a cure.

Rabbinical literature recorded numerous nature miracles: See Epstein, ed., *The Babylonian Talmud*, Seder Nezikin (Volume II), Tractate Baba Mezia, chapter IV, 59b, translated by Salis Daiches (1935), 354; also Seder Nezikin (Volume III), Tractate Baba Bathra, chapter V, 73a–b, translated by Israel W. Slotki (1935), 289–291. On miracles in pagan literature, see the texts in Luck, *Arcana Mundi*, 141–159; and Herzog, *Die Wunderheilungen*, 8–35.

47 On the role of daimonic powers in Judaism and antiquity: Russell, 235–262; Schelkle, II, 71–78; Schillebeeckx, *Christ*, 499–511; Strack-Billerbeck, IV, 501–535: "Zur altjüdischen Dämonologie." Texts relating to such daimonic powers in Judaism include: 1 (Ethiopic Apocalypse of) Enoch 10:4–12, 18:11–19:3, 56:5, found in Charlesworth, I, 17f., 22f., 39, and in Charles, II, 193f., 200f., 222. See also the texts relating to pagan demonology in Luck, *Arcana Mundi*, 176–225, with Luck's introduction, 163–175.

48 According to Mark 3:20–35 (compare Matthew 12:46–50), it appears that Jesus' mother, Mary, along with other members of his natural family, was not in accord with Jesus' mission and that she joined the Jesus-movement only after her son's death (cf. Acts 1:14). See Brown and others, ed., *Mary in the New Testament*, 51–59 (re: the "negative portrait of Mary in Mark's Gospel"); 284 ("her earlier misunderstanding" of Jesus); and 286 ("Mary at this point [Mark 3] stands outside of Jesus' 'eschatological family' "). On the question of the rejection of Jesus see Bornkamm, *Jesus*, 153–155; Fuller, *Introduction to the New Testament*, 82, n. 2; Schillebeeckx, *Jesus*, 294–298.

49 On Jesus' self-evaluation see, for example, Bornkamm, *Jesus*, 169–178, 226–231; Brown, *Jesus God and Man*, 79–99; Fuller, *Foundations*, 102–141; Hahn, *The Titles of Jesus*, 15–53 (Son of Man) and 372–388 (eschatological prophet-like-Moses); Kasper, 100–111; Kümmel, *Theology of the New Testament*, 58–84; Schelkle, II, 178–220. See the bibliography in Küng, *On Being a Christian*, 649, n. 51. Cf. also Fitzmyer, *A Christological Catechism*, 25.

50 See, for example, the Psalms of Solomon (ca. 50 B.C.E.), where the coming messianic Son of David will save or redeem Israel not from its sins but from the pagan nations; as regards "spiritual" salvation, he will (at most) "reprove sinners for the

thoughts of their heart; and he shall gather together a holy people, whom he shall lead in righteousness" (17:27–28 [25–26]: Charles, II, 649=Charlesworth, II, 667).

⁵¹ See n. 14 above and Vermès, *Jesus the Jew*, 160–191, *Jesus and the World of Judaism*, 89–99. Tödt, *The Son of Man in the Synoptic Tradition*, maintains that Jesus envisaged the Son of Man as "the eschatological guarantor of [one's] attachment to Jesus on earth" (295) but that only after Easter did the church arrive at "the earliest Christological understanding (that Jesus will be the coming Son of Man)" (294). Dunn, 82–97, argues: "The earliest datable interpretation of Daniel's 'son of man' as a particular individual is the Christian identification of 'the son of man' with Jesus, whether first made by the post-Easter communities or [n.b.] by Jesus himself" (96).

Lindars, by examining the nine usages of *bar (e)nash(a)* in Q and Mark, shows that *in his own usage* Jesus employed the generic term in a self-referential way ("son of man" = "a man, any man"—including himself; "the generic usage, incorporating a first-personal reference," 160) but never as a christological or messianic title and never with reference to the figure in Daniel 7—not even in Matthew 10:32f. = Luke 12:8f., where the "someone" who will deny the faithless before the angels of God "is Jesus' own words, and therefore in a sense it is Jesus himself" insofar as, in his preaching, he is "the spokesman for God" (182). (See John 12:48: "The word I have spoken will be his judge on the last day.") Moreover, Lindars sees Jesus' idiomatic use of "a man" as ironic insofar as the usage was intended to make his listeners think more profoundly about the kingdom of God: "[T]he authentic sayings convey something of the irony and saltiness of his references to himself. Jesus always wants his hearers to see beyond him and to be ready for the confrontation with God" (189). However, the *messianic-christological use* of "Son of Man" with regard to Jesus stems from the church: "[T]he early history of Christology consists in putting into relation with Jesus, now understood to be the exalted Messiah, more and more of the messianic concepts of the time. . . . Part of this process is the application to him of the Danielic Son of Man" (189). "It may thus be concluded that, insofar as the Son of Man is used as a title in the sayings tradition, it carries with it the [church's] identification [of Jesus] with the Danielic figure. But it is important to realize that this is not due to any supposed currency of the phrase as a title in Jewish thought of the time of [Jesus]" (11). Schillebeeckx, however, does see Jesus as sharing John the Baptist's expectation of the imminent arrival of the Son of Man: *Jesus*, 148.

T. W. Manson, *The Teaching of Jesus*, 175–234, interprets "Son of Man" as collectively designating the faithful Remnant: "In other words, the Son of Man is, like the Servant of Jehovah, an ideal figure and stands for the manifestation of the Kingdom of God on earth in a people wholly devoted to their heavenly King" (227). This position is maintained *juxta modum* also by Meagher, 104–114: "I propose that Jesus' Son of Man is, in the last analysis, the collective body of the righteous" (104). See Perrin, *The Kingdom of God*, 90–111, for a critique of Manson. Pesch, "Zur Entstehung des Glaubens . . . : Ein neuer Versuch," (1983), 94–97, makes the radical assertion that in Luke 12:8–9 Jesus saw himself as identified with the future Son of Man: "Er gibt für sich selbst Zeugnis als denjenigen, mit dem sich der Menschensohn 'identifiziert' " (95). Contrast the more nuanced treatment of the passage in Lindars, 181–184.

⁵² See Schillebeeckx, *Jesus*, 441–449, and his conclusion that even though Jesus never identified himself with the eschatological prophet (*Jesus*, 477), "it is highly

probable, historically speaking, that Jesus understood himself to be the latter-day [= eschatological] prophet" (306), and it is possible that Jesus' followers *may* have identified him as such before Easter (187). (Schillebeeckx notes that "prophet" in the late Judaism of Jesus' time meant "someone who calls men to maintain the 'true law' of God" [*Jesus*, 276] and defines "eschatological prophet" theologically as "the prophet who claims to bring a definitive message which is valid for all history" [*Christ*, 802].) See also his *Interim Report*, 64–74.

Pesch argues for the historicity of the core of Simon's confession (Mark 8:27–30) of Jesus as the messiah—not, however, as the Son-of-David messiah (which, in fact, Jesus later condemns: Mark 12:35–37) but as the messiah of the prophetic tradition, the teacher-prophet who was to be sent by God and filled with the Spirit: "Das Messiasbekenntnis des Petrus," especially the second part, 25–31, and *Simon-Petrus*, 37–40.

Berger maintains that "Jesus understood himself as the final proclaimer of God's will, the one who, in a world of error, offers the last and decisive chance for salvation": *Die Auferstehung des Propheten*, 232.

53 The cleansing of the Temple could have taken place on an earlier visit of Jesus to Jerusalem; John 2:13–17 locates the scene during the first Passover of Jesus' ministry. However: "We suggest that the editing of the Gospel [of John] led to the transposition of the scene from the original sequence which related it to the last days before Jesus' arrest": Brown, *The Gospel According to John* I, 118 (see 114–125). See also Schillebeeckx, *Jesus*, 243–249.

54 As regards the date of Jesus' farewell meal, Jaubert, *The Date of the Last Supper*, argues that Jesus followed the *solar* calendar of the Essenes and the *Book of Jubilees*, and celebrated the Passover meal on Tuesday night, April 4, 30 C.E. She finds confirmation of this in the *Didascalia* (ca. 200 C.E.), chapter 21, XIV, 5–9: "After eating the Pasch, on Tuesday evening, we went to the Mt. of Olives and, in the night, they took our Lord Jesus. The following day, which is Wednesday, he was kept in the house of the high priest Caiaphas. . . . The following day, Thursday, they brought him to the governor, Pilate. . . . On the morning of the Friday . . . they called upon Pilate to put him to death. They crucified him that same Friday" (cited Jaubert, 71). (See also, Schürer, II, 599–601 and n. 33.) This position is taken up by Mackowski, *Jerusalem, City of Jesus*, 163–166; and by Ruckstuhl, *Chronology*.

Concerning the day and year of the crucifixion, a growing number of scholars agree on the Johannine dating (Friday, 14 Nisan) and on the year 30 C.E.: cf. Bornkamm, "Jesus Christ," 153, column b; Finegan, *Handbook of Biblical Chronology*, 285–301, esp. 300–301; Holzmeister, *Chronologia*, 215, 219–220; Küng, *On Being a Christian*, 329. However, Pesch opts for the Synoptic dating, Friday, 15 Nisan, corresponding to April 7, 30 C.E.: *Das Markusevangelium* II, 323–328, and *Simon-Petrus*, 49 (cf. also *Zwischen Karfreitag und Ostern*, 18).

The attempt of Colin J. Humphreys and W. G. Waddington to date the crucifixion to April 3, 33 C.E., by calculating a relevant lunar eclipse fails because it takes apocalyptic images (Acts 2:20 = Joel 2:31) literally: "Dating the Crucifixion," *Nature* 306 (December 22–29, 1983), 743–746.

Jeremias concludes that astronomical calculations are inconclusive in helping one decide whether Good Friday fell on April 7, 30 C.E., or on April 3, 33 C.E.; he argues that the Last Supper was a passover meal: Jeremias, *The Eucharistic Words of Jesus*, 36–84.

The Talmudic tradition states (but at least part of the record is apocryphal): "On the eve of the Passover Yeshu was hanged. For forty days before the execution took place, a herald went forth and cried, 'He is going to be stoned because he has practiced sorcery and enticed Israel to apostasy. Anyone who can say anything in his favor, let him come forward and plead on his behalf.' But since nothing was brought forward in his favor he was hanged on the eve of the Passover!": Epstein, ed., *The Babylonian Talmud*, Seder Nezikin (Volume V), Tractate Sanhedrin, chapter VI [no paragraph listed], 43a, translated by Jacob Schachter (1935), 281. See also Herford, *Christianity in Talmud and Midrash*, 83f.

55 Did Jesus see himself as the savior whose death was to be a propitiation for sin? (See the bibliography in Schelkle, II, 324, n. 76, and 324, n. 79.)

(1) Jeremias, *Eucharistic Words* (222–237), answers in the affirmative: "This is therefore what Jesus said at the Last Supper about the meaning of his death: *his death is the vicarious death of the suffering servant, which atones for the sins of the 'many,' the peoples of the world, which ushers in the beginning of the final salvation and which effects the new covenant with God*" (231).

(2) The Catholic exegete Rudolf Pesch likewise answers the question in the affirmative, although he takes the "many" for whom Jesus sees himself as dying to be only Israel and not all humanity: *Das Abendmahl*, 99, 107–109. (For a cautionary review of Pesch's thesis see Hahn, "Das Abendmahl und Jesu Todesverständnis," *Theologische Revue* 76, 4 [1980], 267–272, esp. 270).

(3) Hengel, who agrees with Jeremias and Pesch, presents "a hypothesis" that Jesus at the Last Supper "represented his imminent death as the eschatological saving event which—in connection with Isa. 53—in the context of the dawn of the kingdom of God brought about reconciliation with God for all Israel, indeed for all men, and sealed God's eschatological new covenant with his creatures": Hengel, *Atonement*, 72.

(4) Schillebeeckx takes a more cautious stance: Even though "no certain logion of Jesus is to be found in which Jesus himself might be thought to ascribe a salvific import to his death" or even "[an] authentic saying of Jesus that tells us how he regarded and evaluated his death," nonetheless "the entire ministry of Jesus during the period of his public life was not just an assurance or promise of salvation but a concrete tender of salvation then and there," and in that sense "the conclusion would seem to be justified that Jesus felt his death to be (in some way or other) part and parcel of the salvation-offered-by-God, as a historical consequence of his caring and loving service and solidarity with people," and thus "There is no gap between Jesus' self-understanding and the Christ proclaimed by the Church": *Jesus*, 310 and 311.

56 See above, n. 23.

57 On the legal proceedings against Jesus see: Blinzler, *The Trial of Jesus;* Bornkamm, *Jesus*, 155–168; Schillebeeckx, *Jesus*, 306–319; Tatum, 164–175. On the history of Jewish scholarship on Jesus' trial and death see Catchpole, *The Trial of Jesus*, and Harbury, "The Trial of Jesus in Jewish Tradition."

58 Blinzer, *The Trial of Jesus*, says it is doubtful that "a claim to be he [the messiah, who in fact would be a human being] could be regarded as an infringement of the majesty of God," but he considers the argument that none of the apparent claimants of the title were tried for blasphemy to be "anything but conclusive" (106, with n. 41; further, 106–108). Cf. the story of Bar Kozibah (Bar Cochba) and his declaration of messiahhood: Epstein, ed., *The Babylonian Talmud*, Seder Nezikin (Volume VI),

Tractate Sanhedrin (Volume II), chapter XI, 93b, translated by H. Freedman (1935), 627.

59 Regarding the cries of the crowd Brown writes (*The Gospel According to John* II, 895): "Obviously here both Gospels [Matthew 27:25 and John 19:15] are reflecting apologetic theology rather than history—they are having the audience of the trial give voice to a late 1st-century Christian interpretation of salvation history. The tragedy of Jesus' death is compounded as it is seen through the veil of hostility between the Church and the Synagogue in the 80s or 90s. . . . [cf. Brown, I, lxxiv–lxxv, on the growing hostility after 70 C.E.]. And the tragedy will be compounded still further through the centuries as the Matthean and Johannine theological presentations of the crucifixion, wrenched from their historical perspectives and absolutized, will serve both as a goad to and an excuse for anti-Jewish hatred"; cf. Schillebeeckx: "the unhistorical cry . . . 'Crucify him!' [etc.]" (*Jesus*, 317); (the contrary suggestion by J. W. Doeve is noted in Brown, II, 884).

The earliest written record of the Christian polemic against the Jews is found in I Thessalonians 2:14–15: "the Jews, who killed both the Lord Jesus and the prophets." On the question of Jewish-Christian conflict in the Johannine writings see Brown, *The Community of the Beloved Disciple*, 40–43. Further, Küng, *On Being a Christian*, 168–174, and bibliography at 628, n. 1, and at 630, nn. 6–13; Schelkle, II, 322, n. 69. Some of the most vicious language against Jews was employed by Gregory of Nyssa, theologian and bishop (ca. 330–395 C.E.): *kyrioktonoi* (Lord-killers [citing I Thessalonians 2:15]), *theomachoi* (fighters against God), *misotheoi* (God haters), *synēgoroi tou diabolou* (advocates of the devil): *In Christi Resurrectionem*, Oratio V, in Migne, ed., *Patrologia Graeca* XLVI (1863), 685. Compare Blaise Pascal: "It is a wonderful thing, and worthy of particular attention, to see this Jewish people existing so many years in perpetual misery, it being necessary as a proof of Jesus Christ, both that they should exist to prove Him, and that they should be miserable because they crucified Him": *Pensées*, No. 640.

60 Mark 15:15, Matthew 27:26, and John 19:1 mention the scourging of Jesus, whereas Luke (23:16,22) only alludes to the possibility; as Lohfink notes, it is not certain whether the scourging was inflicted "as a punishment accompanying crucifixion *after* the sentence was pronounced [as Mark and Matthew imply] or as the last attempt at placating the excited crowd *before* an eventual death sentence": *The Last Day of Jesus*, 55. II Corinthians 11:24 shows that at least in the Diaspora Jewish authorities were empowered to punish a wrongdoer with thirty-nine lashes. On the cruelty of scourging, cf. Flavius Josephus: *The Jewish War* II (xxi, 5 = Niese 612) in *Josephus* II (Loeb No. 203), 558, 559, translated by H. St. J. Thackeray, 1927. Philo reports that Flaccus, prefect of Egypt (32–38 C.E.), had thirty-eight members of the Jewish Senate in Alexandria so badly scourged that some died at once: *Flaccus* X (= 75) in *Philo* IX (Loeb No. 363), 342, 343, translated by F. H. Colson, 1941.

61 A thorough treatment of the practice of crucifixion is found in Hengel, *Crucifixion*. See also: Brown, *Recent Discoveries*, 79–81; Joseph A. Fitzmyer, "Crucifixion in Ancient Palestine, Qumran Literature, and the New Testament," especially 507–513; Mackowski, 155. Concerning an adult crucifixion victim discovered in Tomb I at Giv'at ha-Mivtar (also called Ras el-Masaref) in June 1968, see N. Haas, "Anthropological Observations on the Skeletal Remains from Giv'at ha-Mivtar," 38–59, especially 49–59 and plates 19–24 (between pages 128 and 129).

TWO: HOW JESUS WAS RAISED FROM THE DEAD

[1] For example, *egeirō* (to arouse, awaken, raise/make to rise) is used in the aorist passive voice (*ēgerthē:* Jesus *was raised* [by God]) in Mark 16:6, Luke 24:6 and 34, Romans 4:25 and 6:4; and in the passive perfect (*egēgertai*) in I Corinthians 15:4 and 17. It is used in the active voice (*egeiren:* God raised Jesus) in, for example, Acts 4:10, 5:30, I Thessalonians 1:10, I Corinthians 6:14. The verb *anistēmi* (to raise up), is used, for example, in Acts 2:24 and 32; 13:32 and 34; and once in Paul: I Thessalonians 4:14. Cf. Albrecht Oepke, "*egeirō*," in Kittel, II, especially 333–337. Kremer argues that *ēgerthē* is in the middle (rather than the "divine passive") voice: "Auferstanden —auferweckt," 97–98. For bibliographies on the resurrection see Bode, 186–200 (to 1970); Schelkle, II, 325, n. 87 (to 1973); Dhanis, 645–745 (to 1974); Perkins, *Resurrection*, 453–479 (to 1984).

[2] For popular histories of Jesus' activities between Easter Sunday and Ascension Thursday see, for example, Edersheim, II, 621–652. For a summary of the most recent mainstream exegetical positions on the question of resurrection and appearances, see Kremer, *Die Osterevangelien*, 18–24.

[3] Since Jesus presumably was buried unclothed (Rabbi Eliezer held that "[a man is hanged] without his clothes": Epstein, ed., *The Babylonian Talmud*, Seder Nezikin [Volume V], Tractate Sanhedrin [Volume I], chapter VI, 46a, translated by Jacob Schachter, 1935, p. 301), and since he reportedly left his burial garments in the tomb (John 20:5–7), the question has been raised whether, according to John 20:14ff., Jesus appeared naked to Mary Magdalen and others ("Erschien der Herr die 40 Tage hindurch immer unbekleidet?": Kastner, 347). Kastner answers in the relative affirmative regarding the appearance to Mary Magdalene: 350–352; Brown dismisses the thesis: *The Gospel According to John* II, 990; cf. 991.

[4] On the discrepancies in the gospel accounts of Easter: Bode, 5–24; Bornkamm, *Jesus*, 181–183, 213, n. 4; Brown, *Virginal Conception* 99–106, 117–125; Marxsen, *Resurrection*, 72–74; Perkins, 91–93. The *ne plus ultra* of postresurrection chronologies of Jesus is found in Matthew Power, *Anglo-Jewish Calendar for Every Day in the Gospels*. Although Father Power got the dates wrong, he certainly got the traditional notion of Easter exactly right when he suggested the following chronology of Jesus' departure from earth: "Thursday, June 7, A.D. 31: *Ascension Day*. Friday, June 8, A.D. 31: In Heaven" (92). Here and throughout the text I use the words "myth" and "legend" in regard to the Easter stories with the *caveat* that Alsup expresses (*The Post-Resurrection Appearance Stories*, 272) and as a stand-in for designating the *Gattung* "appearance story." On the meaning of the word "myth" when used with regard to the Easter accounts, see further: Küng, *On Being a Christian*, 413–414, and Sloyan "'Come, Lord Jesus.'"

[5] Acts 1:22 implies that the necessary condition for taking Judas' place among the Twelve was that one was "a witness of [Jesus'] resurrection" (cf. also 4:33). This did not mean that one had to have seen Jesus exit from his tomb but, as Fitzmyer says, only that Jesus had "appeared" to one: *A Christological Catechism*, 77.

[6] The text of the Gospel of Peter in English translation by Christian Mauer and George Ogg (here slightly revised) is found in Hennecke and Schneemelcher, *New Testament Apocrypha* I, 183–187, and is reproduced in Cameron, ed., *The Other Gospels*, 78–82 (the cited passages are on 80–81). See also Cameron, 76–78 and

187–188; Crossan, *Four Other Gospels*, 125–181, esp. 165–178; Fuller, *Formation*, 189–192; Hennecke and Schneemelcher, 179–183; Küng, *Eternal Life?*, 98–99.

⁷ Cf. Schillebeeckx: "[W]hat would a straight appearance of Jesus in the flesh prove? Only *believers* see the one who appears. . . . Faith is emasculated if we insist on grounding it in pseudo-empiricism": *Jesus*, 710, n. 119. Cf. as well Mark 16:12: Jesus appeared "in another form" *(en heterai morphēi).*

⁸ The New Testament never interprets Jesus' resurrection as a "coming back to life," that is, as any form of resuscitation or reanimation, but always as an entry into eschatological existence. Thomas Aquinas writes: "In rising, Christ did not come back to life in the usual sense of life as we all know it; rather, he entered a life that somehow was immortal and godlike": *Summa Theologiae* III, 55, 2, c. Cf. Küng, *Eternal Life?*, 109, 112–114; Pesch, "Zur Entstehung des Glaubens . . . : Ein neuer Versuch" (1983), 88–89; Fitzmyer, *A Christological Catechism*, 77.

⁹ See Blinzer, "Die Grablegung Jesu in historischer Sicht," in Dhanis, 85–87. The Roman (and, earlier, Greek) custom of leaving crucified corpses on the cross until they corrupted is attested in the extracanonical Tractate Semahot (properly: Ebel Rabbati). The tractate prohibits immediate members of the family of the crucified from living in the city "[u]ntil the flesh has wasted away, the features no longer being discernible from the skeleton": Zlotnik, ed., *The Tractate "Mourning,"* p. 36. The family, however, could plead for the body: "No rites whatsoever should be denied those who were executed by the [Roman] state. At what point should the family begin counting the days of mourning for them? From the time they despair of asking for the body, even though they may still hope to steal it": *ibid.*, 9, p. 35.

Concerning the removal of a hanged or crucified person on the day of death: "If he is left [hanging] overnight, a negative command is thereby transgressed. For it is written, 'His body shall not remain all night upon the tree, but thou shalt surely bury him the same day for he is hanged [because of] a curse against God [cf. Deuteronomy 21:23]' "; Epstein, ed., *The Babylonian Talmud*, Seder Nezikin (Volume V), Tractate Sanhedrin (Volume I), chapter VI, 46a, translated by Jacob Schachter, 1935, p. 304 (cf. also 305).

¹⁰ The Mishnah, in discussing the burial of criminals, notes that outside the walls of Jerusalem there were at one time at least two common graves for executed criminals: "And they did not bury him [the executed person] in his ancestral tomb, but two burial places were prepared by the Beth Din [the Jewish court], one for those who were decapitated or strangled, and the other for those who were stoned or burned. When the flesh was completely decomposed, the bones were gathered and buried in their proper place": Epstein, ed., *The Babylonian Talmud*, Seder Nezikin (Volume V), Tractate Sanhedrin (Volume I), chapter VI, 46a; translated by Jacob Schachter, 1935, p. 305. (Concerning "the other for those who were stoned": "All those who are stoned are [afterward] hanged," *ibid.*, 45b; p. 299, that is, on a cross [*ibid.*, 46a; p. 304].) Likewise, the fact of common graves is mentioned in Jeremiah 26:23 ("the burial place of the common people") and in Matthew 27:7 and Acts 1:19 (the potter's field, known as Akeldama, the Field of Blood, for burying strangers). On the question of the historicity of Matthew 27:7 see Jeremias, *Jerusalem in the Time of Jesus*, 138–140. Blinzer, "Die Grablegung Jesu," in Dhanis, 94, argues that there was only *one* criminal grave outside Jerusalem at Jesus' time.

Various texts of the Gemara on the first sentence cited above (Sanhedrin VI, 46a) observe that "a wicked man may not be buried beside a righteous one" (*ibid.*, 47a; p. 311; cf. Isaiah 53:9) and "Both death and [shameful] burial [n. 4: in the criminals' graveyard] are necessary [for forgiveness]" and, in fact, "The decay of the flesh too is necessary [n. 6: for forgiveness]" (*ibid.*, 47b; p. 314). And: "When is atonement effected? After the bodies have experienced a little of the pains of the grave" (*ibid.*, 47b; pp. 314–315).

Blinzer, "Die Grablegung Jesu," in Dhanis, 93–96, argues that, given the circumstances, Jesus *should* have been given the dishonorable burial of a criminal but that Joseph of Arimathea buried Jesus in Josephus' own tomb because of the nearness of the Sabbath and the distance of the common grave from Jerusalem (94–96). For the point about the distance of the common grave, which is alluded to only in John 19:42, Blinzer adduces the very thin evidence of Jeremiah 22:19, Isaiah 53:9, and two texts from Josephus that pertain to ancient Israel (94) and the even thinner evidence of Acts 14:18, "outside the city" (98) and of a rabbinic text (97) that addresses a dead criminal: "[The] people did not put you in a coffin but dragged you to the grave with ropes": *Midrash Rabbah: Ecclesiastes (Koheleth Rabbah)*, chapter 1 (Freedman-Simon, VIII, 42, translated by A. Cohen), commenting on Ecclesiastes/Qoheleth 1:15. The Mishnah, however, mandated merely that "graves . . . must be kept fifty cubits from a town [n. 6: 'Because of the bad smell']": *The Babylonian Talmud*, Seder Nezikin (Volume III), Tractate Baba Bathra (Volume I), chapter II, 25a; translated by Maurice Simon, 1935, 123.

Brown argues that it is at least "[not] implausible" (*Virginal Conception*, 114) that Jesus was buried in a private rather than a common grave, and "[all] the Gospels make it clear that Jesus was not buried in a common *tomb*" (*The Gospel According to John* II, 943, my emphasis). Brown maintains that the claim that Jesus was buried in "a new tomb where no one had ever been laid" (John 19:41) most likely is an apologetic claim according to which "there was no confusion in the report of the empty tomb, for Jesus was not buried in a common tomb where his body might have been mixed with others" (*The Gospel According to John*, II, 959), although later (*Virginal Conception*, 114) he exempts the claim of the "newness" of the tomb (*mnēmeion kainon*: John 19:41; cf. Matthew 27:60) from apologetics: "[It] may reflect an authentic memory that, although buried privately, the corpse of Jesus, accursed as it was under the Law, could still not be allowed to contaminate other corpses in a family grave. Since there was an element of hurry in the burial of Jesus, the choice of a hitherto unused tomb close to the place of execution (John 19:42) is quite plausible."

[11] All four Gospels (here Mark is the source of Matthew and Luke, whereas John represents a second, and independent, tradition) agree that Joseph of Arimathea buried Jesus. (John alone says that Joseph was assisted by Nicodemus, who brought the spices.) Brown observes: "There is every reason to think that the reminiscence of [Joseph's] role in the burial is historical, since there was no reason for inventing him": *The Gospel According to John* II, 938.

Who was this Joseph of Arimathea? Pesch maintains that even if the original Jerusalem community of believers knew that Joseph had buried Jesus, it is not clear that they knew Joseph personally. The primitive passion account that underlies Mark's Gospel "speaks of Joseph not as a man who became a believing Christian; it portrays him as if from a respectful distance, which allows us to conclude that the community had no contact with this high-ranking figure": "Zur Entstehung des Glaubens . . ." (1973), 206–207; cf. his *Markusevangelium* II, 513.

Mark calls Joseph of Arimathea simply "a respected member of the council [Sanhedrin], who was also himself looking for the kingdom of God" (15:43), whereas the later Gospels tend to promote him to somewhat legendary status. Luke, adding that Joseph was "a good and righteous man," has him disagree with the Sanhedrin's decision to have Jesus killed (23:50–51). Matthew elevates him to the status of "a disciple of Jesus" (27:57), and John adds that he was a disciple "secretly," out of fear of the religious authorities (19:38). Insofar as Joseph was a member of the Sanhedrin, there may be no contradiction between, on the one hand, the Gospels' claim that Jesus was buried by Joseph, and the statement in Acts 13:27, 29 that certain "rulers" (that is, members of the Sanhedrin) interred Jesus—perhaps even in a common grave.

12 Jeremias calculates that the number of pilgrims who came to Jerusalem to celebrate Passover during Jesus' time could have been anywhere between 60,000 and 125,000, over and above the resident population of 25,000 to 30,000 (20,000 of whom lived inside the walls): *Jerusalem in the Time of Jesus,* 77–84, with update of research to 1966.

13 On Jesus' women disciples as the only witnesses of the crucifixion: Pesch, *Das Markusevangelium* II, 503–509; *Zwischen Karfreitag und Ostern,* 20–21, 76. Schenke (21) holds to the historicity of the flight of the disciples from Gethsemane in Mark 14:50 (cf. 14:22).

Did the disciples *flee* to Galilee? Bultmann finds such a flight indicated in Mark 14:28 and 16:7: *Theology of the New Testament* I, 45. Brown supports the idea of a flight, with the qualification that "[t]he exact moment of the flight of the Twelve from Jerusalem is not clear in the N[ew] T[estament]": *Virginal Conception,* 108 and n. 181; in "John 21 and the First Appearance," 257, Brown suggests that "after finding the tomb empty, Peter went back to Galilee puzzled and discouraged and resumed his occupation." In *Virginal Conception* (108–109) Brown leaves open the possibility that Peter and the others may have fled Jerusalem without any discovery of an empty tomb; Brown adds that "news that the body of Jesus was no longer in the tomb would only have increased the puzzlement and fright of the disciples, if they heard it before leaving Jerusalem" (109). See also Fuller, *Formation,* 34f. Marxsen declares such a flight to be a "fiction": *Mark the Evangelist,* 82, n. 101. Pesch says that an *immediate* flight *(sofort nach Galiläa)* is an "unwarranted assumption"; rather, the disciples probably first fled to Bethany (where Jesus and the twelve had been lodged during the last days), and *if* they fled to Galilee, they probably did so on Sunday morning at the earliest: *Simon-Petrus,* 49. Cf. Schenke for those who hold to the flight of the disciples (21, n. 30) and those who do not (22, n. 31). For a survey of the literature to 1970, see Bode, 32, n. 2.

14 For a "biography" of Simon, see Pesch, *Simon-Petrus,* 10–134, with bibliography, 173–179; and "The Position and Significance of Peter," 25–28; Brown et al., *Peter in the New Testament,* 158–162 and passim, with bibliography, 169–177. Concerning Simon's name, see Fitzmyer, *Essays,* 105–112. On the excavations of what may be Simon's house at Capernaum, see Corbo, especially 53–70 and Plan III at the end of the book. (Figures 21–23 [pp. 67, 68, 69] show photographs of two graffiti naming, respectively, Jesus and Peter, and of two fish hooks found on the floor of the house church.) Also Bagatti, *Antichi Villagi,* 94–95, and *The Church from the Circumcision,* 128–132.

[15] Concerning Matthew 14:22–33 Brown notes that "even if the general story [of Jesus' walking on the water] is not easily made post-resurrectional, the incident that Matthew added about Peter may have been post-resurrectional" (*The Gospel According to John* II, 1088) insofar as the story contains "many of the features of a post-resurrectional narrative (and indeed features that have a startling similarity to those in the story related in *John* 21)": Brown, "John 21 and the First Appearance," in Dhanis, 252–253.

[16] The thesis that Easter faith first arose with Simon through a "first appearance" (or protophany) of the risen Jesus to him is based on such texts as I Corinthians 15:5, Mark 16:7, and John 21:1ff., taken in conjunction with Matthew 16:18, Luke 22:32 and 24:34. (On the relation of this last text and earlier kerygmas, see Alsup, 61–64.) The thesis is presented by, for example: Bornkamm, *Jesus*, 182; Brown, *The Gospel According to John* II, 1082–1092, *Virginal Conception*, 108–111, and "John 21 and the First Appearance," in Dhanis, 246–265; Fuller, *Formation*, 34f.; Kremer, *Das älteste Zeugnis*, 67–71; Marxsen, *Resurrection*, 81–97; Pesch, "Zur Entstehen des Glaubens . . . ," (1973), 211–212, *Simon-Petrus*, 49–59, and "Zur Entstehung des Glaubens . . . : Ein neuer Versuch" (1983), 91–92; Schillebeeckx, *Jesus*, 385–390; Wilckens, *Resurrection*, 112. In "John 21 and the First Appearance" Brown holds that John 21:1–17 is "basically the lost account of the (first) appearance of the risen Jesus to Peter mentioned elsewhere in the NT" (248).

It is also possible that *chronologically* (but not "officially," that is, not in terms of the commissioning of official witnesses) the first "appearance" of Jesus was to Mary Magdalen. See Pesch, *Simon-Petrus*, 51, and *Zwischen Karfreitag und Ostern*, 77–79; Benoît, "Marie-Madeleine," esp. 150–152.

The popular Catholic notion that Jesus first appeared to his mother, Mary, goes back to the Christian poet Coelius Sedulius, *Carmen Paschale* (ca. 392 C.E.; a prose version is called *Pascale opus*), Book 5, lines 361–362: Migne, *Patrologia Latina* XIX (1846), 743.

There are good grounds for locating the protophany to Simon in Galilee. Cf.: Brown, in Dhanis, 250, n. 15, and 251; *Virginal Conception*, 108–111. Nickelsburg, "Enoch, Levi, and Peter," esp. 590–600, connects the commissioning of Simon at Caesarea Philippi (Matthew 16:13–19) with a tradition about Galilee as the locus of divine revelation that Nickelsburg finds in I Enoch 12–16 and Testament of Levi 2–7. Günter Stemberger rejects the thesis in Davies, *The Gospel and the Land*, 409–438, esp. 429–431.

[17] On the late-Jewish genre of conversion-visions see Schillebeeckx, *Jesus*, 380–385; also 281, 321, 329. Compare the conversion of the pagan woman Asaneth in the Jewish "novel" (written between 200 B.C.E. and 100 C.E.) *Joseph and Aseneth*, 10–17, especially 14:1ff (Charlesworth, II, 214–231, especially 224ff.).

[18] Pesch holds that the grounds for the disciples' readiness to believe Peter's claim that Jesus had appeared was their pre-Easter belief in the implied promise *(Verheissung)* that Jesus would be raised: *Simon–Petrus*, 52–55; "Zur Entstehung des Glaubens . . . : Ein neuer Versuch" (1983), 86–87.

[19] Cf. Brown, *Virginal Conception*, 109. Also Schillebeeckx, who follows Alsup in maintaining that "the empty tomb had a merely negative effect: it did not lead to triumphant hope in resurrection, but to confusion and sorrow": *Interim Report*, 87.

[20] Schillebeeckx presents Simon's experience as a "conversion experience"—a

new experience of forgiveness after Jesus' death—that eventually led Simon (and the other disciples) to believe in God's renewed offer of salvation after the crucifixion because of God's startling vindication of the prophet: *Jesus*, 379–392. (For a brief criticism of Schillebeeckx see Fuller and Perkins, *Who Is This Christ?*, 28–40.)

However, Rudolf Pesch has argued that even before Jesus died, his disciples were already prepared for his "resurrection" (i.e., eschatological rescue). In his earlier article "Zur Entstehung des Glaubens . . ." (1973), Pesch, following Berger's 1971 dissertation published in 1976 as *Die Auferstehung des Propheten* (especially Part One, 42–52 and 109–141), held that the disciples probably were familiar with—and had already begun to interpret Jesus with the aid of—the then current idea of the resurrection of individual men of God who suffered martyrdom (cf. "Zur Entstehung des Glaubens . . . : Ein neuer Versuch" [1983], 82–84). According to Berger's thesis, it was believed that after his death an individual prophet or martyr could be lifted up like Elijah and Moses (cf. Revelation 11:11–12) or translated into heaven and appointed the Son of Man like Enoch (I [Ethiopic Apocalypse of] Enoch 70:1–3 [cf. Genesis 5:24] and 71:1–17, in Charlesworth, I, 49–50; Charles, II, 235–237). Therefore, since the disciples presumably knew this tradition, they needed no "conversion experience" after Jesus' death in order to come to believe that Jesus had been raised—their earlier faith was enough. Simply by reflecting on Jesus' life and its implicit promise of divine rescue, Simon and the disciples could and did come to the conviction that Jesus had been raised up by God and taken into the eschatological future; hence there was no real difference between their faith before and after Jesus died. (For discussion and critique of Pesch's early position, see Fiorenza, *Foundational Theology*, 18–28; Küng, *On Being a Christian*, 370–381; Schillebeeckx, *Interim Report*, 90–91; Vögtle and Pesch, *Wie kam es zum Osterglauben?*; and the bibliography on the debate in "Zur Entstehung des Glaubens . . . : Ein neuer Versuch" [1983], 80, n. 8; 88, n. 13; and in the footnotes to Fiorenza, 51–52.)

In later statements of his position in *Simon-Petrus*, "Zur Entstehung des Glaubens . . . : Ein neuer Versuch" (1983), and *Zwischen Karfreitag und Ostern*, Pesch does not rely on Berger's (somewhat insecure) hypothesis, and he holds to the historicity of the appearances as ecstatic visions (not simply "legitimation formulae") in which the disciples "saw" Jesus as the Son of Man. On these matters, see below.

In this chapter I generally follow Pesch, but without intending to exclude Schillebeeckx's hypothesis. What they have in common lies at the center of my presentation: that the disciples required no special "risen-Jesus events" in order to come to Easter faith.

²¹ Schillebeeckx, like many others, rejects the "standpoint adopted since Bultmann and Käsemann, that there was one primal kerygma, i.e., the resurrection, which then gave rise to divergent developments. . . . In this tunnel period [30–50 C.E.], the 'Easter experience,' common to all traditions, was interpreted in a variety of ways, and in any case not *per se* in the form of the Pauline resurrection kerygma": *Interim Report*, 41 and 43 (cf. *Jesus*, 392–397). Regarding Q, which he calls "[a] Parousia *kerygma* without a resurrection," Schillebeeckx notes: "Not only is the resurrection not proclaimed [in Q]; it is nowhere mentioned in the Q tradition": *Jesus*, 408, 409. Thus Schillebeeckx raises the question "whether for some Jewish Christians the resurrection was not a 'second thought,' which proved the best way to make explicit an earlier spontaneous experience"; and he holds that "the *reality* denoted by 'Easter experience' is independent both of the traditions centred around the Jerusalem tomb

and of that of the appearances (which in my view already presuppose the Easter faith)": (*Jesus,* 396 and 397; cf. 394 on "empty tomb" and "appearances" as "already an interpretation of the resurrection faith"). Cf. also Wilckens, in Moule, 74; and Marxsen, in Moule, 47–48.

[22] On the variety of possible ways of expressing eschatological rescue in the martyr-tradition, see Berger, *Auferstehung,* 109–124 and 593, n. 472 (with textual references): "Often in these cases no distinction is made between being swept up [to heaven: *Entrücktsein;* cf. *raptus*], being bodily raised up, and the mere sojourning of the soul in heaven." See also Schillebeeckx, *Jesus,* 518–523. *Raptus*-texts in the Jewish scriptures include Genesis 5:24 (Enoch), II Kings 2:11 (Elijah), Wisdom 4:10–11 (the "person pleasing to God"), Sirach/Ecclesiasticus 44:16 (Enoch), 48:9 (Elijah), 49:14 (Enoch), I Maccabees 2:58 (Elijah).

[23] Bornkamm, *Jesus of Nazareth,* 183, points out that "what is certainly the oldest view held by the Church made no distinction between the resurrection of Christ and his elevation to the right hand of the Father" (citing as examples Acts 2:33 and 5:30; Philippians 2:9; Hebrews 1:3–13 and 8:1; cf. as well John 3:14 and 12:32). Cf. Schillebeeckx: "In the oldest strata of the early Christian son of man tradition there is no explicit reference to resurrection, but there is reference to Jesus' being exalted to the presence of God. . . . So when we hear tell of Jesus' exalted dwelling with God, without any mention of the resurrection at all (as in the Q tradition), there is no ground whatever for simply postulating the resurrection; after all, the same thing can be envisaged in terms of other categories. A broad late-Jewish tradition finds it easy to envisage the exaltation of the suffering righteous one to God's presence without the idea of resurrection": *Jesus,* 537 (see further, 533–538). Cf. Fitzmyer, *A Christological Catechism,* 75f.: "[T]he earliest levels of the tradition speak at times of his [Jesus'] 'exaltation' to glory from his death on the cross, omitting all reference to the resurrection" (for example, in Philippians 2:8–11 and I Timothy 3:16); cf. also p. 79 on exaltation.

[24] Concerning the rabbinical traditions on the resurrected body, cf.: "Thus all shall be healed, save that as a man departs [this life] so will he return resurrected. If he departs blind, he will return blind; if he departs deaf, he will return deaf; if he departs dumb, he will return dumb; if he departs lame, he will return lame. As he departs clothed, so will he return clothed. . . . Why does a man return as he went? So that the wicked of the world should not say: 'After they died God healed them and then brought them back! Apparently these are not the same but others.' 'If so,' says God to them, 'let them arise in the same state in which they went, and then I will heal them. . . .' After that animals too will be healed": *Midrash Rabbah: Genesis (Bereshith Rabbah),* chapter 95 (Vayyigash), 1 (Freedman–Simon, II, 880), commenting on Genesis 46:28 in the light of Isaiah 35:5–6.

"[W]hen [the dead] arise, shall they arise nude or in their garments?—He [Rabbi Meir] replied, 'Thou mayest deduce by an *a fortiori* argument [the answer] from a wheat grain: if a grain of wheat, which is buried naked, sprouteth forth in many robes, how much more so the righteous, who are buried in their raiment!' ": Epstein, ed., *The Babylonian Talmud,* Seder Nezikin (Volume VI), Tractate Sanhedrin (Volume II), chapter XI, 90b, translated by H. Freedman, 1935, p. 607. Also: "They shall rise with their defects and then be healed": *ibid.,* 91b, p. 612, glossing Jeremiah 31:8 and Isaiah 35:6.

"R[abbi] Hiyya b[en] Joseph [after 200 C.E.?] further stated: The just in the time to come will rise [appareled] in their own clothes [n. 9: 'Which they wore during their lifetime']. [This is deduced] *a minori ad majus* from a grain of wheat. If a grain that is buried naked sprouts up with many coverings how much more so the just who are buried in their shrouds": Epstein, ed., *The Babylonian Talmud*, Seder Nashim (Volume IV), Tractate Kethuboth (Volume II), chapter XIII, 111b, translated by Israel W. Slotki, 1936, p. 720.

It may be the case (although Berger, *Auferstehung*, disagrees) that "[t]he idea of the resurrection of a single individual in advance of the events at the end of time was not generally known in [first-century] Judaism" (Wilckens, *Resurrection*, 125); and in that case one can understand why Matthew's Gospel, as John P. Meier points out, multiplies apocalyptic events surrounding the crucifixion and the empty tomb (27:51–54, 28:2–4) so as to present the death and resurrection of Jesus as the definitive "turn of the ages": Brown and Meier, *Antioch and Rome*, 60. Cf. Helmut Koester: "Resurrection is thus a mythological metaphor for God's victory over the powers of unrighteousness.... The preaching of Jesus' resurrection was thus the proclamation that the new age had been ushered in": "The Structure and Criteria of Early Christian Beliefs" in Robinson and Koester, *Trajectories*, 223, 224.

Resuscitation-texts in the Scriptures include: I Kings 17:17–24; II Kings 4:18–37; Mark 5: 35–43; Luke 7:11–17; John 11:1–44; Acts 9:40.

25 If "resurrection" is an interpretation, what is it that is being interpreted? Whereas Bultmann holds that resurrection interprets the meaning of Jesus' *death* ("Indeed, faith in the resurrection is really the same thing as faith in the saving efficacy of the cross": "New Testament and Mythology," in *Kerygma and Myth*, 41, italicized in the original), Marxsen (in Moule, 30) holds that resurrection is an interpretation of *experiences the disciples had after Jesus' death*. On the other hand, Pesch holds that "resurrection" was the disciples' interpretation of *Jesus*—his words and deeds and the promise of God that they had perceived in him—in and through "revelatory experiences" in which they "saw" Jesus as the Son of Man: "Zur Entstehung des Glaubens . . . : Ein neuer Versuch" (1983), 84, *Zwischen Karfreitag und Ostern*, 61, and *Simon-Petrus*, 55.

26 Cf. the slightly different hypothesis of Schelkle, II, 113: "Perhaps the development of the kerygma can be set forth as follows: The primitive experience is attested to as *(a)* an appearance of Jesus in circumstances in which, since it is described by use of the term *ōphthē* (1 Cor[inthians] 15:3–8 and elsewhere), *(b)* this appearance is explained as a divine theophany. Another interpretation by means of apocalyptics says: *(c)* He was raised up, he is risen. *(d)* The former terminology emphasizes the work of God in the event, the latter, the proper action of Christ. *(e)* Further inspection designates the raising up as exaltation. The Gospel accounts of the resurrection [some forty to sixty years later] depict *(f)* encounters with the risen Christ *(g)* in the face of the evidence of the empty tomb. *(h)* The corporeality of the risen Christ is made more and more certain by experientially demonstrative evidence. *(i)* The exaltation is graphically portrayed in the account of the ascension into heaven. *(j)* The three days of resting in the grave are first computed *(k)* and then, by theological reflection, are filled up with activities. *(m)* Preaching expounds upon the meaning that Christ's resurrection has for salvation."

27 On the centrality of the resurrection for the Hellenistic Jewish Christians (who had not witnessed Jesus' mission or teaching and who needed to establish the identity

of the risen and the historical Jesus by a quasi-historicization of the resurrection and appearances), see Wilckens, in Moule, 74f.

[28] Would the discovery of Jesus' corpse have argued against his being eschatologically rescued ("raised") by God? Brown, following Pannenberg, holds: "If the tomb was visited and it contained the corpse or skeleton of Jesus, it is difficult, if not impossible, to understand how the disciples could have preached that God raised Jesus from the dead, since there would have been irrefutable evidence that He had not done so" (*Virginal Conception*, 126). But Anton Vögtle concludes that "on closer inspection the argument that the 'raising' of Jesus could not have been successfully proclaimed in Jerusalem without the emptiness of his grave being able to be checked proves to be, at the very least, uncompelling": in Vögtle and Pesch, *Wie kam es zum Osterglauben?*, 97 (originally in Vögtle, "Wie kam es zur Artikulierung des Osterglaubens? [III]," *Bibel und Leben* 15 [1974], 119). Cf. Schillebeeckx, *Jesus*, 381: "[A]n actual bodily resurrection does not require as its outcome a vanished corpse"; and 704, n. 45: "An eschatological, bodily resurrection, theologically speaking, has nothing to do, however, with a corpse."

Some fifty years ago in Jerusalem E. L. Sukenik discovered a first-century ossuary inscribed with the dead man's name: *Yeshua bar Yehoseph* (Jesus son of Joseph). As Fitzmyer points out, Sukenik "drew no conclusions from it about any New Testament personage, realizing that 'Jesus' and 'Joseph' were commonly used names for Palestinian Jews in the first century": *A Christological Catechism*, 76.

[29] This assertion would not be incompatible with, for example, the orthodox Catholic position, so long as "Easter" in the sense of God's rescue of Jesus from death was understood "as something prior to the [believer's] faith itself, albeit only apprehensible *in* that faith": Rahner, "Remarks on the Importance of the History of Jesus," in *Theological Investigations* XIII, 207.

[30] On the date of Paul's conversion I follow Hengel, *Between Jesus and Paul*, 31, and his *Acts and the History of Earliest Christianity*, 83 and 137. On I Corinthians 15:3–8 see, besides, for example, the works cited in Dhanis, 660–664: Alsup, 55–61; Brown, *Virginal Conception*, 78–96; Fuller, *Formation*, 9ff; Perkins, 88–91; Schelkle, II, 113–114.

[31] Against Bultmann's position on Paul and the empty tomb ("The accounts of the empty grave, of which Paul still knows nothing, are legends": *Theology of the New Testament* I, 45; cf. *Kerygma and Myth*, 42: "the legend of the empty tomb"), see Lehmann, 78–86, especially 82f., where Lehmann argues correctly that Paul's silence on the question of the tomb cannot be taken as proof that the stories of the empty tomb are legends. See "What Really Happened," below. For bibliography on the question of the empty tomb, see Lehmann, 86, n. 187.

[32] On the "third day" as used in I Corinthians 15:4, see Lehmann, passim, but especially 260–272, and his conclusion that the "third day" in I Corinthians 15 is not a chronological but a salvation-history statement (280, 287, 323f., 343, 349): "der dritte Tag ist also der Tag der Heilswende, der Errettung aus grosser Not und drohender Gefahr" (264 ["the day of the turning point of salvation, of deliverance from dire need and imminent danger"]), that is, "Rettungstag" (267 [the "day of deliverance/salvation"]). So too Bode, 181 ("the day of divine salvation, deliverance and manifestation"); Fuller, *Formation*, 25–27 ("not a chronological datum, but a

dogmatic assertion: Christ's resurrection marked the dawn of the end-time, the beginning of the cosmic eschatological process of resurrection").

See *Midrash Rabbah: Genesis (Bereshith Rabbah)*, chapter 56 (Vayera), 1 (Freedman-Simon edition, I, 491), and chapter 91 (Mikketz), 7 (Freedman-Simon edition, II, 843); also *Midrash Rabbah: Esther*, chapter 9, 2 (Freedman-Simon, IX, 112, translated by Simon), and Strack-Billerbeck, I, 747, for similar texts.

The phrase "third day" in I Corinthians is to be kept distinct from the Gospels' *supposed* dating of the resurrection to the Sunday after Jesus' death; that is, the phrase in I Corinthians 15:4 refers to the resurrection itself, not the day on which the tomb was supposedly found empty (Lehmann, 260); see also Brown, *Virginal Conception*, 124 (cf. 119, n. 198). Cf. Schenke, 97, n. 15. Also Schillebeeckx, *Jesus*, 725, nn. 27 and 32; and Schubert, in Dhanis, 224.

33 Cf. Rahner's *theological* assessment: "The resurrection which is referred to in the resurrection of Jesus . . . means the final and definitive salvation of a concrete human existence by God and in the presence of God": *Foundations*, 266; also: "[Resurrection is] the handing over of the whole bodily man to the mystery of the merciful loving God": "Dogmatic Questions on Easter," *Theological Investigations* IV (1966), translated by Kevin Smyth, 128.

34 Cf. Bultmann: "If the Easter-event is in any sense a historical event [*ein historisches Ereignis*] in addition to the event of the cross, it is nothing else than the rise of faith in the risen Lord. . . . The resurrection itself is not an event of past history": "The New Testament and Mythology," in *Keryma and Myth*, 42, translation slightly revised here.

35 That is to say, I use the term "[alleged] appearances" in the sense of Pesch's phrase "*Visionsbehauptungen*," "claims" or "assertions" of a vision: *Simon-Petrus*, 52.

36 Some scholars hold that these formulaic sentences may have served primarily to legitimize the apostolic mission of those mentioned in them. See Schillebeeckx, *Jesus*, 352–360. Wilckens, *Resurrection*, asserts that "the *tradition* about the appearances was concerned with the authorization of the witnesses by the authority of the risen Christ. The appearances are thus not really *testimonies* to the resurrection, but rather *credentials* proving the identity and authority of the men who because of their heavenly authorization had permanent authority in the Church" (114) and that "the appearances of the risen Christ were experienced by the witnesses essentially as their vocation to their task, their call to mission" (130). Fuller, *Formation*, distinguishes between the "church-founding appearances" to Peter and the Twelve and "the later appearances, whose function is the call and sending of apostles to fulfill a mission" (35; cf. 41f.). On the connection between appearance and vocation to preach, see also Küng, *On Being a Christian*, 376.

37 For this and the following paragraphs see Wilhelm Michaelis, "*horaō*," in Kittel, V, 315–367, especially 355–361. Also: Alsup, 246–251, for discussion of *ōphthē* texts in the Jewish scriptures and intertestamental literature; Brown, *Virginal Conception*, 89–92; Fuller, *Formation*, 30–34; Marxsen, in Moule, 26–30; Rigaux, 340–346; Schelkle, II, 114–116; Schillebeeckx, *Jesus*, 346–354, and 706, n. 68 (for texts).

38 The hypothesis of a "hallucination" on the part of the disciples, which goes back to David Strauss (*The Life of Jesus Critically Examined*), postulates that Jesus' followers had a dream or ecstasy during which they thought they saw Jesus alive.

But this hypothesis is too much tied to the ocular definition of *ōphthē*, which, as we have seen, is not the essential meaning of the word in the Bible. In its looser forms the hypothetical hallucination is defined broadly enough to include *any* experience other than a space-time encounter with Jesus in the flesh, and hence does not illuminate very much. In both forms, the hypothesis fails to engage the ancient Jewish and biblical understanding of divine or eschatological appearances. Cf. Alsup, 273, on how the appearance stories, because of their literary genre, "seem to resist probing inquiry into the 'how did it happen question.' This deals, of course, a severe blow to the parapsychological explanation of the appearance stories."

[39] For the early believers, Jesus rose into the eschatological future ("Jesus rose into the final judgment of God": Wilckens, in Moule, 70) and appeared from that future. Cf. Fuller, in *Interpretation* 29 (1975), 325: "These appearances are to be interpreted not as encounters with a resuscitated Jesus prior to an ascension, but as eschatological disclosures 'from heaven' [read: 'from the eschatological future'] of an already exalted One." See also Wilckens, *Resurrection*, 67, and Fitzmyer, *A Christological Catechism*, 77–78.

[40] Cf. Schillebeeckx, *Jesus*, 346: "Only we suffer from the crude and naïve realism of what 'appearances of Jesus' came to be in the later tradition, through unfamiliarity with the distinctive character of the Jewish-biblical way of speaking."

[41] Schillebeeckx, *Jesus*, 385–392, argues for Simon's Easter experience as a "conversion experience" after Simon had denied Jesus. In what follows I offer my own, very different interpretation of what constituted Simon's denial and conversion.

[42] Cf. Wilckens, in Moule, 74: The original, pre-Marcan (see below) resurrection story, which was to develop into Mark 16:1–8, "was the only place in the living tradition of the primitive [Jerusalem] community in which the resurrection of Jesus formed the *theme* in a narrative context. Apart from this, it was used merely as the starting point of authentication formulae, which stated the authority of particular witnesses of the risen Jesus." On the question of authentication (or legitimation) formulae, see n. 36, above.

[43] On Mark 16: Pesch, *Das Markusevangelium* II, 519–559; Kremer, *Die Osterevangelien*, 30–54 (45–49 on redaction); F. Neirynck, "Marc 16,1–8, Tradition et Rédaction," *Ephemerides Theologicae Louvaniensis* 56 (1980), 56–88. Cf. also: Bode, 44–48; Brown, *Virginal Conception*, 97–98 with n. 166; and 123; Fuller, *Formation*, 155–159; Kremer, in Dhanis, 146–153; Marxsen, *Mark the Evangelist*, 81; and *The Resurrection*, 42 and 63; Perkins, 114–124; Schillebeeckx, *Jesus*, 334–337.

[44] On the possibility that Mark's story of the finding of the empty tomb is related to the *raptus*-tradition, see Pesch, *Das Evangelium des Urgemeinde*, 219–221, with text references; also Hamilton, "Resurrection Tradition," 420.

[45] On the question of the meaning of the reference to Galilee in 16:7 (which we do not touch upon here), see Bode, 31–35 and 183 (not the parousia but the resumption of evangelical work); Brown, *Virginal Conception*, 123, n. 209 (generally against Lohmeyer); Fuller, *Formation*, 57–64 (considers Lohmeyer's position possible, but finally opts against it); Lohfink, "Der Ablauf," 163 (the angel's command "justifies" the prior flight to Galilee); Ernst Lohmeyer, *Galiläa und Jerusalem*, Göttingen: Vandenhoeck & Ruprecht, 1936 (reference to the parousia in Galilee); Marxsen, *Mark the Evangelist*, 83–95 (partial agreement with Lohmeyer: Mark's audience did expect the parousia in Galilee); Perkins, 120; Pesch, *Das Markusevangelium* II, 534

(a confirmation-appearance in Galilee; no later ascension is anticipated); Schillebeeckx, *Jesus*, 419; 707, n. 71 ("very probably" refers to the parousia). See Günter Stemberger, "Galilee—Land of Salvation?," in Davies, ed., *The Gospel and the Land*, 409–438, with attention to Lohmeyer's hypothesis at 411–414.

46 See Bode, 39–41, for theories on why Mark has the women retreat into silence (to explain why the empty tomb legend was so long unknown: Bousset; in keeping with the Marcan "messianic secret": Wilckens, Dechamps; apologetics, to keep official witnesses free from the empty tomb report: Bode). Kremer, *Die Osterevangelium*, 54, suggests that Mark wanted to indicate that the women lacked faith and understanding even in face of the angel's announcement, just as the disciples had misunderstood Jesus during his lifetime. For a further summary of views: Neirynck (see n. 43, above), 64–72.

47 See, for example, Fuller, *Formation*, chapters 4 and 5; Schillebeeckx, *Jesus*, 338–344; Wilckens, *Resurrection*, 44–48.

48 Concerning the question of the redaction of Mark 16:1–8, see the literature on Mark 16 listed above; also: Fuller, *Formation*, 52–57; Schenke, 56–93, on the original tradition and its *Sitz im Leben*. On the question of the pre-Marcan primitive passion narrative (which Pesch attributes to the Galileans living in Jerusalem: "Zur Entstehung des Glaubens . . . : Ein neuer Versuch" [1983], 90), see Brown, *The Gospel According to John* II, 787–791; Bultmann, *The History of the Synoptic Tradition*, 275–284; Jeremias, *The Eucharistic Words*, 89–96. The majority of scholars (e.g., Alsup, 85f.; Brown, *Virginal Conception*, 118–119, 123; Bultmann [see immediately above]; Schenke, 20–30) hold that the primitive passion narrative ended with the burial of Jesus (cf. Mark 15:47) and that the story of the empty (or open) tomb arose independently and was connected to the primitive passion narrative either before Mark or (Alsup, 90) by Mark. As evidence of the independence of the two narratives these scholars offer the facts that different women are named (Mark 15:47 and 16:1) and that 15:46 gives no evidence that the burial was incomplete. A minority hold that the primitive passion account ended with the story of the empty/open tomb: e.g., Pesch, "Zur Entstehung des Glaubens . . ." (1973), 205; *Das Markusevangelium* II, 518–520 (see Perkins, 115); *Das Evangelium der Urgemeinde*, 221; and Wilckens, in Moule, 72–73.

49 See Schenke, 57, 62f., 78–83, 86–89; Schillebeeckx, *Jesus*, 331–337, 702–703, nn. 30–32; van Iersel, 54–67; Bode disagrees but summarizes the position: 127–150.

50 The discussion of the narrations of Jesus' appearances has been significantly enhanced by Alsup, who, through an investigation of the history of the tradition of the genre "appearance story" in the New Testament, (a) establishes the genre's literary independence vis-à-vis kerygmatic statements, "blaze-of-light" (*Lichtglanz*) conversion stories, and empty tomb stories; (b) argues (147–213; see his helpful "Text Synopsis") for a complex sevenfold structure common to the four kinds of New Testament appearance stories (group appearances, the Emmaus story, the Galilee appearance in John 21, and the appearance to Mary Magdalene in John 20); and (c) traces the origin of the genre to Old Testament anthropomorphic theophanies.

51 Schillebeeckx, *Christ*, 879, n. 120, holds that the tradition of Jesus' appearance to the women in Matthew (Schillebeeckx, not unproblematically, includes John as well) is relatively late and probably derived from the Marcan story of the *angel's* appearance to the women in the tomb.

[52] Cf. Lehmann, 84; also Schenke, who concludes from this fact that "the 'empty tomb' is not the chief object of the angel's proclamation to the women" (76) and "only after the angel's message do the women notice the empty tomb-site" (81). Note that Luke 24:3–7 later reverses the order: first the women discover that the tomb is empty, and *then* they hear the angel's announcement.

[53] See note 45 above.

[54] Cf. Schillebeeckx, *Jesus*, 703, n. 32: "[S]ome important commentators trace the tradition of 'the tomb' back to a very early tradition of an actual confirmation that the tomb was empty (thus i[nter] a[lios]: L. Cerfaux, J. Jeremias, E. Lohse, J. Héring, J. Weisz, J. Dupont, K. Rengstorf, J. Blank). But these exegetes are defending the *antiquity* of the tomb tradition against a number of interpretations according to which that tradition is said to be very late. The antiquity of this tradition is now more generally accepted than heretofore. The new problem is whether we have a tradition of an 'empty tomb' or a tradition of the 'holy tomb' (in other words, a cultic tradition)."

[55] The various Gospels list the women as: Mary Magdalene and "the other Mary" (Matthew 28:1); Mary Magdalene, Mary the mother of James, and Salome (Mark 16:1); Mary Magdalene, Joanna, Mary the mother of James, and "the other women with them" (Luke 24:10); Mary Magdalene alone (John 20:1), but note "we" in 20:2. See Bode, 160–161, with references in 161, n. 1, concerning the disallowance of women as witnesses in Palestine, but not in the Hellenistic Diaspora. Also Pesch, *Zwischen Karfreitag und Ostern,* 76. Strack-Billerbeck, III, 217, cites the Tanhuma (or Yelammedenu) Midrash on Genesis 18:12–15, as it appears in the Vilna edition of the *Yalkut Shim'oni* Midrash, I, section 82: "From this passage [Sarah's lie about having laughed at God's announcement that she will bear a child in her old age] it has been taught that women are unfit to give evidence." Also 251: "[S]he is not certified to give testimony (must not come before a court as a witness)"—because she led Adam into sin (Genesis 3); and 560: because Deuteronomy 19:17 ("both parties to the dispute shall appear") was taken to mean: both *men,* not women.

[56] Jeremias, *Heiligengräber,* studies forty graves in Palestine (and nine outside, in Nabatea, Egypt, Mesopotamia) and concludes (114–117) that, according to the tradition, at least ten sacred graves were in evidence in ancient times and that the dead were thought to be somehow present in those graves (127–129). Jeremias studies the tradition of pilgrimages to and acts of reverence for graves (138–143) but does not mention liturgical ceremonies. He concludes (144) that the Jerusalem community knew Jesus' grave. Likewise Schenke, 97–103, strongly argues that the early community knew the grave. But Blinzer, in Dhanis, 96, n. 127, points out that one may not argue from Acts 2:27–31 that the Jerusalem community knew the tomb of Jesus, because the text mentions only the tomb of David, not that of Jesus.

[57] See Schenke, 98: "The women are witnesses not of the burial but of the place of the tomb." Whereas Mark 15:47 says that the two women saw only *where* Jesus was laid *(pou tithetai)*—which could mean that they were not present at the actual burial—Luke 23:55 attempts to decide the point by adding: "They saw the tomb and *how* his *body* was laid [*hōs etethē to sōma autou*]."

[58] "We go out to the cemetery and examine the dead within three days and do not fear [being suspected of] superstitious practices. It once happened that [a man who was buried] was examined [and found to be living], and he lived for twenty-five

years and then died. Another [so examined lived and] begat five children before he died." (There is a note on the word "examine": "To see if by chance there is life in them. This was the practice in ancient times when the dead were buried in caves and it was only necessary to lift the lid of the coffin to make an inspection."): Cohen, ed., *The Minor Tractates of the Talmud*, Volume I, Tractate Semahot (or Ebel Rabbathi), chapter VIII, rule 1, translated by J. Rabinowitz, 1965, p. 363. (All material within brackets above is bracketed in the text itself.) However, a different translation of Chapter VIII, rule 1, reads "for thirty days" instead of "within three days": Zlotnik, ed., *The Tractate "Mourning,"* p. 57.

59 The custom in ancient Israel was to mourn the dead for seven days (cf. Genesis 50:10, I Samuel 31:13, I Chronicles 10:12, Judith 16:29, Ecclesiasticus 22:12). The first three were "days of weeping," followed by four "days of lamentation." A midrash on Genesis 50:10 ("and [Joseph] made a mourning for his father [Israel] seven days") reveals a Jewish belief that the soul lingered around the grave for three days and departed on the fourth day, at which point, it was thought, decomposition set in and the soul no longer could reenter and animate the body (cf. Brown, *Virginal Conception*, 116, n. 194; Fuller, *Formation*, 25f.; Mackowski, 158–159; Schillebeeckx, *Jesus*, 528; Schubert, in Dhanis, 222). The text runs as follows:

"[Rabbi Eliazar*] Bar Kappara [of Caesarea, ca. 200 C.E.*] said: He [the mourner*] may not work at all even on the third day [after the death*], because mourning is then at its height. Bar Kappara taught: Until three days [after death], the soul keeps on returning to the grave, thinking that it will go back [into the body] but when it sees that the facial features have become disfigured, it departs and abandons it [the body]": *Midrash Rabbah: Genesis (Bereshith Rabbah)*, chapter C [100], Vayechi, 7 (Freedman-Simon, II, 995, translated by Freedman); also p. 992f., for seven days of mourning. (Note: Bracketed matter marked with * is my own addition.) Cf. also *Midrash Rabbah: Ecclesiastes (Koheleth Rabbah)*, chapter I, 15, §1, commenting on Ecclesiastes 1:15 (Freedman-Simon, VIII, 42f., translated by L. Rabinowitz): "you were a repulsive object after your death for three days."

Wilhelm Bousset, *Die Religion des Judentums* (Berlin: Reutner & Richard), second edition (1906), 341f., n. 1 (third edition, 1966, 297, n. 1), observes that this belief that the soul hovered for three days may have given rise to a later custom of burying the corpse only after three days. Cf. *Testament of Job* (100 B.C.E.–100 C.E.), 53:5–7: "And as soon as they brought the body to the tomb, all the widows and orphans circled about, forbidding it to be brought into the tomb. But after three days they laid him in the tomb in a beautiful sleep": Charlesworth, I, 868. Also *Testament of Abraham*, Recension A (first–second century C.E.), 20:11: "And they tended the body of the righteous Abraham with divine ointments and perfumes until the third day after his death. And they buried him": Charlesworth, I, 895. Bousset notes as well the alternative tradition that the soul departed the body only on the *seventh* day: *The Books of Adam and Eve [Vita]* (first century C.E.), 43:1 ("Six days hence his soul shall leave his body") and 51:2 ("Man of God, mourn not for thy dead more than six days, for on the seventh day is the sign of the resurrection"): Charles, II, 144 and 153; see *Life of Adam and Eve [Apocalypse]*, 43:3 ("And do not mourn more than six days; on the seventh day rest and be glad in it, for on that day both God and we angels rejoice in the migration from the earth of a righteous soul"): Charlesworth, II, 295.

Bode concludes (180): "The Jewish notion of a soul hovering near the tomb for three days would not have served to found the three-day theme—Jesus' resurrection was not conceived as the return of a dead man to former life; [and] the resurrection of Jesus would have had to wait until the fourth day to show its divine singularity." On the question of the relation between the "third day" and the "first day of the week," see Schenke, 97, n. 15: "Regardless of how the issue [of the third day in I Corinthians 15:4] is decided, it is clear that Mark 16:2 can have no influence on its outcome. In no way is the time-indication of Mark 16:2 to be taken as a historical remembrance. Rather, it points to the fact that already in the earliest days [of its existence] the community celebrated the resurrection of Jesus on 'the third day." Also Bode, 105–126; Schillebeeckx, *Jesus,* 527f.

[60] Fuller, *Formation,* 51–52: "First, the embalming of bodies was apparently not in accord with contemporary Jewish custom. [In a footnote Fuller observes that Strack and Billerbeck, II, 52–53, are unable to give a single example.] Second, the completion of the burial rites on a Sunday morning after burial on Friday night is inconceivable in the Palestinian climate, in which decomposition would already have set in (cf. John 11:39)." Cf. Brown to the contrary: "Little credence should be given to the objection that in a hot country no one would come to anoint a body that would have begun to rot. Actually, it can be quite cool in mountainous Jerusalem in early spring; moreover, those who recounted the story presumably knew local weather and customs and would scarcely have invented a patently silly explanation": *The Gospel According to John* II, 982. If the motive for visiting the tomb was to anoint Jesus' body, why did the women not do so on the evening after the Sabbath (the night between Saturday and Sunday, April 8 and 9, 30 C.E.)? The answer Schubert gives in Dhanis, 221–222 (that, first-century Jews feared ghosts in the graveyard), is not very credible—even with Schubert's reference to the Talmud, since in that story the pious man on three separate occasions spent the night in the cemetery!: Epstein, ed., *The Babylonian Talmud,* Seder Zeraim (Volume I), Tractate Berakoth, chapter III, 28b, translated by Maurice Simon, 1958, pp. 110–112.

[61] Josephus remarks: "the Jews are so careful about funeral rites that even malefactors who have been sentenced to crucifixion are taken down and buried before sunset": *The Jewish War* IV, (v, 2 = Niese 317), in *Josephus* III (Loeb No. 210), 92, 93, translated by H. St. J. Thackeray, 1928.

[62] "John gives no indication that there were to be further burial procedures [after the sabbath]; and certainly the staggering amount of spices and oils used on Friday would make otiose the bringing of oils on Sunday": Brown, *The Gospel According to John* II, 957; on the "royal burial" see II, 960, and *Virginal Conception,* 116.

Concerning Matthew 28:1, where the women go to the tomb merely to *see* it and not to anoint the body: Matthew may have omitted the anointing motif because earlier (27:63) he wrote that the chief priests and Pharisees had heard that Jesus claimed he would rise from the dead after three days; hence, why would the women (who, we may deduce from Matthew, presumably also knew of this report) go to anoint a body that they expected to be raised?

[63] See, for example, Benoît, *The Passion and Resurrection,* 226–227.

[64] Bode: "The narrative of the guard develops an apologetic against the accusation that the body of Jesus had been stolen by the disciples. The guard is set on the passover itself ([Matthew] 27:62–66), is present at the removal of the stone (28:3–4) and is

bribed to falsify a report of theft by the apostles (28:11–15). . . . Matthew defends the apostles against the Jewish charge that Jesus' followers had stolen his body" (52). "As the need arose to construct an apologetic taking into consideration the local setting, the empty tomb assumed a supporting role and was altered to bring out the innocence of the Christian community in regard to any tampering with the tomb" (178).

65 The Talmud distinguishes between the *golel*, the large "covering stone" that is rolled in front of the grave to cover the entrance, and the *dofek*, or buttressing stone, that is, the very rock into which the tomb is carved and on which the *golel* rests. However, the *dofek* has also been interpreted as a "wedge stone" that holds the *golel* in place: "The covering stone and the buttressing stone [of a grave] defile by contact": Epstein, ed., *The Babylonian Talmud*, Seder Tohoroth (Volume II), Tractate Oholoth, chapter II, 4 (Mishnah), translated by H. Bornstein, 1959, p. 156. Compare: "When do the mourning rites commence? From the closing of the grave with the grave stone [*golel*]": *The Babylonian Talmud*, Seder Nezikin (Volume V), Tractate Sanhedrin (Volume I), chapter VI, 47b, translated by Jacob Schachter, 1935, p. 314. Cf. also Brown, *The Gospel According to John* II, 982–983; and *Virginal Conception*, 121, n. 203: "[T]he bare fact of the stone being rolled away may be ancient." On the types of tombs in Palestine at the time, see Hachlili and Killebrew, especially 115–119. Regarding the historicity of the burial in general, and therefore implicitly of the stone, Bultmann declares: "This is an historical account which [apart from the women as witnesses] creates no impression of being a legend": *The History of the Synoptic Tradition*, 274.

66 Schonfield, *The Passover Plot*, argues that Jesus planned his own "death" and "resurrection." He plotted to have himself drugged on the cross and then removed (alive) and entombed by Joseph of Arimathea so that, when he later revived from the drug, he might present himself as resurrected. The plot was foiled when the Roman soldier pierced Jesus' side with a lance. Mortally wounded, Jesus was indeed buried, did briefly revive, and then died. His remains were buried elsewhere. When a witness to his death attempted to inform the disciples, they mistook that person for the risen Jesus. For the "trance theory" see John Cheek, "The Historicity of the Markan Resurrection Narrative," *Journal of Bible and Religion* 27 (1959), 191–201.

67 Brown, *Virginal Conception*, 121, n. 203, asks: "[W]as the suggestion that the body had been stolen part of the original narrative about the empty tomb? Or was it a later apologetic addition—an actual Jewish objection set into Mary Magdalene's mouth [John 20:2, 13] in order that it might be clearly refuted by what follows? I see no way to answer with certitude."

68 The "double tomb" theory is presented by G. Baldensperger, "Le tombeau vide," *Revue d'Histoire et de Philosophie Religieuses* 12 (1932) 413–443 (esp. 426, 435, 439); 13 (1933) 105–144 (esp. 111, 119, 122); 14 (1934) 97–125. Baldensperger, who bases himself in part on the fact that the gospels use two names for tomb (*taphos* and *mnēma / mnēmeion*), argues that Joseph of Arimathea secretly reburied Jesus without telling the disciples. A variation is the "wrong tomb" theory: Kirsopp Lake, *The Historical Evidence for the Resurrection of Jesus Christ*, New York: Putnam, 1907, 68–69; 250–252, and Percival Gardner-Smith, *The Narratives of the Resurrection: A Critical Study*, London: Methuen, 1926, suggest that the women came to the wrong tomb and that, when a cemetery worker tried to point them to the right tomb, they fled in fear.

[69] Wilckens, *Resurrection,* 117, puts the matter succinctly and correctly: "The way Jesus's tomb became empty is a question to which history cannot supply the answer." See also Kremer, *Die Osterevangelien,* 49–51, and the reference, 49, n. 56, to the discovery of the anointed bones of a first-century crucified Jew in a rock tomb: P. Stuhlmacher, "Kritischer müssten mir die Historisch–Kritischen sein," *Theologische Quartelschrift* 153 (1973), 245–251, here 247f. Concerning the *Shroud of Turin,* note the following arguments:

(A) in favor of its authenticity: Francis L. Filas, *The Dating of the Shroud of Turin From Coins of Pontius Pilate,* third edition, Youngtown, Arizona: Cogan, 1984; John H. Heller, *Report on the Shroud of Turin,* Boston: Houghton Mifflin, 1983; Kenneth E. Stevenson and Gary R. Habermas, *Verdict on the Shroud,* Ann Arbor, Michigan: Servant Books, 1981; Ian Wilson, *The Shroud of Turin: The Burial Cloth of Jesus Christ?* Garden City, N.Y.: Doubleday, 1978;

(B) against authenticity: Jack A. Jennings, "Putting the Shroud to Rest," *The Christian Century* 100 (June 1, 1983), 552–554; Joe Nickell ("in collaboration with a panel of scientific and technical experts"), *Inquest on the Shroud of Turin,* Buffalo, N.Y.: Prometheus, 1983; Robert A. Wild, S.J., "The Shroud: Probably the Work of a 14th-Century Artist or Forger," *Biblical Archaeology Review* 10:2 (March-April, 1984), 30–46;

(C) cautiously negative: Brown judges that the shroud is *"a priori* suspect" (*The Gospel According to John* II, 942; cf. 941–942); and in a more circumspect conclusion: "If it is genuine, it tells us virtually nothing about Christ's death that is not already known from the Scriptures. As for Christian faith, those who receive the blessing of John 20:29 for believing in Jesus without seeing his risen body will scarcely need the support of having seen an image of his dead body, however that image was produced": *Recent Discoveries and the Biblical World,* 82–83. On the burial clothes of Jesus, as reported in John's Gospel: Brown, *The Gospel According to John* II, 986–987, 1007–1008.

[70] Bode, 178: "Hence, the reality of the events would include that some Christian women visited the tomb of Jesus on the first day of the week, found it empty, left perplexed and apparently kept the matter to themselves." Wilckens, *Resurrection,* 117: "Accordingly, it must be accepted that the core of the narrative is indeed that the women found Jesus's tomb empty in the early morning of the first day of the week." Benoît, "Marie-Madeleine," sees in John 20:1–2 (note "we" in verse 2) a reflection of an early account of the historical core of the events at the tomb.

[71] "In itself the fact of the empty tomb did not originally convey the idea of resurrection; the subsequent appearances of Jesus clarified the *meaning* of the empty tomb": Brown, *The Gospel According to John* II, 998. Cf. Wilckens, *Resurrection,* 117: "The possibility must be left open that the women's discovery [of the open/empty tomb] was only later given an Easter explanation in the light of the disciples' belief in the resurrection."

[72] Brown, *Virginal Conception,* 121–122: "The bare historical fact that on the Sunday after his crucifixion Jesus' tomb was found empty could have been interpreted in many ways, but it was woven into a narrative that became the vehicle of the basic Christian proclamation of Jesus' victory: *Jesus was raised."* On the question of Jesus' absence in Mark 16, see Schillebeeckx, *Jesus,* 417–423.

[73] On the legendary nature of the story of the angel in the tomb, see: Bode, 178: "Did [the women who came to the tomb] experience an apparition of an angel and

receive a heavenly message? The answer has to be 'no' because of the kerygmatic and redactional nature of the angelic message." Cf. Benoît, *The Passion and Resurrection*, 261; also Brown, *The Gospel According to John* II, 975, and *Virginal Conception*, 123; Fuller, *Formation*, 51; Kremer, in Dhanis, 150–151.

74 Cf. Berger's judgment, *Auferstehung*, 232, that the pseudolocalization of the resurrection only *appears* to be pious *(nur scheinbar fromm)* and in fact distorts the meaning of the faith affirmation.

75 See, for example, Schillebeeckx, *Jesus*, 644–650; 645: "[N]o Easter experience of renewed life was possible without the personal resurrection of Jesus—in the sense that Jesus' personal-cum-bodily resurrection (in keeping with a logical and ontological priority; a chronological priority is not to the point here) 'precedes' any faith-motivated experience." *Interim Report*, 77: "The resurrection itself is a real event, accomplished by God in Jesus."

76 Marxsen, in Moule, 50; *Resurrection*, 77, 78, etc.

77 See Origen, *Commentaria in Ezechiel, de prima visione ejusdem*, Homelia I, 11, *Patrologia Graeca* XIII, 677a (1862): "I think often of the maxim, 'It is dangerous to speak of God, even when what you say is true'—and I believe that the man who uttered it was wise in the faith. False things said about God are dangerous, but so too are the true, if said when the time is not right." Also Martin Heidegger, *Unterwegs zur Sprache*, Neske: Pfullingen, 1965, p. 152 ("Geschwiegen vor allem über das Schweigen").

THREE: HOW JESUS BECAME GOD

1 The main works I draw upon for Part Three of this book include: Berger, "Zum traditionsgeschichtlichen Hintergrund"; Brown, *Jesus God and Man, The Birth of the Messiah, The Community of the Beloved Disciple, The Churches the Apostles Left Behind*; Brown and Meier, *Antioch and Rome*; Bultmann, *Theology of the New Testament* I, *Primitive Christianity, The Presence of Eternity*; Conzelmann, *History of Primitive Christianity*; Dunn, *Christology in the Making*; Elizabeth Fiorenza, ed., *Aspects of Religious Propaganda*; Fuller, *The Foundations of New Testament Christology*; Hahn, *The Titles of Jesus in Christology*; Hengel, *Between Jesus and Paul, The Son of God, Acts and the History of Early Christianity*; Küng, *On Being a Christian*; Kümmel, *The Theology of the New Testament*; Longenecker, *The Christology of Early Jewish Christianity*; Meagher, *Five Gospels*; Neusner, *Judaism in the Beginning of Christianity*; Perrin, *The New Testament*; Robinson and Koester, *Trajectories Through Early Christianity*; Schillebeeckx, *Jesus, Christ, Interim Report*; Schelkle, *Theology of the New Testament* II; Tobin, *The Creation of Man*; Wilken, ed., *Aspects of Wisdom in Judaism and Early Christianity*. Cf. also above, Introduction, n. 9. For summaries of current positions in christology within the Roman Catholic tradition (a matter not covered in this book), see Fitzmyer, "The Biblical Commission and Christology," with the accompanying document of the Pontifical Biblical Commission on "Scripture and Christology."

2 On the "Council of Jerusalem" see, for example, Brown and others, *Peter*, 49–56; Conzelmann, 82–90; Hengel, *Acts and the History of Early Christianity*, 111–126 (with background, 92–110).

3 On the structure of synagogue services in first-century Palestine see Dalman,

Jesus—Jeshua, 38–44. For historical and archaeological information on the Jewish Christian communities of the first century, including Galilee, see Bagatti, *The Church from the Circumcision*, especially 3–93.

⁴ See Pesch, *Simon-Petrus*, 55–65; Conzelmann, 32–62.

⁵ See Schillebeeckx, *Jesus*, for the thesis that four early and divergent Christian creeds ("maranatha," or parousia, christologies; "divine man" christologies [cf. also Alsup, 221]; wisdom christologies; and death-and-resurrection christologies) stem from the earliest unified interpretation of Jesus as the eschatological prophet: 403–438 (the four creeds), 439–515. Cf. Fuller, *Foundations*, chapter 2, 142ff.; Longenecker, 32–38.

⁶ *On the Heavens* I, v, 271 b, 8–9 (Loeb No. 338), 32, 33, translated by W.K.C. Guthrie, 1939.

⁷ The deemphasis of eschatology may have been influenced in part by political realities. Perkins, *Resurrection*, 23, notes that "the Jewish community of those [Hellenistic] cities [of the Diaspora] looked upon Roman imperial power as beneficient (as in Rom[ans] 13:1–7) and not as the embodiment of evil shortly to be overthrown by divine intervention." Meier, in Brown and Meier, *Antioch and Rome*, 16, notes that the (somewhat later) community for whom Matthew's Gospel was written had already come to terms with the delay of the parousia by means of a "realized eschatology" of Jesus within the Church for a period with an indefinite future. However, the *Didache*, or *Teaching of the Twelve Apostles* (Syria, first or second century C.E.), still concludes its Eucharistic Prayer with "May grace come and this world pass away. . . . Maranatha": Rordorf and Tuilier, ed. and trans., *La Doctrine des douze apôtres* X, 6 (lines 23 and 27), pp. 180, 182; cf. also the eschatological discourse that terminates the work: XVI, 1–8 (lines 1–23), pp. 194–199.

⁸ Cf. Dunn, passim; Fitzmyer "Pauline Theology," in *Jerome Biblical Commentary* II, 800–827, and *A Christological Catechism*, 84–89; Fuller, *Foundations*, chapter 7; Hengel, *Between Jesus and Paul*, 48–96; Longenecker, 63–136; Schelkle, II, 177–220; Schillebeeckx, *Jesus*, 424–429, and (for the topic of grace in Saint Paul) *Christ*, 112–179. Berger, "Zum traditionsgeschichtlichen Hintergrund," argues that higher christological titles of Hellenistic Jewish Christianity. such as "Christ" and "Kyrios," originated in the community's deepening understanding (with the use of Jewish categories) of its belief that Jesus had been sent as the eschatological prophet and normative envoy of God (see 424).

⁹ On this "backwards migration" see Brown's summary presentations in *The Birth of the Messiah*, 29–32, 135–137, 141, 313–316; and the developed treatments in Fuller, *Foundations*, and Hahn, *The Titles of Jesus*, which I follow in this chapter.

¹⁰ In *A Christological Catechism*, 63f., Fitzmyer notes briefly that Paul's epistles are focused on functional or soteriological christology ("the significance of Christ Jesus for human beings," 63) and have little that is truly constitutive or ontological christology (63), even though there are texts in Paul (Philippians 2:6–11; Romans 1:3, and 8:32; I Corinthians 15:24–28) that fall somewhere between functional and ontological christology.

¹¹ On interpretations of Jesus' death in early Christianity see Fitzmyer, *A Christological Catechism*, 91–94; Hengel, *The Atonement*, 33–75; Schillebeeckx, *Jesus*, 274–294, *Christ*, 166–168.

¹² Tertullian still employs this dating of the christological moment when, refer-

ring to Jesus' baptism (Luke 3:1, 21–22), he writes: "In the fifteenth year of Tiberius, Christ Jesus deigned to descend from heaven": *Adversus Marcionem* I, 19, in Migne, *Patrologia Latina* II (1844), 267. Earlier in the same work (I, 15; p. 263) Tertullian says that "the Lord was revealed in the 12th [*sic;* = 15th?] year of Tiberius Caesar."

13 For early Patristic texts in which the conception christology (without incarnation or preexistence) of Matthew and Luke is combined with the preexistence/incarnation christology of John, see Brown, *The Birth of the Messiah*, 141, n. 27, and 314, n. 48. Cf. Schillebeeckx's suggestion, *Jesus*, 454 (referring to Qumran text 4 Q Mess ar), that "when all is said and done, a virgin birth of a messiah descending out of heaven was perhaps already a pre-Christian, Jewish concept, associated with Davidic messianism."

14 See Schillebeeckx, *Christ*, 182–184, 195–204.

15 See Alexander of Aphrodisias (ca. 200 C.E.), *On Fate* (Peri Heimarmenēs), edited and translated by R. W. Sharples, London: Duckworth, 1983, 41–93 (English translation), and 179–229 (Greek, with fragments). Seneca's text is a citation from some lost verses of the Greek Stoic philosopher Cleanthes (331–232 B.C.E.): Fragment 527, in Johann von Arnim, ed., *Stoicorum Veterum Fragmenta*, Leipzig: Teubner, 1921, I, 119. The text (here: Ducunt volentem fata, nolentem trahunt) is quoted in Latin in *Seneca* VI, *Ad Lucilium Epistulae Morales*, Vol. III, (Loeb No. 77), Letter 107, no. 11, translated by Richard M. Gummere (1925), 228. Saint Augustine cites the same Latin verses and attributes them to Seneca: *The City of God Against the Pagans* II, (Loeb No. 412), V, 8, translated by William Green (1963), 164.

On the question of cyclical time, cf. Empedocles' dictum that the cosmic elements (?) remain "unmoved in circularity" (*akinētoi kata kyklon*): Fragment 26, in Hermann Diels, *Die Fragmente der Vorsokratiker*, 2nd ed., Berlin: Weidmann, 1906, I, 183; cf. also Origen's interpretation of how, according to Greek cyclical theories, the history of salvation would have to repeat itself: *Peri Archōn*, II, 3, no. 4, *Patrologia Graeca* XI (1857), 192.

16 Cf. Fuller, *Foundations*, chapter 8.

17 Today New Testament scholars tend to discount earlier hypotheses (e.g., Bultmann's) about Gnostic origins of the descending-ascending savior in New Testament texts and rather find intertestamental Jewish elements in those texts: see Schelkle, II, 323, n. 74. George W. MacRae, "The Jewish Background of the Gnostic Sophia Myth," *Novum Testamentum* 12 (1970), 86–101, argues that in contacts between the Jewish and the Gnostic wisdom traditions, it was the Jewish that influenced the Gnostic. Cf. also Schillebeeckx, *Jesus*, 429–432; Charles H. Talbert, "The Myth of a Descending-Ascending Redeemer in Mediterranean Antiquity," *New Testament Studies* 22 (1976), 418–440; and the essays in Wilken, *Aspects of Wisdom*. On Gnosticism especially in relation to early Christianity, cf. R. McL. Wilson, ed. and trans. *Gnosis: A Selection of Gnostic Texts*, 2 vols., Oxford: Clarendon, 1972 (German original, ed. Werner Foerster, 1969); Robert M. Grant, ed., *Gnosticism: A Source Book of Heretical Writings from the Early Christian Period*, New York: Harper and Row, 1961; Hans Jonas, *The Gnostic Religion: The Message of the Alien God and the Beginnings of Christianity*, Boston: Beacon, 1958; and Elaine Pagels, *The Gnostic Gospels*, New York: Random House, 1979.

18 Cf. Fuller, *Foundations*, chapter 8; Schillebeeckx, *Christ*, 168–177.

19 On John's Prologue, see Brown, *The Gospel According to John* I, 3–36.

CONCLUSION: RECOVERING THE KINGDOM

¹ Origen, "Commentaria in Evangelium secundum Matthaeum," *Patrologia Graeca* XIII (1862), 1197: "katho [ho Christos] autobasileia esti."

² Philo, *Allegorical Interpretation of Genesis II, III [Legum Allegoria]* III, xxiv (= 78), in *Philo* I (Loeb No. 226), 352, 353, translated by F. H. Colson and G. H. Whitaker, 1956; emphasis added.

³ T. S. Eliot, *Four Quartets:* The Dry Salvages," V, in *The Complete Poems and Plays of T. S. Eliot,* London: Faber and Faber, 1969, p. 190.

Selected Bibliography

Alexander, Paul J. *The Byzantine Apocalyptic Tradition.* Edited by Dorothy deF. Abrahamse. Berkeley: University of California Press, 1985.

Alsup, John E. *The Post-Resurrection Appearance Stories of the Gospel Tradition: A History-of-Tradition Analysis, With Text-Synopsis.* Stuttgart: Calwer, and London: SPCK, 1975.

Bagatti, Bellarmino. *The Church from the Circumcision: History and Archaeology of the Judaeo-Christians.* Translated by Eugene Hoade. Jerusalem: Franciscan Printing Press, 1971 (French original, 1965).

――――. *Antichi Villaggi Cristiani di Galilea.* Jerusalem: Franciscan Press, 1971.

Karl Barth. *The Epistle to the Romans.* Translated from the sixth edition (1929) by Edwyn C. Hoskyns. London: Oxford University Press, 1933 (German original, 1919).

Bellinzoni, Arthur J., Jr., editor. *The Two-Source Hypothesis: A Critical Appraisal* Macon, Ga.: Mercer University Press, 1985.

Benoît, Pierre. "Marie-Madeleine et les Disciples au Tombeau selon Joh 20[,] 1–18." In Walther Eltester, editor, *Judentum, Urchristentum, Kirche: Festschrift für Joachim Jeremias,* 141–152. Berlin: Alfred Töpelmann, 1960.

――――. *The Passion and Resurrection of Jesus Christ.* Translated by Benet Weatherhead. New York: Herder and Herder, and London: Darton, Longman, Todd, 1969 (French original, 1966).

Berger, Klaus. "Zum traditionsgeschichtlichen Hintergrund christologischer Hoheitstitel." *New Testament Studies* 17 (1971), 391–425.

――――. *Die Gesetzesauslegung Jesu: Ihr historischer Hintergrund im Judentum und im Alten Testament* I: Markus und Parallelen. Neukirchen-Vluyn: Neukirchener Verlag des Erziehungsvereins, 1972.

————. *Die Auferstehung des Propheten und die Erhöhung des Menschensohnes: Traditionsgeschichtliche Untersuchungen zur Deutung des Geschickes Jesu in frühchristlichen Texten.* Göttingen: Vandenhoeck & Ruprecht, 1976.

Bickerman, Elias. *From Ezra to the Last of the Maccabees: Foundations of Post-Biblical Judaism.* Translated in part by Moses Hadas. New York: Schocken, 1947, 1949, 1963.

Blinzler, Josef. *The Trial of Jesus: The Jewish and Roman Proceedings Against Jesus Christ Described and Assessed From the Oldest Accounts.* No translator listed. Westminster, Md.: Newman, 1959 (second German edition, 1955).

————. *Die Brüder und Schwestern Jesu.* 2nd ed. Stuttgart: Katholisches Bibelwerk, 1967.

Bode, Edward Lynn. *The First Easter Morning: The Gospel Accounts of the Women's Visit to the Tomb of Jesus.* Rome: Biblical Institute Press, 1970.

Bornkamm, Günther. *Jesus of Nazareth.* Translated by Irene and Fraser McLuskey with James M. Robinson. New York: Harper, 1960 (German original, 1956).

————. "Jesus Christ." In *The New Encyclopaedia Britannica*, Macropaedia, X, 145–155. Chicago: Benton, 1974.

Bousset, Wilhelm. *The Antichrist Legend: A Chapter in Christian and Jewish Folklore.* Translated by A. H. Keane. London: Hutchinson, 1896 (German original, 1895). Reissued: New York: AMS, 1985.

Braaten, Carl E., and Roy A. Harrisville, editors and translators. *The Historical Jesus and the Kerygmatic Christ: Essays on the New Quest of the Historical Jesus.* Nashville and New York: Abingdon Press, 1964.

Broer, Ingo. *Die Urgemeinde und das Grab Jesu: Eine Analyse der Grablegungsgeschichte im Neuen Testament.* Munich: Kösel, 1972.

Brown, Raymond E. *The Gospel According to John.* 2 vols. Garden City, N.Y.: Doubleday, 1966 and 1970.

————. *Jesus God and Man: Modern Biblical Reflections.* New York: Macmillan, 1967.

————. "Jewish Law From Ezra to the Talmud—Rabbinic Literature." In *Jerome Biblical Commentary* II, 558–560.

————. *The Virginal Conception and Bodily Resurrection of Jesus.* New York: Paulist Press, 1973.

————. *Biblical Reflections on Crises Facing the Church.* New York: Paulist Press, 1975.

————. *The Birth of the Messiah: A Commentary on the Infancy Narratives in Matthew and Luke.* Garden City, N.Y.: Doubleday, 1977.

————. *The Community of the Beloved Disciple.* New York: Paulist Press, 1979.

————. *The Critical Meaning of the Bible.* New York: Paulist Press, 1981.

————. *Recent Discoveries and the Biblical World.* Wilmington, Del.: Michael Glazier, 1983.

————. *The Churches the Apostles Left Behind.* New York: Paulist Press, 1984.

————. "Liberals, Ultraconservatives, and the Misinterpretation of Catholic Biblical Exegesis." *Crosscurrents* 34 (1984), 311–328.

Brown, Raymond E., Karl P. Donfried, and John Reumann, editors. *Peter in the New Testament.* Minneapolis: Augsburg; New York: Paulist Press, 1973.

Brown, Raymond E., Karl P. Donfried, Joseph A. Fitzmyer, and John Reumann, editors. *Mary in the New Testament.* Philadelphia: Fortress; New York: Paulist Press, 1978.

Brown, Raymond E., Joseph A. Fitzmyer, and Roland E. Murphy, editors. *The Jerome Biblical Commentary.* Englewood Cliffs, N.J.: Prentice-Hall, 1968.

Brown, Raymond E., and John P. Meier. *Antioch and Rome: New Testament Cradles of Catholic Christianity.* New York: Paulist Press, 1983.

Bultmann, Rudolf. *History of the Synoptic Tradition.* Translated by John Marsh. New York: Harper & Row, 1963 (German original, 1921).

————. *Jesus and the Word.* Translated by Louise Pettibone Smith and Erminie Huntress Lantero. New York: Scribner's, 1934 (German original 1926).

————. *Theology of the New Testament.* Volume I. Translated by Kendrick Grobel. New York: Scribner's, 1951 (German original, 1948).

————. *Primitive Christianity in Its Contemporary Setting.* Translated by R. H. Fuller. Cleveland and New York: Meridian, 1956 (German original, 1949).

————. *The Presence of Eternity: History and Eschatology* (Gifford Lectures, 1955). New York: Harper, 1957.

Bultmann, Rudolf, and others. *Kerygma and Myth: A Theological Debate.* Edited by Hans Werner Bartsch, translated by Reginald H. Fuller. 2nd ed. London: SPCK, 1957 (first English edition, 1953).

Buttrick, George Arthur, editor. *The Interpreter's Bible.* Volume I. New York and Nashville: Abingdon, 1952.

————. *The Interpreter's One-Volume Commentary on the Bible.* New York and Nashville: Abingdon, 1971.

Cameron, Ron, editor. *The Other Gospels: Non-Canonical Gospel Texts.* Philadelphia: Westminster, 1982.

Catchpole, David R. *The Trial of Jesus: A Study in the Gospels and Jewish Historiography from 1770 to the Present Day.* Leiden: Brill, 1971.

Charles, R. H., editor. *The Apocrypha and Pseudepigrapha of the Old Testament in English.* Various translators. 2 vols. Oxford: Clarendon, 1913 (reissued 1963).

Charlesworth, James H., editor, *The Old Testament Pseudepigrapha.* Various translators. 2 vols. Garden City, New York: Doubleday, 1983 and 1985.

Cohen, A., editor. *The Minor Tractates of the Talmud: Massektoth Ketannoth.* Translated into English with Notes, Glossary, and Indices. 2 vols. London: Soncino Press, 1965.

Collins, John J. "The Son of Man and the Saints of the Most High in the Book of Daniel." *Journal of Biblical Literature* 93 (1974), 50–66.

————. *The Apocalyptic Imagination: An Introduction to the Jewish Matrix of Christianity.* New York: Crossroad, 1984.

————, editor. *Semeia* 14 (1979): *Apocalypse: The Morphology of a Genre.*

Conzelmann, Hans. *History of Primitive Christianity.* Translated by John E. Steely. Nashville and New York: Abingdon, 1973 (German original, 1971).

Corbin, Henry. "Cyclical Time in Mazdaism and Ismailism." In *Man and Time: Papers from the Eranos Yearbooks,* edited by Joseph Campbell, translated by Ralph Manheim, 115–126. Bollingen Series XXX, 3. Princeton, N. J.: Princeton University Press, 1957 (French original, 1951).

Corbo, Virgilio. *The House of St. Peter at Capharnaum: A Preliminary Report of the*

First Two Campaigns of Excavations, April 16–June 19, Sept. 12–Nov. 26, 1968. Translated by Sylvester Saller. Jerusalem: Franciscan Printing Press, 1969.

Crehan, F. J. "The Bible in the Roman Catholic Church from Trent to the Present Day." In *The Cambridge History of the Bible,* Volume 3: The West from the Reformation to the Present Day, edited by S. L. Greenslade. Cambridge: Cambridge University Press, 1963.

Crossan, John Dominic. *In Parables: The Challenge of the Historical Jesus.* New York: Harper & Row, 1973.

————. *Four Other Gospels: Shadows on the Contours of Canon.* Minneapolis, Chicago, New York: Winston-Seabury, 1985.

Dalman, Gustaf. *The Words of Jesus: I. Introduction and Fundamental Ideas.* Translated by D. M. Kay. Edinburgh: T. & T. Clark, 1902 (German original, 1898).

————. *Jesus—Jeshua: Studies in the Gospels.* Translated by Paul P. Levertoff. New York: Macmillan, 1929 (German original, 1922). Reissued New York: KYAV, 1971.

Davies, W. D. *Introduction to Pharisaism.* Philadelphia: Fortress, 1967.

————. *The Gospel and the Land: Early Christianity and Jewish Territorial Doctrine.* Berkeley: University of California Press, 1974.

Denzinger, Henry, editor. *Enchiridion symbolorum, definitionum et declarationum de rebus fidei et morum.* 30th ed., revised by Karl Rahner. Freiburg: Herder, 1954; English translation: *The Sources of Catholic Dogma.* Translated by Roy J. Deferrari. St. Louis and London: Herder, 1957.

Devisch, M. "La source dite des Logia et ses problèmes." *Ephemerides Theologicae Louvaniensis* 51 (1975), 82–89.

Dhanis, Édouard, editor. *Resurrexit: Actes du Symposium International sur la Résurrection de Jésus (Rome 1970).* Rome: Libreria Editrice Vaticana, 1974.

Dibelius, Martin. *From Tradition to Gospel.* Translated by Bertram Lee Woolf. New York: Scribner's, 1935 (German original, 1919).

Dodd, C. H. *The Parables of the Kingdom.* 3rd ed. London: Nisbet, and New York: Scribner's, 1961 (1st ed., 1935).

Duchesne-Guillemin, J. *La Religion de l'Iran ancien.* Paris: Presses Universitaires de France, 1962.

————. "Zoroastrianism and Parsiism." In *The New Encyclopaedia Britannica,* Macropaedia, XIX, 1171–1176. Chicago: Benton, 1974.

Dunn, James D. G. *Christology in the Making: A New Testament Inquiry Into the Origins of the Doctrine of the Incarnation.* Philadelphia: Westminster, 1980.

Edersheim, Alfred. *The Life and Times of Jesus the Messiah.* 2 vols. 3rd ed. New York: Herrick, 1886.

Eliade, Mircea. *Cosmos and History: The Myth of the Eternal Return.* Translated by Willard R. Trask. New York: Harper & Row, 1954, 1959 (French original, 1949).

Epstein, Isidore, editor. *The Babylonian Talmud.* Various translators. 34 vols. and index. London: Soncino Press, 1935–1952.

Farmer, William R. *The Synoptic Problem: A Critical Analysis.* New York: Macmillan, 1964.

Finegan, Jack. *Handbook of Biblical Chronology: Principles of Time Reckoning in the Ancient World and Problems of Chronology in the Bible.* Princeton, N. J.: Princeton University Press, 1964.

Fiorenza, Elisabeth Schüssler, editor. *Aspects of Religious Propaganda in Judaism and Early Christianity.* Notre Dame, Ind., and London: University of Notre Dame Press, 1976.

Fiorenza, Francis Schüssler. *Foundational Theology: Jesus and the Church.* New York: Crossroad, 1984.

Fitzmyer, Joseph A. *Essays on the Semitic Background of the New Testament.* London: Chapman, 1971.

————. *A Christological Catechism: New Testament Answers.* New York: Paulist Press, 1982.

————. "The Biblical Commission and Christology." *Theological Studies* 46 (1985), 407–479. (This article, pp. 408–443, contains "Scripture and Christology," the English translation of the Pontifical Biblical Commission document on christology, *Bible et christologie,* Paris: Cerf, 1984.)

————. "Crucifixion in Ancient Palestine, Qumran Literature, and the New Testament." *Catholic Biblical Quarterly* 40 (1978), 493–513.

Fitzmyer, Joseph A., and Raymond E. Brown. "Danger Also from the Left." *The Bible Today* 23 (1985), 105–110.

Freedman, H., and Maurice Simon, editors and translators. *Midrash Rabbah.* 10 vols. 3rd ed. London and New York: Soncino, 1983 (1st ed., 1939).

Freyne, Séan. *Galilee From Alexander the Great to Hadrian, 323 B.C.E. to 135 C.E.: A Study of Second Temple Judaism.* Wilmington, Del.: Michael Glazier, and Notre Dame, Ind.: Notre Dame University, 1980.

Fuller, Reginald H. *The New Testament in Current Study.* New York: Scribner's, 1962.

————. *Interpreting the Miracles.* London: SCM, 1963.

————. *The Foundations of New Testament Christology.* New York: Scribner's, 1965.

————. *A Critical Introduction to the New Testament.* Corrected ed. London: Duckworth, 1971.

————. *The Formation of the Resurrection Narratives.* New York and London: Macmillan-Collier, 1971.

Fuller, Reginald H., and Pheme Perkins. *Who Is This Christ?: Gospel Christology and Contemporary Faith.* Philadelphia: Fortress, 1983.

Grant, Michael. *Herod the Great.* New York: American Heritage Press, 1971.

Haas, N. "Anthropological Observations on the Skeletal Remains from Giv'at ha-Mivtar." *Israel Exploration Journal* 20 (1970), 38–59, 128–129.

Hachlili, Rachael, and Ann Killebrew. "Jewish Funerary Customs During the Second Temple Period, in the Light of the Excavations at the Jericho Necropolis." *Palestinian Exploration Quarterly* 115 (1983), 109–132.

Hahn, Ferdinand. *The Titles of Jesus in Christology: Their History in Early Christianity.* Translated by Harold Knight and George Ogg. New York and Cleveland: World Publishing Co., 1969 (German original, 1963).

————. *Historical Investigation and New Testament Faith.* Edited by Edgar Krentz and translated by Robert Maddox. Philadelphia: Fortress, 1983 (German original, 1972 and 1974).

————. "Das Abendmahl und Jesu Todesverständnis." *Theologische Revue* 76 (1980), 267–272.

Hamilton, Neill Q. "Resurrection Tradition and the Composition of Mark." *Journal of Biblical Literature* 84 (1965), 415–421.

Harbury, William. "The Trial of Jesus in Jewish Tradition." In *The Trial of Jesus: Cambridge Studies in honour of C.F.D. Moule*, 103–121. Naperville, Ill.: Allenson, 1970.

Harnack, Adolf von. *What Is Christianity?* Translated by Thomas Bailey Saunders. New York: Putnam's, 1901 (German original, 1900).

Harrington, Daniel J. *Interpreting the New Testament: A Practical Guide.* Wilmington, Del.: Glazier, 1979.

Heitmüller, W. "Zum Problem Paulus und Jesus." *Zeitschrift für die neutestmentliche Wissenschaft* 13 (1912), 320–337.

Hengel, Martin. *Judaism and Hellenism: Studies in Their Encounter in Palestine During the Early Hellenistic Period.* Translated by John Bowden. 2 vols. Philadelphia: Fortress, 1974 (German original, 1968, 2nd ed., 1973).

—. *Between Jesus and Paul: Studies in the Earliest History of Christianity.* Translated by John Bowden. London: SCM 1983 (German essays, 1971–1983).

—. *The Son of God: The Origin of Christology and the History of Jewish-Hellenistic Religion.* Translated by John Bowden. Philadelphia: Fortress, 1976 (German original, 1975).

—. *Jews, Greeks and Barbarians: Aspects of the Hellenization of Judaism in the Pre-Christian Period.* Translated by John Bowden. Philadelphia: Fortress, 1980 (German original, 1976).

—. *Crucifixion in the Ancient World and the Folly of the Message of the Cross.* Translated by John Bowden. London: SCM, and Philadelphia: Fortress, 1977 (German original, 1976, with later additions).

—. *Acts and the History of Earliest Christianity.* Translated by John Bowden. Philadelphia: Fortress, 1979 (German original, 1979).

—. *The Atonement: A Study of the Origins of the Doctrine in the New Testament.* Translated by John Bowden. London: SCM, 1981 (German original, 1980).

Hennecke, Edgar, and Wilhelm Schneemelcher. *New Testament Apocrypha.* 2 vols. Translated by R. McL. Wilson, et al. Philadelphia: Westminster, 1963 and 1965 (from the German ed., 1959).

Herford, R. Travers. *Christianity in Talmud and Midrash.* Clifton, N. J.: Reference Book Publishers, 1966.

Herzog, Rudolf. *Die Wunderheilungen von Epidauros: Ein Beitrag zur Geschichte der Medizin und der Religion.* In *Philologus*, Supplementband XXII, Heft III. Leipzig: Dieterichsche Verlagsbuchhandlung, 1931.

Hoehner, Harold W. *Herod Antipas.* Cambridge: Cambridge University Press, 1972.

Holland, David Larrimore. "History, Theology and the Kingdom of God: A Contribution of Johannes Weiss to 20th-Century Theology." *Biblical Research* 13 (1968), 54–66.

Holzmeister, Urban. *Chronologia Vitae Christi.* Rome: Pontifical Biblical Institute, 1933.

Humphreys, Colin J., and W. G. Waddington. "Dating the Crucifixion." *Nature* 306 (December 22–29, 1983), 743–746.

Iersel, Bas van. "The Resurrection of Jesus—Information or Interpretation?" In Pierre Benoît and Roland Murphy, editors, *Immortality and Resurrection*. New York: Herder and Herder, 1970.

Jaubert, Annie. *The Date of the Last Supper.* Translated by I. Rafferty. Staten Island, N.Y.: Alba House, 1965 (French original, 1957).

Jeremias, Joachim. *Jerusalem in the Time of Jesus: An Investigation into Economic and Social Conditions During the New Testament Period.* Translated by F. H. and C. H. Cave. Philadelphia: Fortress, 1969 (German original, 1923, 3rd ed., 1967).

————. *The Parables of Jesus.* 3rd, rev. ed. Translated by S. H. Hooke. New York: Scribner's, 1972 (German original, 1947, 8th ed., 1970).

————. *Heiligengräber in Jesu Umwelt (Mt. 23,29; Lk. 11,47): Eine Untersuchung zur Volksreligion der Zeit Jesu.* Göttingen: Vandenhoeck & Ruprecht, 1958.

————. *The Eucharistic Words of Jesus.* Translated by Norman Perrin (from the 3rd German ed., 1960, with author's revisions to July 1964). London: SCM, 1966.

————. *The Central Message of the New Testament.* London: SCM, 1965.

The Jerome Biblical Commentary. See Brown, Raymond E., Joseph A. Fitzmyer, and Roland E. Murphy, editors.

Kähler, Martin. *The So-Called Historical Jesus and the Historic, Biblical Christ.* Translated (from the 2nd ed., 1896) by Carl E. Braaten. Philadelphia: Fortress, 1964 (German original, 1892).

Kaiser, Otto. *Introduction to the Old Testament: A Presentation of Its Results and Problems.* Translated by John Sturdy. Minneapolis: Augsburg, 1975 (German original, 1969).

Kasper, Walter. *Jesus the Christ.* Translated by V. Green. New York: Paulist Press, 1977 (German original, 1974).

Kastner, Karl. "Noli me tangere." *Biblische Zeitschrift* 13 (1915), 344–353.

Kittel, Gerhard, and Gerhard Friedrich, editors. *Theological Dictionary of the New Testament.* English translation and edition by Geoffrey W. Bromiley. 10 vols. Grand Rapids, Mich.: Eerdmans, 1964–1976 (German original, 1933); also in 1-vol. abridged ed., 1985.

Kraeling, Carl H. *Anthropos and Son of Man: A Study in the Religious Syncretism of the Hellenistic Orient.* New York: Columbia University Press, 1927.

Kremer, Jacob. *Das älteste Zeugnis von der Auferstehung Christi: Eine bibeltheologische Studie zur Aussage und Bedeutung von 1 Kor 15,1–11.* 2nd ed. Stuttgart: Katholisches Bibelwerk, 1967 (1st ed., 1966).

————. *Die Osterevangelien—Geschichten um Geschichte.* Stuttgart and Klosterneuburg, Austria: Katholisches Bibelwerk, 1977.

————. "Auferstanden—auferweckt." *Biblische Zeitschrift* 23 (1979), 97–98.

Krentz, Edgar. *The Historical-Critical Method.* Philadelphia: Fortress, 1975.

Küng, Hans. *On Being a Christian.* Translated by Edward Quinn. Garden City, N.Y.: Doubleday, 1976 (German original, 1974).

————. *Eternal Life: Life After Death as a Medical, Philosophical, and Theological Problem.* Translated by Edward Quinn. Garden City, N.Y.: Doubleday, 1984 (German original, 1982).

Kümmel, Werner Georg. *The New Testament: The History of the Investigation of Its Problems.* Translated by S. McLean Gilmour and Howard C. Kee. Nashville-New York: Abingdon Press, 1972 (German original, 1958).

————. *The Theology of the New Testament, According to Its Major Witnesses: Jesus-Paul-John.* Translated by John E. Steely. Nashville: Abingdon, 1973.

Kwiran, Manfred. *Index to Literature on Barth, Bonhoeffer and Bultmann.* Basel: Friedrich Reinhardt, 1977.

Lehmann, Karl. *Auferweckt am dritten Tag nach der Schrift: Früheste Christologie, Bekenntnisbildung und Schriftauslegung im Lichte von 1 Kor. 15,3–5.* 2nd, rev. ed. Freiburg, Basel, Vienna: Herder, 1969.

Lessing, Gotthold Ephraim. *Gesammelte Werke.* 10 vols. Edited by Paul Rilla. 2nd ed. Berlin and Weimar: Aufbau, 1968 (1st ed., 1956).

Lindars, Barnabas. *Jesus Son of Man: A Fresh Examination of the Son of Man Sayings in the Gospels in the Light of Recent Research.* London: SPCK, 1983.

Loeb Classical Library. Various editors and translators. Cambridge, Mass.: Harvard University Press, and London: Heinemann, 1912ff.

Lohfink, Gerhard. "Der Ablauf der Osterereignisse und die Anfänge der Urgemeinde." *Theologische Quartelschrift* 160 (1980), 163–176.

———. "Hat Jesus eine Kirche gestiftet?" *Theologische Quartelschrift* 162, 2 (1981), 81–97.

———. *The Last Day of Jesus.* Translated by Salvator Attanasio. Notre Dame, Ind.: Ave Maria Press, 1984 (German original, 1981).

Longenecker, Richard N. *The Christology of Early Jewish Christianity.* Naperville, Ill.: Allenson, 1970.

Luck, George. *Arcana Mundi: Magic and the Occult in the Greek and Roman Worlds: A Collection of Ancient Texts Translated, Annotated, and Introduced by Georg Luck.* Baltimore: Johns Hopkins University Press, 1985.

McCool, Gerald A. *Catholic Theology in the Nineteenth Century: The Quest for a Unitary Method.* New York: Seabury, 1977.

Mackey, James P. *Jesus the Man and the Myth.* New York: Paulist Press, 1979.

McKnight, Edgar V. *What Is Form Criticism?* Philadelphia: Fortress, 1969.

Mackowski, Richard M. *Jerusalem, City of Jesus: An Exploration of the Traditions, Writings, and Remains of the Holy City From the Time of Christ.* Grand Rapids, Mich.: Eerdmans, 1980.

Major, D.H.A., T. W. Manson, and C. E. Wright. *The Mission and Message of Jesus.* London: Nicholson & Watson, and New York: Dutton, 1937.

Manson, T. W. *The Sayings of Jesus.* London: SCM, 1949 (originally published as Part II of Major, et al., *The Mission and Message of Jesus*).

———. *The Teaching of Jesus: Studies of Its Form and Content.* Cambridge: Cambridge University Press, 1963.

Marx, Karl, and Friedrich Engels. *Collected Works.* 40 vols. Moscow: Progress Publishers, 1975–1983.

Marxsen, Willi. *Mark the Evangelist: Studies on the Redaction History of the Gospel.* Translated by James Boyce, Donald Juel, and William Poehlmann with Roy A. Harrisville. Nashville and New York: Abingdon, 1969 (German original, 1956).

———. *The Resurrection of Jesus of Nazareth.* Translated by Margaret Kohl. Philadelphia: Fortress, 1970 (German original, 1968).

Meagher, John C. *Five Gospels: An Account of How the Good News Came to Be.* Minneapolis: Winston, 1983.

Michaelis, Johann David. *Introduction to the New Testament.* Translated by Herbert Marsh. Cambridge: J. Archdeacon (later editions: London: Rivington), 1793–1801.

Migne, J.-P., editor. *Patrologiae Cursus Completus: Series Prima Latina.* 221 vols. Paris: Migne, 1844–1864, with supplements, 1952ff. (Cited as *Patrologia Latina.*)

———, editor. *Patrologiae Cursus Completus: Series Graeca.* 161 vols. Paris: Garnier, 1857ff. (Cited as *Patrologia Graeca.*)

Moule, C.F.D., editor. *The Significance of the Message of the Resurrection for Faith in Jesus Christ.* Translated by Dorothea M. Barton and R. A. Wilson. Naperville, Ill.: Allenson, 1968 (German essays from 1964).

Neill, Stephen. *The Interpretation of the New Testament, 1861–1961.* London: Oxford University Press, 1964.

Neusner, Jacob. *Midrash in Context: Exegesis in Formative Judaism.* The Foundations of Judaism: Method, Teleology, Doctrine, Part One: Method. Philadelphia: Fortress, 1983.

———. *Judaism in the Beginning of Christianity.* Philadelphia: Fortress, 1984.

———. *Torah: From Scroll to Symbol in Formative Judaism.* The Foundations of Judaism: Method, Teleology, Doctrine, Part Three: Doctrine. Philadelphia: Fortress, 1985.

Nickelsburg, George W. E., Jr. *Resurrection, Immortality, and Eternal Life in Intertestamental Judaism.* Cambridge, Mass.: Harvard University Press, 1972.

———. "Enoch, Levi, and Peter: Recipients of Revelation in Upper Galilee." *Journal of Biblical Literature* 100 (1981), 575–600.

Nietzsche, Friedrich. *The Will to Power.* Translated by Walter Kaufmann and R. J. Hollingdale. Edited by Walter Kaufmann. New York: Random House, 1967 (German original, various versions, 1901, 1911).

Ott, Ludwig. *Fundamentals of Catholic Dogma.* Translated by Patrick Lynch. St. Loius: Herder, 1955 (German original, 1952).

Perkins, Pheme. *Resurrection: New Testament Witness and Contemporary Reflection.* Garden City, N.Y.: Doubleday, 1984.

Perrin, Norman. *The Kingdom of God in the Teaching of Jesus.* Philadelphia: Westminster, 1963.

———. *Rediscovering the Teaching of Jesus.* New York: Harper & Row, 1967.

———. *What Is Redaction Criticism?* Philadelphia: Fortress, 1969.

———. *The New Testament: An Introduction. Proclamation and Pareness, Myth and History.* New York: Harcourt Brace Jovanovich, 1974.

———. *Jesus and the Language of the Kingdom: Symbol and Metaphor in New Testament Interpretation.* Philadelphia: Fortress, 1976.

———. *The Resurrection According to Matthew, Mark, and Luke.* Philadelphia: Fortress, 1977.

Pesch, Rudolf. "The Position and Significance of Peter in the Church of the New Testament: A Survey of Current Research." Translated by David Bourke. In *Papal Ministry in the Church,* edited by Hans Küng. *Concilium* 64 (1971), 21–35.

———. "Zur Entstehung des Glaubens an die Auferstehung Jesu: Ein Vorschlag zur Diskussion." *Theologische Quartelschrift* 153 (1973), 201–283.

———. "Stellungnahme zu den Diskussionsbeiträgen." *Theologische Quartelschrift* 153 (1973), 270–283.

———. "Das Messiasbekenntnis des Petrus (Mk 8, 27–30): Neuverhandlung einer alten Frage." *Biblische Zeitung* 17 (1973) 178–195; 18 (1974), 20–31.

———. "The Markan Version of the Healing of the Gerasene Demoniac." No translator listed. *Ecumenical Review* 23 (1976), 349–376.

———. *Das Markusevangelium.* 2 vols. 2nd ed. Freiburg: Herder, 1977.

———. *Das Abendmahl und Jesu Todesverständnis.* Quaestiones Disputatae, No. 80. Freiburg: Herder, 1978.

———. *Das Evangelium der Urgemeinde.* Freiburg: Herder, 1979.

————. *Simon-Petrus: Geschichte und geschichtliche Bedeutung des ersten Jüngers Jesu Christi*. Stuttgart: Anton Hiersemann, 1980.

————. "Zur Entstehung des Glaubens an die Auferstehung Jesu: Ein neuer Versuch." *Freiburger Zeitschrift für Philosophie und Theologie* 30 (1983), 73–98.

————. *Zwischen Karfreitag und Ostern: Die Umkehr der Jünger Jesu*. Zürich: Benziger, 1983.

(See also below: Anton Vögtle and Rudolf Pesch. *Wie kam es zum Osterglauben?*)

Pesch, Rudolf, E. Gerhart, and F. Schilling. " 'Hellenisten' und Hebräer: Zu Apg 9, 29 und 6, 1." *Biblische Zeitschrift* 23 (1979), 87–92.

Pfeiffer, Robert H. *History of New Testament Times, With an Introduction to the Apocrypha*. Westport, Conn.: Greenwood Press, 1972 (originally New York: Harper, 1949).

Pidoux, Georges. "À propos de la notion biblique du temps." *Revue de Théologie et de Philosophie* 2 (1952), 120–125.

Pixner, Bargil (Virgil). "Tabgha on Lake Gennesareth: The Eremos of Jesus." *Christian News From Israel*. Special Issue, June 1985, 18–26.

Pontifical Biblical Commission. "Scripture and Christology." Translated from the Latin and French by Joseph A. Fitzmyer. In Fitzmyer, "The Biblical Commission and Christology." *Theological Studies* 46 (1985), 408–443, q.v., supra. (In French: *Bible et christologie*, Paris: Cerf, 1984.)

Power, Matthew. *Anglo-Jewish Calendar for Every Day in the Gospels: Being an Introduction to the Chief Dates in the Life of Christ (An Essay Towards a Final Determination of the Gospel Chronology)*. London: Sands, 1902.

Rad, Gerhard von. *Old Testament Theology*. Volume II: The Theology of Israel's Prophetic Tradition. Translated by D.M.G. Stalker. New York: Harper & Row, 1965 (German original, 1960).

Rahner, Karl. *Theological Investigations*. 13 vols. Various translators. Baltimore and New York: Helicon and Crossroads, 1961ff. (German originals, 1954ff.).

————. *Foundations of Christian Faith: An Introduction to the Idea of Christianity*. Translated by William V. Dych, London: Darton, Longman & Todd, and New York: Seabury, 1978 (German original, 1976).

Reimarus, Hermann Samuel. *Reimarus: Fragments*. Edited by Charles H. Talbert and translated by Ralph S. Fraser. Philadelphia: Fortress Press, 1970 (German original, 1774–1778).

————. *The Goal of Jesus and His Disciples*. Translated by George Wesley Buchanan. Leiden: Brill, 1970 (German original, 1778).

Renan, Ernest. *The Life of Jesus*. Translated by Charles Edwin Wilbour. New York: Carleton, 1864 (French original, 1863). Reissued, New York: Random House, 1955.

Riches, John. *Jesus and the Transformation of Judaism*. London: Darton, Longman & Todd, 1980.

Rigaux, Béda. *Dieu l'a ressuscité: Exégèse et théologie biblique*. Gembloux: Duculot, 1973.

Ritschl, Albrecht. *The Christian Doctrine of Justification and Reconciliation: The Positive Development of the Doctrine*. Translated by H. R. Mackintosh and A. B. Macaulay. Edinburgh: T. & T. Clark, 1900 (German original, Volume III, 1874). Reissued, Clifton, N.J.: Reference Book Publishers, 1966.

————. *Unterricht in der christlichen Religion*. Bonn: Marcus, 1875. Reissued: Gerhard Ruhbach, editor, Gütersloh: Mohn, 1966. (English translation in the following work, 221–291.)

————. *Three Essays*. Philip Hefner, editor and translator. Philadelphia: Fortress, 1972 (German originals, 1875, 1877, 1881).

Robinson, James M. *A New Quest of the Historical Jesus*. London: SCM, 1959.

Robinson, James M., and Helmut Koester. *Trajectories Through Early Christianity*. Philadelphia: Fortress, 1971.

Rohde, Joachim. *Rediscovering the Teaching of the Evangelists*. Translated by Dorothea M. Barton. Philadelphia: Westminster, 1968 (German original, 1966, with author's revisions to 1968).

Rordorf, Willy, and André Tuilier, editors and translators. *La Doctrine des douze apôtres (Didachè)*. Sources Chrétiennes, No. 248. Paris: Cerf, 1978.

Ruckstuhl, Eugen. *Chronology of the Last Days of Jesus: A Critical Study*. Translated by Victor J. Frapela. New York: Desclee, 1965 (German original, 1963).

Russell, D. S. *The Method and Message of Jewish Apocalyptic, 200 BC–AD 100*. Philadelphia: Westminster, 1964.

Safrai, S., and M. Stern, editors, in cooperation with D. Flusser and W. C. van Unnik. *Compendia Rerum Iudaicarum ad Novum Testamentum*. Section One, in 2 vols.: *The Jewish People in the First Century: Historical Geography, Political History, Social, Cultural and Religious Life and Institutions*. Philadelphia: Fortress, 1974 and 1976.

Sanders, E. P. *Jesus and Judaism*. Philadelphia: Fortress, 1985.

Schelkle, Karl Hermann. *Theology of the New Testament*. Volumes II and III. Translated by William A. Jurgens. Collegeville, Minn.: Liturgical Press, 1976 and 1973 (*sic*; German original, 1973).

Schenke, Ludger. *Auferstehungsverkündigung und leeres Grab: Eine traditionsgeschichtliche Untersuchung von Mk 16,1–8*. 2nd ed. Stuttgart: Katholisches Bibelwerk, 1969 (1st ed., 1968).

Schillebeeckx, Edward. *Jesus: An Experiment in Christology*. Translated by Hubert Hoskins. New York: Seabury, 1979 (Dutch original, 1974).

————. *Christ: The Christian Experience in the Modern World*. Translated by John Bowden. New York: Seabury, 1980 (Dutch original, 1977).

————. *Interim Report on the Books "Jesus" and "Christ."* Translated by John Bowden. New York: Seabury, 1980 (Dutch original, 1978).

Schleiermacher, Friedrich. *The Life of Jesus*. Edited by Jack C. Verheyden, translated by S. Maclean Gilmour. Philadelphia: Fortress, 1975 (posthumous German original, 1862, from lectures delivered in 1832).

Schmidt, Karl Ludwig. *Der Rahmen der Geschichte Jesu: Literarkritische Untersuchungen zur ältesten Jesusüberlieferung*. Berlin: Trowitzsch, 1919. Reissued, Darmstadt: Wissenschaftliche Buchgesellschaft, 1969.

Schonfield, Hugh J. *The Passover Plot: New Light on the History of Jesus*. London: Hutchinson, 1965.

Schoof, Ted Mark. *A Survey of Catholic Theology, 1800–1970*. Translated by N. D. Smith. New York: Paulist Newman, 1970.

Schubert, Kurt. "Die Entwicklung der Auferstehungslehre von der nachexilischen bis zur frührabbinischen Zeit." *Biblische Zeitschrift* 6 (1962), 177–213.

Schürer, Emil. *The History of the Jewish People in the Age of Jesus Christ (175*

B.C.–A.D. 135). 2 vols. New English version revised and edited by Géza Vermès and Fergus Millar. Edinburgh: T. & T. Clark, 1973 and 1979 (first English edition, 1885).

Schweitzer, Albert. *The Quest for the Historical Jesus: A Critical Study of Its Progress from Reimarus to Wrede.* Translated by W. Montgomery. London: A. & C. Black, 1910 (German original, 1906). Reissued, New York: Macmillan, 1968.

Scobie, Charles H. H. *John the Baptist.* Philadelphia: Fortress, 1964.

Sloyan, Gerard S. *Is Christ the End of the Law?* Philadelphia: Westminster, 1978.

———. " 'Come, Lord Jesus': The View of the Post-Resurrection Community." In Francis A. Eigo, editor, *Who Do People Say I Am?* Proceedings of the Theology Institute of Villanova University, Volume XII, 91–121. Villanova, Pa.: University of Villanova Press, 1980.

Speiser, E. A. *Genesis.* Anchor Bible Series, No. 1. Garden City, N.Y.: Doubleday, 1964.

Steiner, George. *In Bluebeard's Castle: Some Notes Towards the Redefinition of Culture.* New Haven: Yale University Press, 1971.

Steinmann, Jean. *St. John the Baptist and the Desert Tradition.* Translated by Michael Boyes. New York: Harper, 1958 (French original, 1955).

Stemberger, Günter. "Galilee—Land of Salvation?" In W. D. Davies, editor, *The Gospel and the Land,* 409–438. Berkeley, Los Angeles, London: University of California Press, 1974.

Stone, Michael, editor. *Jewish Writings of the Second Temple Period: Apocrypha, Pseudepigrapha, Qumran Sectarian Writings, Philo, Josephus.* Assen: Van Gorcum, and Philadelphia: Fortress, 1984.

Strack, Hermann L. *Introduction to the Talmud and Midrash.* No translator listed. New York: Meridian, and Philadelphia: Jewish Publication Society of America, 1959 (5th German ed., 1921; 1st English ed., 1931).

Strack, Hermann L., and Paul Billerbeck. *Kommentar zum Neuen Testament aus Talmud und Midrasch.* 11th ed., 5 vols. in 6. Munich: Beck, 1956.

Strauss, David Friedrich. *The Life of Jesus, Critically Examined.* Translated by George Eliot. London: Chapman, 1846 (German original, 1835–1836). Reissued, New York: Macmillan, 1968.

Streeter, Burnett Hillman. *The Four Gospels: A Study of Origins.* London: Macmillan, 1924.

Strobel, August. *Kerygma und Apokalyptik: Ein religionsgeschichtlicher und theologischer Beitrag zur Christusfrage.* Göttingen: Vanderhoeck & Ruprecht, 1967.

Tatum, W. Barnes. *In Quest of Jesus: A Guidebook.* Atlanta, Ga.: John Knox Press, 1982.

Taylor, Vincent. *The Gospel According to St. Mark.* 2nd ed. London: Macmillan, and New York: St. Martin, 1966 (1st ed., 1950).

Teeple, Howard M. *The Mosaic Eschatological Prophet.* Philadelphia: Society of Biblical Literature, 1957.

Tobin, Thomas H., S.J., *The Creation of Man: Philo and the History of Interpretation.* Washington, D.C.: Catholic Biblical Association of America, 1983.

Tödt, Heinz-Eduard. *The Son of Man in the Synoptic Tradition.* Translated by Dorothea M. Barton. London: SCM, 1965 (German original, 1959).

Vermès, Géza. *Jesus the Jew: A Historian's Reading of the Gospels.* London: Collins, 1973; Philadelphia: Fortress, 1981.

————, translator. *The Dead Sea Scrolls in English.* 2nd ed. New York: Penguin, 1975.

————. *Jesus and the World of Judaism.* Philadelphia: Fortress, 1984.

Vögtle, Anton, and Rudolf Pesch. *Wie kam es zum Osterglauben?* Düsseldorf: Patmos, 1975.

Weiss, Johannes. *Jesus' Proclamation of the Kingdom of God.* Translated by Richard Hyde Hiers and David Larrimore Holland. Philadelphia: Fortress, 1971 (German original, 1892).

Wifall, Walter. "David—Prototype of Israel's Future?" *Biblical Theological Bulletin* 4 (1974), 94–107.

————. "Son of Man—A Pre-Davidic Social Class?" *Catholic Biblical Quarterly* 37 (1975), 331–340.

Wilckens, Ulrich. *Resurrection: Biblical Testimony to the Resurrection: An Historical Examination and Explanation.* Translated by A. M. Stewart. Atlanta: Knox, 1978 (German original 1970).

Wilken, Robert L., editor. *Aspects of Wisdom in Judaism and Early Christianity.* Notre Dame, Ind., and London: University of Notre Dame Press, 1975.

Wink, Walter. *John the Baptist in the Gospel Tradition.* Cambridge: Cambridge University Press, 1968.

Winter, Paul. *On the Trial of Jesus.* Berlin: de Gruyter, 1961.

Wrede, William. *The Messianic Secret.* Translated by J.C.C. Greig. Cambridge and London: James Clark, 1971 (German original, 1901).

Wright, Addison G. *The Literary Genre of Midrash.* Staten Island, N.Y.: Alba House, 1967.

Zaehner, R. C. *The Dawn and Twilight of Zoroastrianism.* London: Weidenfeld and Nicolson, 1961.

Zlotnik, Dov, editor and translator. *The Tractate "Mourning" (Semahot): (Regulations Relating to Death, Burial, and Mourning).* Yale Judaica Series, Volume XVII. New Haven and London: Yale University Press, 1966.

ABOUT THE AUTHOR

THOMAS SHEEHAN is professor of philosophy at Loyola University in Chicago. He received his doctorate from Fordham University and has taught in Italy as well as in the United States. Sheehan has been the recipient of research and translation grants from the Ford Foundation, the Mellon Foundation, and the National Endowment for the Humanities. He is the editor of *Heidegger: The Man and the Thinker* and the author of the forthcoming *Karl Rahner: The Philosophical Foundations*.